ISBN 978-1-331-84460-0
PIBN 10241179

This book is a reproduction of an important historical work. Forgotten Books uses
state-of-the-art technology to digitally reconstruct the work, preserving the original format
whilst repairing imperfections present in the aged copy. In rare cases, an imperfection in
the original, such as a blemish or missing page, may be replicated in our edition. We do,
however, repair the vast majority of imperfections successfully; any imperfections that
remain are intentionally left to preserve the state of such historical works.

1 MONTH OF
FREE
READING

at

www.ForgottenBooks.com

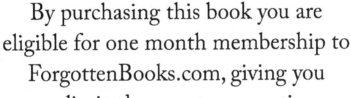

By purchasing this book you are eligible for one month membership to ForgottenBooks.com, giving you unlimited access to our entire collection of over 700,000 titles via our web site and mobile apps.

To claim your free month visit:

www.forgottenbooks.com/free241179

The Dialogues of Saint Gregory, surnamed the Great: Pope of Rome & the First of that Name.

Divided into Four Books, wherein he entreateth of the Lives and Miracles of the Saints in Italy and of the Eternity of Men's Souls. Translated into our English Tongue by P. W. and printed at Paris in mdcviii. Re-edited with an Introduction and Notes by Edmund G. Gardner, M.A. With Illustrations after the Old Masters annotated by G. F. Hill

London: Philip Lee Warner
vii Grafton St., Bond St., W. mdccccxi

ST. BENEDICT DELIVERS HIS RULE

The Dialogues of Saint Gregory, surnamed the Great: Pope of Rome & the First of that Name.

Divided into Four Books, wherein he entreateth of the Lives and Miracles of the Saints in Italy and of the Eternity of Men's Souls. Translated into our English Tongue by P. W. and printed at Paris in mdcviii. Re-edited with an Introduction and Notes by Edmund G. Gardner, M.A. With Illustrations after the Old Masters annotated by G. F. Hill

London: Philip Lee Warner
vii Grafton St., Bond St., W. mdccccxi

The binding of this volume
is reproduced from a fine
Italian example dating
from the XVIth Century

Contents

The First Book

The Second Book
Of the Life and Miracles of St. Bennet

v

Contents

vi

Contents

The Third Book

Contents

The Fourth Book

Contents

ix

Contents

Contents

List of Illustrations

With Notes by G. F. Hill

Plates in Colour

The manuscript is a Latin Psalter, written and illuminated most probably at Christ Church, Canterbury, between 1012 and 1023, in a style which had its origin at Winchester.   The miniature of St. Benedict, which shows a combination of outline and full illumination, comes between the Psalter and the Canticles.   The Saint, enthroned, points to an open book inscribed " Ausculta, o fili, precepta," which a monk holds up to him.   His brooch is inscribed " Iustus," the fillet on his head, "Timor Dei" ; the border of his nimbus, "Sanctus Benedictus pater monachorum et dux."   The girdle of the prostrate monk who kisses his right foot bears the words "Zona humilitatis." In the spandril between the two arches which form the background is the hand of God, holding a stole, inscribed " Qui vos audit me audit" and "Obedientes cstote preposito vestro."   The miniature closely resembles another in the Benedictional of St. Æthelwold.

G. F. Warner, *Illuminated Manuscripts in the British Museum* (1903), pl. 7.

This picture was painted in 1511 for the church of S. Maria Assunta at Monte Oliveto in Barbiano, the final payment to the artist being made on February 9, 1512.   The original commission specified that the two Saints should be Benedict and Bernard.   The former has been replaced by a Pope, probably Gregory the Great.   The Madonna is seated on white clouds in a mandorla of blue edged with white, with cherubs' heads.   St. Gregory is represented without any particular attributes ; his tiara rests on the ground beside the mitre of St. Bernard, who wears the white habit and holds his pastoral staff. Landscape background of the kind typical of Pintoricchio.

C. Ricci, *Pintoricchio*, transl. by F. Simmonds (1902), p. 229.

Illustrations

Illustrations

of Federigo of Urbino, fourteen are now in the Louvre, the others in
the Palazzo Barberini. The distinction between his work and that of
Melozzo da Forlì has been much disputed, and this particular figure is
claimed by Schmarsow, in his work on Melozzo, for that artist; but
the general opinion seems now to be on the other side. Boëthius
seems to be represented as the author of the *de institutione arithmetica*,
and traditional founder of mediæval arithmetic, reckoning on his
fingers; or possibly the action may be merely that of a philosopher
checking off the heads of an argument. The eulogy under the portrait
was "L. Boetio, ob cuius commentationes Latini M. Varronis scholas
non desiderant, Fed. Urb. princeps pos."

St. Gregory the Great. By Justus of Ghent. Barberini Palace,
Rome 6

Another of the twenty-eight fancy portraits painted for the library
at Urbino (*see* above). The Pope, in tiara and cope, holds a book;
Gothic architectural background. The eulogy reads: "Gregorio in
coelum relato, ob morum sanctitatem, librorum quoque elegantiam
testatam, gratitudo Christiana memor erexit."

St. Benedict. By Perugino. Vatican Gallery, Rome 48

From the same altar-piece as the St. Scholastica (*see* above). The
Saint holds a bundle of rods, indicating the severity of his rule, and a
book.

St. Benedict leaving his father's house. By Spinello Aretino.
San Miniato al Monte, Florence 52

A scene from the frescoes in the sacristy of San Miniato, painted
about 1387 (*see* above). The Saint, mounted on a horse, bids farewell
to his relations; in the background, the town of Nursia; on the right,
two travellers.

St. Maurus. By Perugino. San Pietro, Perugia . . . 60

Another relic of the great altar-piece of 1496 (*see* above).

Maurus saving Placidus from drowning. By Giov. Antonio
Bazzi (Sodoma). Monte Oliveto Maggiore 64

From the series of thirty-one frescoes executed by Bazzi between
August 1505 and August 1508. It was revealed to St. Benedict in his
study that a young monk named Placidus, who had gone to draw
water, had fallen into the river. On the left, the abbot is seen in his
study despatching Maurus to the rescue; on the right, Maurus,
walking on the waters, brings Placidus to land.

The women sent by Florentius. By Giov. Antonio Bazzi.
Monte Oliveto Maggiore 68

From the same series of frescoes as the preceding. Florentius,
having failed to poison St. Benedict, endeavoured to debauch his
disciples, and "took seven maidens, all naked, and sent them into the
garden to dance and carol for to move the monks to temptation." To

the seven women correspond, on the other side, seven monks and an ass ; St. Benedict looks on in horror from the balcony above. The story goes that Bazzi in the first instance followed the legend exactly, and painted the women nude, and that he was afterwards obliged, by the indignation of his employers, to add clothes. This, however, is refuted by the fact that there is no trace here, as elsewhere, of anything being added in a second painting ; such additions are easily detected in a fresco.

From the series of frescoes in the sacristy of San Miniato mentioned above. . The scene is practically the same as that represented by Neroccio (*see* above) ; but the composition is naturally simpler, and the conception more dignified.

From the same altar-piece as the St. Scholastica (*see* above). St. Placidus, with hands joined in prayer, and holding a palm, is a characteristically sentimental Peruginesque type.

Benedetto Bonfigli's chief work was the decoration of the chapel of the Palazzo del Comune at Perugia with frescoes representing scenes from the life of St. Herculanus and St. Louis of Toulouse (begun in 1454 and continued at intervals until his death in 1496). The body of St. Herculanus, having been found uncorrupted, after it had been decapitated, flayed and exposed for forty days at the order of Totila, is here being carried in procession by the clergy, accompanied by lay-folk ; on the right, two women kneel as it passes. In the background, the buildings of Perugia.

The Virgin, holding her Son, is enthroned beneath a lemon-tree. On the left is St. Laurence Justinian, holding book and cross ; the Child presents a girdle to him. On the right is S. Zeno, with book and crozier, from which is suspended a fish, his symbol. Below are three angels making music. Painted in 1526, and inscribed "XXVI. Men. Mar. XXVIIII. Hieronimus a Libris pinxit." Oil on canvas.

· Painted about 1306. Faith, who wears a tall mitre and veil, rests the shaft of her cross on the torso of a fallen idol, which she spurns with her right foot, and holds a scroll inscribed with the creed. The key of heaven hangs from her girdle, and her left foot tramples upon cabalistic books. Above, two angels bend down to her.

Illustrations

Painted by Ghirlandaio before 1485 in the chapel of Santa Fina in
the Collegiate Church of S. Gimignano; the chapel itself was
consecrated in 1488. One of Santa Fina's attendants raises her head
so that she may see the vision, which warns her of her approaching
death.

Of twenty-eight bronze statues round the cenotaph of the Emperor
Maximilian in the Franciscan church at Innsbruck, two were supplied
by the foundry of Peter Vischer, and it is universally admitted that these
two were the statues of Theodoric and Arthur of Britain. The latter
is sometimes ascribed to Peter's son, of the same name, but there is
general agreement that the Theodoric is the elder artist's own work.
The payment for the statues was made in 1513. Theodoric rests in a
somewhat affected attitude on his battle-axe, supporting his shield with
his left hand; a curious contrast to the swaggering self-confidence of
the King Arthur.

The picture was completed in February 1413 for the high altar of the
Church of the Monastery degli Angeli. Removed thence in the sixteenth
century, it was rediscovered at Cerreto in 1830, and has been in the
Uffizi since 1866. It was restored by Franchi.

In the centre is the coronation of the Virgin by her Son, among a
crowd of angels; below kneel two angels, censing, and a third (mostly
destroyed) accompanies the choir on an organ. The wings contain
each ten saints. On the left, counting from the left, are in the first
row Benedict, Peter, John Baptist; in the second row, Stephen, Paul,
James, Matthew. On the right, counting from the right, in the first
row, Romuald, Andrew, John the Evangelist; in the second row,
Laurence, Bartholomew, Augustine, Giovanni Gualberto. Above the
middle, in the pinnacle, is a half-figure of Christ blessing between two
cherubim; over the wings is the Annunciation. (These are not
included in the illustration.) Of the six panels of the predella, the
two in the middle represent the Nativity and the Adoration of the
Magi. The other four, counting from the right, show (1) Benedict
reviving one of the brethren, killed by a falling wall during the building
of the Abbey of Monte Cassino; (2) Benedict forced to remain with his
sister Scholastica, whose prayer has induced a storm which prevents
him from leaving her; and Benedict sending Maurus to rescue Placidus
from drowning; (3) the death of Benedict; (4) Benedict curing a
monk of his inability to continue in prayer; and Benedict in his cave
in the wilderness, with Romanus letting down food to him by a
string.

O. Siren, *Don Lorenzo Monaco* (1905), pp. 77 ff.

Illustrations

The Mass of St. Gregory. By Andrea Sacchi (1600–1650).
Vatican Gallery,.Rome 240

The Pope, standing before the altar (on which is his tiara), pierces with a knife the fragment of linen cloth from the shroud of St. John the Evangelist, which exudes blood. Two deacons assist, one of them opening a cup to catch the blood as it falls. The ambassador of the Empress Constance and two soldiers of his retinue kneel in astonishment. A dove hovers round the Pope's head.

[*In the title of the Plate facing p.* 16, " *St. Benedict* " *should be printed* " *St. Bernard.*"]

Justus of Ghent   *Anderson*

BOETHIUS
(Barberini Palace, Rome)

Introduction

The four books of *Dialogues* of Saint Gregory the Great, "concerning the life and miracles of the Italian Fathers and the eternity of souls," were written in 593, three years after his elevation to the papacy, at the request of certain monks of his household.

"My brethren who dwell familiarly with me," writes Gregory to Maximianus, Bishop of Syracuse, "would have me by all means write something in brief fashion concerning the miracles of the Fathers, which we have heard wrought in Italy. For this purpose I earnestly need the help of your charity, that you should briefly inform me of all those which come back to your memory, or which you have happened yourself to know. For I remember that you related certain things, which I have forgotten, concerning the lord abbot Nonnosus, who lived near the lord Anastasius de Pentumis. I beseech you, therefore, to put down this, and whatever others there are, in your letters, and forward them to me with speed, unless you yourself are coming to me shortly."[1]

There is no other book that gives us so vivid a picture of religious life in Italy during the sixth century: the century that witnessed the brief epoch of Gothic

---

[1] *Gregorii I. Registrum, Epist.* iii. 5 (ed. Ewald and Hartmann, I. p. 206). Cf. *Dialog.* i. 7, 8, iii. 36. The title "lord" (*domnus*) is given to an abbot in accordance with the *Rule of St. Benedict* (cap. 63): "Abbas autem, quia vices Christi agere creditur, Domnus et Abbas vocetur."

domination, the restoration of the imperial Byzantine
power, and finally the invasion of the Lombards, that
"barbarous and cruel nation," writes Gregory, which,
"drawn as a sword out of a sheath," wrought such
unutterable havoc and devastation in the peninsula that
many, with Bishop Redemptus, held verily that "the
end of all flesh was come."[1] It is the century that
closed the period of classical civilisation, and ushered
in that dreariest epoch in the history of mankind known
as the Dark Ages.

Inevitably, men turned from the spectacle of a world
"fraught with so many miseries and divers afflictions,"[2]
to prepare in the solitude of the cloister for the end
which they deemed fast approaching, if it were not
already come. They naturally sought eagerly to grasp
such phenomena as seemed to them miraculous, as
visible signs that God had not utterly abandoned His
creation, and to find proofs that the soul, at least, was
immortal, and might look forward to a better life hereafter by forgiveness of injuries, and by offering herself
up before death as a sacrifice to Him that had made
her.[3] It is this that gives pathos even to the apparent
triviality of some of the miracles that Gregory records,
and deeper significance to the note on which the work
ends.

Three great figures illumine the general darkness of
the sixth century in Italy : Boëthius, the last philosopher
of the classical world ; Benedict, the organiser of
western monasticism ; and Gregory himself, the chief
agent in the building up of the mediæval ideal of the
papacy.

The Roman senator, Anicius Manlius Severinus
Boëthius, whom Gibbon calls "the last of the Romans
whom Cato or Tully could have acknowledged for their
countryman," was tortured to death by the orders of

[1] *Dialog.* iii. 38.   [2] *Ibid.* iii. 38.   [3] *Ibid.* iv. 60.

King Theodoric the Goth, in 524 or 525. Dante was
to meet him among the glowing spirits of great teachers
in the fourth sphere of Paradise : "In the vision of all
good there rejoiceth the holy soul, who unmasks the
world's deceit to whoso giveth good heed to it. The
body whence it was hunted lieth below in Cieldauro,
and it from martyrdom and from exile came unto this
peace."[1] Though a martyr for the liberty of Rome
rather than for the faith of Christ, Boëthius was (as we
now know for certain) an advocate of Christianity, albeit
from the philosophical rather than the religious standpoint ; but his famous work, *De Consolatione Philosophiae*,
composed in his prison at Pavia under the shadow of
death, attempts to "assert eternal Providence and
justify the ways of God to men" from the standpoint
of human reason alone. It is somewhat curious that
his name, which rings through the literature of the
Middle Ages from Alfred to Dante, occurs nowhere in
the *Dialogues*, although his fellow-victims under the
tyranny of the last years of Theodoric's rule, John the
Pope and Symmachus the Senator, are mentioned more
than once, and the monkish legend of their persecutor's
terrible end is related in full.[2]

Some four or five years after the death of Boëthius,
Benedict of Nursia founded the great monastery of
Monte Cassino, about 529. Here in 543, fourteen
years later, he died. Even in the west, Benedict was
naturally not without precursors ; such as Martin of
Tours, Cassianus of Marseilles, Cesarius of Arles,
Equitius, who, "by reason of his great holiness of life,
was the father and governor of many abbeys in the
province of Valeria,"[3] and some others ; but it was
more especially the work of the great Italian monk,

---

[1] *Par.* x. 124-129. *Cieldauro* is the church of San Pietro in Ciel
d'Oro (the Golden Roof) at Pavia, where Boëthius was buried.
[2] *Dialog.* iii. 2, iv. 30.   [3] *Ibid.* i. 4.

whose face Dante so ardently desired to behold unveiled
in Paradise, to elevate this western monastic life into a
system, with fixed laws and an ideal, like the object of
hope according to the scholastic definition, "arduous
but not impossible of attainment." The famous rule,
the *Regula Sancti Benedicti*, which he wrote and promul-
gated from Monte Cassino (based, in part, upon the
eastern rule of St. Basil), for all its apparent simplicity,
is one of the few great constructive works of the sixth
century. Although, from the standpoint of the *Divina
Commedia*, Dante makes the Saint declare that his *regola*
remained on earth solely to waste the parchment on
which it was written, *per danno delle carte*, it became the
norm according to which generations of men and women
throughout the western world devoted themselves to
the highest spiritual life, and became "kindled by that
heat which gives birth to flowers and holy fruits."[1]

The second book of the *Dialogues*, *De vita et miraculis
venerabilis Benedicti*, is the earliest and most authoritative
account of St. Benedict that we possess. Indeed, it, together with his Rule, is our only source for the story of
his life and the understanding of his character. As has
been well said, it is "the biography of the greatest Monk,
written by the greatest Pope (himself also a Monk.)"[2]

Gregory was born probably a year or two before the
death of St. Benedict. The son of the Roman senator,
Gordianus, and a scion of the noble house of the
Anicii, he inherited vast possessions in the Roman
Campagna and in the territory of Tivoli, stretching
almost to the gates of Praeneste (Palestrina), and a
palace on the Caelian Hill. His childhood was passed
amidst the disastrous events of the struggle between
Justinian's generals and the Goths, when Rome was
taken and retaken again and again by the Goths and the

[1] *Par.* xxii. 46–48, 73–75.
[2] Hodgkin, *Italy and her Invaders*, vol. iv., p. 411.

barbarian armies of the Empire. In his early manhood, after the death of Justinian and the recall of Narses to Constantinople, came the even more disastrous invasion and partial conquest of Italy by the Lombards. "Late and long," he writes, "I put off the grace of conversion, and, after I had been inspired with celestial desire, I thought it better to be clothed in the secular habit."[1] In 573, when still a young man, he was prefect of Rome. A few years later, he became a monk, turned his palace into a monastery, made over his lands to the monks, and disposed of his property to religious and public uses. After serving as *apocrisiarius,* or papal legate, to the imperial court of Byzantium, for Pope Pelagius II., he was, on the latter's death during the terrible pestilence that devastated Rome at the beginning of 590, elected Pope, and, in spite of his resistance, was compelled to accept the choice of the Romans, which (in accordance with the usage of the times) was confirmed by the Emperor Mauritius.

This is not the place to tell again the story of Gregory's pontificate. Physically a complete invalid, suffering from almost incessant pain, he held the see for fourteen years (dying on March 12, 604), with an indefatigable vigour and an incessant activity, in times of wellnigh unqualified difficulty and gloom. Convinced in his own mind that the end of the world was at hand (he had announced it to the people in his first public homily as Pope in St. Peter's, and the conviction abode with him until his death),[2] he nevertheless did not neglect even the care of temporal things, when these were forced upon him by the duties of his state and the pressure of the times. His conception of the temporal power of the papacy, and the relations of Church and State, was poles asunder from that of the Popes of

[1] *Moralia, Epistola missoria* (to Leander of Seville), cap. i.
[2] *Homilia I. in Evangelia* (Migne, P.L., lxxvi. coll. 1077-1081).

Introduction

Dante's century, and essentially the same as that of the poet himself. Of the vast territorial possessions of the Church, the administration of which he thoroughly reformed, he regarded the Pope, "not as possessor, but as dispenser of the fruits for the poor of Christ, on behalf of the Church."[1] Compelled to act as a secular ruler in defence of Rome against the Lombards, he regarded himself, in the temporal field, as the subject of the State. Like Dante, he conceives of the Church and State as mutually co-operating, but ruling over different spheres, and the Emperor is God's vicar and representative on earth in all things temporal : " What he does, if canonical, we follow ; if it is not canonical, we bear it, as far as we can without sin."[2] In the ecclesiastical sphere, on the other hand, he is uncompromising in asserting the supremacy of Rome over all other Christian churches. His work of converting the English, and preparing the conversion of the Lombards, need not be told here. Gregory was the creator of the spiritual ideal of the mediæval papacy, even as Benedict had created that of western monasticism.

The *Dialogues* were translated into Greek by one of St. Gregory's successors, Pope Zaccharias I. (741–752) : " that so the Grecians might be instructed in the rules of good living," as Platina's seventeenth-century translator puts it. With a similar desire for the edification of the English, an Anglo-Saxon version was made, about 890, by Bishop Werferth of Worcester, at the instigation of Alfred the Great.[3] The *Dialogues* were among the most popular reading of the Middle Ages, and early translations exist in almost every European language. In the fourth book, we find the first rudi-

[1] *De Monarchia*, iii. 10.
[2] *Epist.* xi. 29 (Ewald and Hartmann, II. pp. 299–300).
[3] *Bischofs Waerferth von Worcester Übersetzung der Dialoge Gregors des Grossen.* Ed. Hans Hecht. Leipzig, 1900.

xxiv

ments of the mediæval conception of the three states of souls in the other world. The story of the vision seen by a certain soldier[1] is practically the first in the west of those more or less fictitious visions of Hell, Purgatory, and Heaven, which inspired so many imitations throughout the Middle Ages, from Venerable Bede's legends of Fursaeus and Drythelm to the visions of Tundal, Alberic of Monte Cassino, and the monk Edmund of Eynsham—the long series which (speaking superficially) may be said to culminate in the *Divina Commedia.* Dante himself knew the *Dialogues* well. His account of St. Benedict in the sphere of Saturn, and his own vision of the nothingness of the world in his ascent to the Stellar Heaven, were directly suggested by St. Gregory's words.[2] From Gregory, too, came his doctrine of the " Mansions of Beatitude," albeit its significance had for him acquired a deeper and intenser note by the passage through the mystical mind of Bonaventura. Echoes of the *Dialogues* may likewise be discerned in the *De Monarchia* and in the *Letter to Can Grande.* The influence of Gregory's earlier work, the *Moralia,* or *Exposition of the Book of Job,* is also very marked in many passages of the *Divina Commedia.*

The translation of the *Dialogues,* here offered to the reader, was published at Paris in 1608—seventeen years, that is, before the first English version of Boccaccio's *Decameron.* It was dedicated " to the high and excellent princess Anne: by God's singular providence, Queen of great Britain, France, and Ireland "; that is, to Anne of Denmark, the consort of King James I. The translator claims to be the first thus to present a book to her : " For whereas divers, of divers professions, have directed their works to our most dread Sovereign,

---

[1] *Dialog.* iv. 36. *See* Notes.
[2] Cf. *Par.* xxii. 37–45, *Dialog.* ii. 8 ; *Par.* xxii. 133–153, *Dialog.* ii. 35.

and one also to our young Prince (your dear son, and
the orient object of our country's joy), so none at all,
for aught that I can learn, much less that professeth
the religion of St. Gregory, hath hitherto presented any
book to your Princely person." His "epistle dedica-
tory" is dated "the first of January, 1608," and signed
"Your Majesty's most devoted servant, and daily orator,
P.W." This "P. W." has not been identified ; the
Jesuit father, Henry James Coleridge, who edited
his translation, in a somewhat modernised form, in
1874, suggested that he was "an English Catholic,
desirous to interest the Queen in favour of the ancient
religion." The *Dialogues* are further introduced by a
lengthy preface "to the courteous and virtuous Christian reader," and followed (with an independent title-
page) by " A short Relation of divers Miracles wrought
at the memories or shrines of certain martyrs, especially
St. Stephen, the Protomartyr of Christ's Church," the
contents of which are mainly taken from the *City of
God* of St. Augustine and the Life of St. Bernard. The
present re-issue of the translation, save for the spelling,
follows verbally the edition of 1608. The Latin text
cited is that given by Migne (P.L. lxxvii.).

The *Dialogues* of St. Gregory have exercised a certain
influence upon Christian iconography. Spinello Aretino
at San Miniato, Luca Signorelli and Giovanni Antonio
Bazzi at Mont' Oliveto Maggiore, Fra Filippo Lippi,
Neroccio of Siena, Benedetto Bonfigli, and many
other Italian masters found subjects ready to their hand
in its pages ; while the pilgrim to Subiaco and the
other sanctuaries of the Roman Campagna, hallowed by
the footsteps of these " fathers of the olden time," will
still find the words of the great pontiff of the sixth
century the most vivid of guides.

EDMUND G. GARDNER

August 15, 1911

The Dialogues of Saint Gregory, surnamed the Great

The First Book

The Dialogues of Saint Gregory the Great, Pope of Rome

The First Book

Being upon a certain day too much over-charged with the troubles of worldly business, in which oftentimes men are enforced to do more than of duty they are bound, I retired myself into a solitary place, very fit for a sad and melancholy disposition ; where each discontentment and dislike concerning such secular affairs might plainly show themselves, and all things that usually bring grief, mustered together, might freely be presented before mine eyes. In which place after that I had sat a long while, in much silence and great sorrow of soul, at length Peter, my dear son and deacon, came unto me ; a man whom, from his younger years, I had always loved most entirely, and used him for my companion in the study of sacred scripture : who, seeing me drowned in such a dump of sorrow, spake unto me in this manner : " What is the matter ? or what bad news have you heard ? for certain I am, that some extraordinary sadness doth now afflict your mind." To whom I returned this answer : " O Peter, the grief which continually I endure is unto me both old and new : old through common use, and new by daily increasing. For mine unhappy soul, wounded with worldly business, doth now call to mind in what state it was, when I lived in mine Abbey, and how then it was superior to all earthly matters, far above all transitory and corruptible pelf, how it did usually think upon nothing but heavenly things ; and though it was enclosed in mortal body, yet did it by contemplation pass far beyond earthly bounds, and penetrate to the very height of heaven ; and as for death, the memory whereof is almost to all men grievous, that it did love and desire, as the end of all misery, the reward of her labours, and the very entrance to an everlasting and blessed life. But now, by reason of my pastoral charge, my poor soul is enforced to endure the burden of secular men's business, and after so excellent and sweet a kind of rest, defiled it is with the dust of worldly conversation : and when it doth, at the request of others, attend to outward affairs, no question but it returneth back, far less fit to think upon those that be inward, spiritual, and heavenly. Wherefore, at this present, do I meditate what I suffer, and consider what my soul hath lost : and the memory of my former loss doth make that more grievous which I do now endure. For do you not behold at this present, how I am tossed with the waves of this wicked world, and see the ship of my soul beaten with the storms of a terrible tempest ? and therefore, when I remember my former state of life, I cannot but sigh to look back, and cast mine eyes upon the forsaken shore.

" And that which doth yet grieve me more is because I see myself so carried away amain with the boisterous blasts of this troublesome world, that I cannot now scarce behold the port from whence I did first hoist sail ; for such be the downfalls of our soul, that first it loseth that goodness and virtue which before it possessed ; yet so that it doth still remember what it hath lost ; but afterwards, carried away more and more, and straying further from the path of virtue, it cometh at length to that pass, that it doth not so much as keep in mind what before it did daily practise : and so in conclusion, it falleth out as

I said before, that sailing farther on, we go at length so far, that we do not so much as once behold the sweet harbour of quiet and peace from whence we first set forth. Sometime also my sorrow is increased, by remembering the lives of certain notable men, who with their whole soul did utterly forsake and abandon this wicked world : whose high perfection when I behold, I cannot also but see mine own infirmities and imperfection : very many of whom did, in a contemplative and retired kind of life, much please God : and lest by dealing with transitory business they might have decayed in virtue, God's goodness vouchsafed to free them from the troubles and affairs of this wretched world. But that which I have now said will be far more plain, and the better perceived, if the residue of my speech be dialogue wise distinguished, by setting down each of our names, you asking what you shall think convenient, and I by answer, giving satisfaction to such questions as you shall demand at my hands."

Peter. I do not remember any in Italy, that have been very famous for virtue ; and therefore ignorant I am who they be, that, comparing your life to theirs, you should be so much inflamed to imitate their steps ; for although I make no doubt but that there have been many good men, yet do I verily think that none of them wrought any miracles, or at least they have been hitherto so buried in silence that, whether any such thing hath been done or no, not any one man can tell.

Gregory. If I should, Peter, but report only those things which myself alone have understood by the relation of virtuous and credible persons, or else learned by myself, concerning the life and miracles of perfect and holy men, I should sooner in mine opinion lack day to talk in, than matter to speak of.

Peter. Desirous I am that you would vouchsafe to make me partaker of some of them : and not to think much, if, upon so good an occasion, you interrupt your other study of interpreting the scripture, because no less edification doth grow by the relation of miracles. For as by the exposition of that, we learn how virtue is to be found and kept : so by recounting the miracles of holy men, we know how that which is found out and possessed, is declared and made manifest to the world. And some there are that be sooner moved to the love of God by virtuous examples than by godly sermons : and often-times, by the lives of holy fathers, the heart doth reap a double commodity ; for if, by comparing of his own life with theirs, he findeth himself inflamed with the love of heaven, although before he had haply a good opinion of himself, yet seeing now how far others do excel him, he becometh also more humble, and is brought to have a more lowly conceit of his own actions and virtue.

Gregory. Such things as venerable and holy men have told me, I will now, without any further delay, make you partaker of, and that following the example of sacred scripture : for sure I am that St. Luke and St. Mark learned that gospel which they wrote, not by sight but by the relation of others : yet lest any in reading should have occasion to doubt whether such things as I write be true or no, I will set down by what means and of whom I have learned them : yet in some of them you have to know that I remember not all the particulars, but only the matter : in other some, both the matter and also the words. And besides, if I should have been so curious as to have kept in mind each man's particular words, many, uttered after the country manner, would have made the style of my discourse nothing handsome nor seemly. That story which I mean first to begin with, I had by the report of passing reverent men and of great years.

Chapter One: of Honoratus, Abbot of the Monastery of Funda. ¶ In times past one Ven-antius, a noble man, had a living in the country of

5

Justus of Ghent

ST. GREGORY THE GREAT
(Barberini Palace, Rome)

Anderson

Samnium; the farmer whereof had a son called
Honoratus, who from his very childhood by the virtue
of abstinence did thirst after the joys of heaven : and
as in other things he led an holy life, and refrained from
all idle talk, so did he much, as I said before, subdue
his body by means of abstinence. His parents, upon a
certain day, had invited their neighbours to a banquet
which consisted altogether of flesh, whereof because
for the love of mortification he refused to eat, his father
and mother began to laugh at him, willing him to fall
to that which they had : " For can we," quoth they,
" get you any fish here in these mountains ? " (for in
that place they used sometimes to hear of fish, but sel-
dom to see any.) But whiles they were thus jesting, and
mocking at their son, suddenly they lacked water :
whereupon a servant with a wooden bucket (as the
manner is there) went to the well to fetch some : into
which, as he was a drawing, a fish entered in, which upon
his return, together with the water, he poured forth
before them all. And the fish was so great, that it
served Honoratus very well for all that day. At this
strange chance all were stroken in admiration, and his
parents abstained now from further scoffing at his virtue,
and began to have him in reverence for his abstinence,
whom before for that very cause they did mock and
scorn : and by this means, the fish, brought miraculously from the well, discharged God's servant from
that shame, which he had endured through their uncivil
jesting. Honoratus, proceeding forward in virtue, at
length was made free by the foresaid Lord Venantius :
and afterward, in that place which is called Funda, he
built an Abbey, wherein he was the father almost of
two hundred monks : and he lived in so great holiness
that he gave good example to all the country round
about. Upon a certain day, it fell so out, that a stone
of an huge greatness, which was digged out of the

mountain that hung over the top of his Abbey, tumbled
down by the side of the hill, threatening both the ruin
of the house and the death of all the monks within
which danger the holy man seeing ready to come upon
them, called often upon the name of Christ, and, putting
forth his right hand, made against it the sign of the
cross, and by that means did he stay it, and pin it fast
to the side of that steep hill : which thing Lawrence, a
religious man, affirmed to be most true.   And because
it found not there any place upon which it might rest,
it hangeth at this time in such sort, that all which now
look upon it do verily think that it would continually
fall.

Peter. I suppose so notable a man as he was, and who
afterward became master to so many scholars, had himself some excellent teacher of whom he was instructed.

Gregory. I never heard that he was scholar to any :
but the grace of the Holy Ghost is not tied to any law.
The usual custom of virtuous men is, that none should
take upon him to rule, who first hath not learned to obey :
nor to command that obedience to his subjects, which
before he hath not given to his own superiors.   Yet
some there be which are so inwardly taught by the
doctrine of God's holy spirit, that although they have
no man to instruct them outwardly, yet do they not
want the direction of an inward teacher : which liberty
of life notwithstanding is not to be taken for an example
by such as be weak and infirm, lest, whiles each one
doth in like manner presume to be full of the Holy
Ghost, and contemn to learn of any, they become themselves erroneous masters. But that soul which is full of
God's holy spirit, hath for proof thereof most evident
signs, to wit, the other virtues, and especially humility,
both which if they do perfectly meet in one soul,
apparent it is that they be testimonies of the presence
of heavenly grace.   And so we read not that John Baptist

had any master, nor yet that Christ, who by his corporal presence taught his Apostles, took him in amongst the number of his other disciples, but vouchsafed to instruct him inwardly, and left him, as it were, in the sight of the world to his own liberty. So Moses, likewise, was taught in the wilderness, and learned by the Angel what God gave him in charge, which by means of any mortal man he knew not : but these things, as before hath been said, are of weaklings to be reverenced, and not by any means to be followed.

Peter. I like very well of your opinion : yet I beseech you to tell me, whether so notable a father as he was, left not some scholar behind him, that did imitate his master's steps.

Chapter Two : of Libertinus, Prior of the same Abbey. ¶ Gregory.

The reverent man, Libertinus, who, in the time of Totilas, king of the Goths, was Prior of the same Abbey of Funda, was brought up and taught by him : of whom, albeit the certain report of passing many hath made his sundry virtues known to the world, yet the foresaid religious man, Lawrence, who still liveth and that time had very familiar acquaintance with him, hath often told me many things, whereof some few, which now come to my mind, I will here set down. In the same province of Samnium, as Libertinus was in his journey about business of the Abbey, it so fell out that Darida, captain of the Goths, with his army, met him, by whose soldiers the man of God was thrown from his horse ; which injury he taking very patiently, offered them also his whip, saying : "Take this, that you may make him the better to go"; and having said so, he betook himself to his prayers. The army marched on very fast, and quickly came to the river called Vulturnus, where they began to beat their horses both with their lances and also to spur them, till the blood came, and all this to

9

The Dialogues of St. Gregory

make them take the water ; but yet no beating nor
spurring could enforce them forward : for they were as
much afraid to enter the river as though it had been
some deep downfall. At length, when they were all
wearied with beating, one amongst the rest said, that
the reason why they were thus punished was for taking
away the horse from God's servant : whereupon
returning straightways back, they found Libertinus
prostrate at his prayers ; and calling upon him to rise
and take his horse, he bade them go on a God's name,
saying that he needed him not ; but for all that they
alighted and set him perforce upon his own beast, and
so in all haste departed, and returning back to the
river they passed over so quickly as though in the
channel there had been no water at all ; and so it fell
out that God's servant having restitution made him of
his one horse, that all the soldiers came likewise to
enjoy the use of their own.

At the same time one Buccellinus entered Campania
with an army of French men, and because it was commonly said that the Abbey in which the holy man lived
had great store of money, the French men, very greedy
of so good a booty, came thither, and with raging minds
went into his oratory (where he lay prostrate at his
prayers) seeking and crying out for Libertinus ; and a
strange thing it was, for though they came in, and
stumbled upon him, yet could they not see him, and
so, deceived through their own blindness, away they
departed as empty as they came.

At another time likewise upon business of the monastery, at the commandment of the Abbot who succeeded
his master Honoratus, he took his journey to Ravenna.
And for the great love which he bare to venerable
Honoratus, always did he bear about him in his bosom
one of his stockings. Being in his way it fell so out
that a certain woman was carrying the corpse of her

10

dead son; who no sooner saw the servant of God, but, for the love of her child, she laid hold upon his bridle, protesting with a solemn oath that he should not depart, before he had raised up her dead son. The holy man, not acquainted with so strange a miracle, was much afraid to hear her make such a request, and willing to have got away, yet seeing no means how to effect his desire, greatly did he doubt what was best to be done. Here it is worth the noting to consider what a conflict he had in his soul: humility and the mother's piety striving together : fear to presume upon so un-usual a miracle, and grief not to help the desolate mother. At length, to the greater glory of God, piety and compassion overcame that virtuous soul, which therefore may truly be called invincible, because it did yield and was conquered ; for a virtuous soul it had not been, if piety and compassion had not overcome it · wherefore, lighting from his horse, he fell upon his knees, lift up his hands to heaven, drew the stocking out of his bosom, laid it upon the breast of the dead corpse ; and behold, whiles he was at his prayers, the soul of the child returned into the body, which he perceiving, took it by the hand and delivered it alive to his sorrowful mother, and so went on the rest of his journey.

Peter. What is to be said in this case ? For was it the merit of Honoratus, or the prayers of Libertinus, that wrought this miracle ?

Gregory. In the working of so notable a miracle, to-gether with the faith of the woman, the virtue of both did concur ; and therefore, in mine opinion, Libertinus had power to raise up that dead child, because he had learned to trust more upon the virtue of his master than his own : for when he laid his stocking upon the child's breast, no doubt but he thought that his soul did obtain that for which he did then pray. For we read the like of Heliseus, who carrying his master's cloak, and coming to the river of Jordan, stroke the waters once, and yet divided them not ; but when straight after he said, *Where is now the God of Helias?* and then stroke the river with the same cloak, he made a way open for himself to pass through.[1] Whereby you perceive, Peter, how much humility availeth for the working of miracles, for then the merit of the master had force to do that which he desired, when he called upon his name ; and when with humility he did submit himself to his master, he wrought the same miracle which his master had done before him.

Peter. I am well pleased with your answer : but is there, I pray you, anything else of him yet remaining, which may serve for our edification ?

Gregory. Surely there is, if there be yet any that list to imitate so notable an example : for I make no doubt, but that the patience of so worthy a man did far excel all his signs and miracles, as you shall now hear. Upon a certain day, the Abbot, who succeeded Honoratus, fell so pitifully out with venerable Libertinus, that he stroke him with his fists : and because he could find never a staff, up he took a footstool, and with that did so strike his head and his face, that they both swelled and became black and blue. Being thus unreasonably beaten, without giving any words, he went quietly to bed. The next day, he was to go forth about business of the Abbey, and therefore, when matins were ended, he came to his Abbot's bedside, and humbly demanded of him leave. The Abbot, knowing how greatly all did honour and love him, supposed that he would for the former injury have forsaken the Abbey : and therefore he asked him, whither he meant to go : to whom he answered : "Father," quoth he, "there is a certain matter concerning the Abbey to be handled, where I must needs

---

[1] 4 Kings 2.

12

be, for yesterday I promised to come, and therefore I am determined to travel thither." Then the Abbot, considering from the bottom of his heart his own austerity and hard dealing, and the humility and meekness of Libertinus, suddenly leapt out of his bed, gat hold of his feet, confessed that he had sinned and done wickedly, in presuming to offer unto so good and worthy a man so cruel and contumelious an injury. Libertinus, on the contrary, prostrate upon the earth, fell down at his feet, attributing all that he had suffered, not to any cruelty of his, but to his own sins and demerits. And by this means, the Abbot was brought to great meekness; and the humility of the scholar became a teacher to the master. Going afterward abroad about the foresaid business of the Abbey, many gentlemen of his acquaintance, that had him in great reverence, much marvelled, and diligently enquired by what means he came by such a swollen and black face: to whom he answered: "Yesterday," quoth he, "at evening, for punishment of my sins, I met with a footstool, and gat this blow which ye see." And thus the holy man, preserving both truth in his soul and the honour of his master, did neither bewray the fault of his father, nor yet incurred the sin of lying.

Peter. Had not so venerable a man as this Libertinus was, of whom you have told so many miracles and strange things, in so great a convent, some that did imitate his holy life and virtues?

Chapter Three: of a certain monk, that was gardener to the same Abbey. ¶ Gregory. Felix,

called also Corvus, one whom you know very well, and who not long since was Prior of the same Abbey, told me divers very strange things, some of which I will pass over with silence, because I hasten to other, but one there is which by no means I can omit. This it was.

13

In the same Abbey there lived a certain monk, very virtuous, who was the gardener. A thief likewise there was, that used to climb over the hedge, and so to steal away the worts. The holy man, seeing that he did set many which afterward he could not find, and perceiving that some were trodden down, and other stolen away, walked round about the garden to find the place where the thief came in, which when he had found, by chance also as he was there, he lighted upon a snake, which he willed to follow him, and bringing him to the place where the thief entered, gave him this charge :_" In the name of Jesus," quoth he, " I command thee to keep this passage, and not to suffer any thief to come in." Whereupon the snake forthwith, obeying his commandment, laid itself across in the way, and the monk returned to his cell. Afterward in the heat of the day, when all the monks were at rest, the thief, according to his custom, came thither, and as he was climbing over the hedge and had put one leg on the other side, suddenly he saw the snake, which stopped the way, and for fear falling backward, he left his foot hanging there by the shoe upon a stake, and so he hung with his head downward, until the return of the gardener ; who, coming at his usual hour, found the thief hanging there in the hedge, whom when he saw, he spake thus to the snake : " God be thanked, thou hast done what I bade thee, and therefore now go thy way " : upon which licence, the snake by and by departed. Then, coming to the thief, he spake thus unto him · " What meaneth this, good brother ? God hath delivered you, as you see, into mine hands : why have you been so bold as so often to rob away the labour of the monks ?" and speaking thus, he loosed his foot, without doing him any harm, willing him also to follow him ; who brought him to the garden gate, and gave him those worts which he desired to have stolen, speaking also to him in sweet manner after this sort: "Go your way, and steal no more; but when you have need, come hither to me, and what sinfully you would take, that will I willingly bestow upon you for God's sake."

Peter. I have hitherto, as I now perceive, lived in an error: for never did I think that there had been any holy men in Italy, which had wrought miracles.

Chapter Four: of Equitius, Abbot in the Province of Valeria. ¶ Gregory.

By the relation of venerable Fortunatus, Abbot of the Monastery which is called Cicero's Bath, and also of other reverent men, I have come to the knowledge of that which now I mean to tell you. There was a passing holy man called Equitius, dwelling in the province of Valeria, who, for his virtuous life, was in great admiration with all men, with whom Fortunatus was familiarly acquainted. This Equitius, by reason of his great holiness of life, was the father and governor of many Abbeys in that province. In his younger years, many and sore carnal temptations he endured, which made him more fervent and diligent in prayers, and to persevere continually in that holy exercise, which he did, craving most instantly of God to afford him some remedy. Living in that manner, it fell so out, that in vision, upon a certain night, he saw an Angel come unto him, who made him an eunuch, and so delivered him from all those carnal motions in such sort that never after he felt any more, as though he had not been any man at all. Trusting now upon this great grace received by the special goodness of God, as before he was a governor of men, so afterward he took charge likewise of women, and yet, for all that, did he continually admonish his scholars not easily to credit themselves herein, nor to follow his example, nor yet to trust upon that gift, which they had not in themselves, lest it turned to their own ruin and destruction.

At such time as divers witches were here in this city of Rome apprehended, one Basilius, that was a principal man in that wicked art, put upon him the habit of a monk, and so fled away to Valeria ; and coming to the reverent Bishop of the city of Amirtin, he desired his help, that he would, for the good of his soul, commend him to Abbot Equitius. The Bishop went with him to the Abbey, where he made suit to the servant of God, that he would vouchsafe to receive into his convent that monk which he brought, whom so soon as the holy man beheld, he said to the Bishop : "This man, good brother," quoth he, "whom you commend unto me, seemeth in mine eyes to be a devil, and not any monk" ; whereunto the Bishop replied and said, that he sought excuses not to grant his petition. "Not so," quoth the servant of God, "but I do denounce him to be such a one as I see him, and because you shall not think that I will be disobedient, what you command I will perform." Whereupon he was received into the Abbey. Not many days after, God's servant travelled far off to preach unto the people in the country ; after whose departure it fell out that, in the monastery of virgins which was under his charge, one of them, which in respect of her corruptible carcase seemed beautiful, fell into an ague, to be afflicted with sore fits, and not so much to speak as pitifully to cry out in this manner : "I shall die forthwith, unless Basilius come unto me, and by his skill in physic restore me to my health." But, in the absence of their father, none of the monks durst presume to enter into the monastery of virgins, much less was he permitted, that was yet but a novice, and whose life and conversation was not known to the rest of the brethren. A messenger, therefore, with all speed was dispatched to the servant of God, Equitius, to let him understand how such a Nun was fallen into a terrible burning ague, and how she did earnestly

Pintoricchio

THE MADONNA IN GLORY WITH ST. GREGORY AND ST. BENEDICT
(San Gimignano)

desire to be visited of Basilius : which news so soon as the holy man did hear, in an anger he smiled, and said : "Did I not say beforehand that this companion was a devil and not a monk ? Go your ways, and turn him out of the Abbey ; and as for the virgin that is so sick of a fever, take no further care, for hereafter it shall not trouble her any more, nor she make any further inquisition after Basilius." The monk that was the messenger returning back, understood that the Nun was at that very hour restored to her health, in which the servant of God, Equitius, far distant, affirmed that she should : no question but by special miracle, like to the example of our Saviour, who, being desired to visit the son of a lord, did by his only word restore him to his health, so that the father at his return knew his son to be restored to life at that very hour in which he heard so much from the mouth of truth itself.[1] The monks, putting their father's commandment in execution, turned Basilius out of the Abbey, who being so expulsed did often say, that he had by his incantations hanged Equitius his cell in the air, and yet that he could not hurt any of his monks. This wretch not long after, in this city of Rome, through the zeal of good people, for his wickedness was burnt, and so ended his life.

Upon a certain day, one of the Nuns of the same monastery, going into the garden, saw a lettice that liked her, and forgetting to bless it before with the sign of the cross, greedily did she eat it : whereupon she was suddenly possessed with the devil, fell down to the ground, and was pitifully tormented. Word in all haste was carried to Equitius, desiring him quickly to visit the afflicted woman, and to help her with his prayers : who so soon as he came into the garden, the devil that was entered began by her tongue, as it were, to excuse himself, saying : "What have I done ? What have I done ?

[1] John 4, 53.

I was sitting there upon the lettice, and she came and did eat me." But the man of God in great zeal commanded him to depart, and not to tarry any longer in the servant of almighty God, who straightways went out, not presuming any more to touch her.

A certain noble man likewise called Felix, of the province of Nursia, father to Castorius, who now dwelleth here with us in Rome, understanding that Equitius had not received holy orders, and yet that he did visit many places and preach unto divers, upon a day very boldly went and asked him, how he durst presume to preach, not having received holy orders, nor yet licence of the Bishop of Rome, under whom he did live ; upon which demand, the holy man, being thus compelled, gave him to understand by what means he had obtained licence to preach : speaking thus unto him : " What you say unto me, myself have seriously thought upon ; but, on a certain night, a young man in vision stode by me, and touched my tongue with such an instrument as they use in letting of blood, saying : ' Behold, I have put my word into thy mouth, go thy way and preach.' And since that day, though I would, I can not but talk of God."

Peter. Desirous I am to know, what manner of life he led, who is said to have received such gifts at God's hand.

Gregory. The work, Peter, proceedeth of the gift, and not the gift from the work, otherwise grace were not grace : for God's gifts do go before all works of ours, although the gifts by the works which follow do increase ; but to the end that you may understand what lite he led, which was known to the reverent man Albinus, Bishop of Reatino ; and many there be yet alive, which might very well remember the same. But what do you seek for further works, when as his purity of life was answerable to his diligence in preaching ? for

18

such a zeal to save souls had inflamed his heart, that albeit he had the charge of many monasteries, yet did he diligently travel up and down, and visit churches, towns, villages, and particular men's houses, and all this to stir up the hearts of his auditors to the love of heavenly joys. The apparel which he ware was so base and contemptible, that such as knew him not would have thought scorn so much as to have saluted him, though himself had first offered that courtesy. And whithersoever he went, his manner was to ride, but that upon the most forlorn beast which could be found ; his bridle was but an halter, his saddle no better than plain sheep's skins. His books of divinity were put into leather bags, and those he did carry himself, some hanging on the right side of his horse, and some upon the left : and to what place soever he came, he did so open the fountains of sacred scripture, that he watered their souls with the heavenly dew of his sermons. Whose grace in preaching was so great, that the fame thereof came even to Rome itself : and as the tongues of flatterers do with their glorious words kill the souls of such as give them the hearing, at the same time some of the Roman clergy did in flattering sort complain unto the Bishop of this Apostolic see, saying : "What manner of rustical companion is this, that hath taken upon him authority to preach, and, being without learning, presumeth to usurp unto himself the office of our Apostolical Lord ? wherefore, if it please you, let him be sent for before your presence, that he may taste of the severity of ecclesiastical discipline." And as it falleth out, that he which hath much business is overcome sometime by flattery, if that pleasing venom be not speedily dispatched from the soul, at the persuasion of his clergy the Pope gave his consent that he should be sent for to Rome, to understand what talent and gift he had received from God. And so one Julianus, who afterward was made Bishop of Sabinum, was sent,

having yet commandment given him to bring him up
with great honour, to the end that the servant of God
might not thereby sustain any injury or detriment in his
fame : who, to gratify the Pope's clergy, went in post to
the Abbey, and finding there in his absence certain anti-
quaries writing, demanded of them for the Abbot ; who
told him that he was in the valley at the bottom of the
Abbey, mowing of hay. Julianus had a man very proud
and stubborn, and such a one that he could scarce rule
him. This man he sent in all haste for the Abbot ; who
in an angry mood went his way, and coming quickly into
the meadow where beholding all that were there cutting
of grass, he demanded which of them was Equitius ; and
when they shewed him where he was, being yet far off,
he fell into a great fear, and became therewith so faint,
that he could scarce go upon his legs : trembling in
that manner he came to the man of God, and humbly
bowing down his head, he embraced his knees and kissed
them, telling him that his master was desirous to speak
with him. After God's servant had saluted him again,
he willed him to take up some of the grass, and to carry
it home for their horse, "and I will," quoth he, "straightways come, when I have dispatched this little work
which remaineth."

In this meantime, Julianus much marvelled what the
matter was, why his man tarried so long, and seeing him
at length to come laden with grass upon his neck, in great
rage he cried out to him, saying : "Sirrah, what meaneth
this ? I sent you to fetch me the Abbot, and not to
bring meat for mine horse." "Sir," quoth his man, "he
will come to you by and by": and forthwith the man
of God came in base apparel and a pair of shoes beaten
full of nails, carrying his scythe upon his neck ; and
being yet far off, his man told him that he was the Abbot.
So soon as Julianus beheld him attired in that base sort,
he contemned him, and devised with himself how to

speak unto him in the most cross and crooked manner he could. But when God's servant drew nigh, such an intolerable fear came upon Julianus, that he fell a trembling, and his tongue so faltered, that he could scarce deliver the message for which he came : whereupon he fell down at his feet, and desired that he would vouchsafe to pray for him ; and withal gave him to understand, that his Apostolical father the Pope was desirous to see him. Upon the receipt of which news the venerable man, Equitius, gave almighty God most hearty thanks, saying that heavenly grace had visited him by means of the highest Bishop ; and straightways he called for some of his monks, commanding horse to be made ready in all haste : but Julianus, weary of his journey, told him that he could not travel so soon, but of necessity must rest himself that night. "I am very sorry for that," quoth the holy man, "for if we go not to-day, to-morrow we shall not" : and thus, by reason of the other's weariness, he was enforced that night to remain in the Abbey. The next morning, about the dawning of the day, came a post with a tired horse, bringing letters to Julianus, commanding him not to presume to molest or to draw the servant of God out of his monastery. And when he required the reason of this counter-command, the messenger told him that, the next night after his departure, the Pope was terribly frighted in a vision, for presuming to send for the man of God : whereupon Julianus, rising suddenly out of his bed, and commending himself to the venerable man's prayers, spake thus unto him : "Our father desireth you not to trouble yourself any further, but to stay in your monastery" : which when God's servant heard, very sorry he was, and said : "Did not I tell you, that if we did not set forward on our journey by and by, that afterward we should not ?" Then upon charity he entertained his messenger a little while with him in his Cloister, and though by all means he refused, yet he enforced upon him a reward for the pains he had taken. See therefore, Peter, how God doth preserve and keep them, who in this life do contemn themselves, and how they are secretly honoured of the citizens in heaven, who are not ashamed outwardly to be little esteemed in this world ; and on the contrary, in the sight of God they be of no account, who in the eyes of their own friends and neighbours do swell through desire of vain glory. And therefore our Saviour Christ, who was truth itself, said to certain : *You are they that justify yourselves before men, but God knoweth your hearts, for that which is high to men is abominable in the sight of God.*[1]

Peter. I marvel very much how so great a Bishop could be deceived in so worthy a man.

Gregory. Why do you marvel, Peter ? for the reason why we are deceived is, because we be men. What ? have you forgotten how David, who usually had the spirit of prophecy, pronounced sentence against innocent Mephibosheth, the son of Jonathan, when he gave credit to the lying words of his servant Siba ?[2] which thing notwithstanding because it was done by David, we both believe to be just in the secret judgment of God, and yet by human reason how it was just we cannot perceive. What marvel then is it, if we, that be not prophets, be sometimes by lying tongues abused, and otherwise transported than charity and justice would : for it is much to be considered, that every Bishop hath his mind troubled with a world of business, and it cannot be, when the mind is distracted about many things, but that it is the less able sufficiently to examine those that be particular, and so much the sooner is he deceived in some special case, by how much he is busied with the multitude of many.

Peter. It is most true that you say.

Gregory. But I must not pass over with silence that which the reverent man Valentinus, some time mine

[1] Luke 16, 15. [2] 2 Kings, 16 and 19.

22

Abbot, told me concerning Equitius. For he said, that his body being buried in the oratory of St. Lawrence the martyr, a certain country man set upon his grave a chest full of wheat, little considering or respecting how worthy and notable a man lay there buried. Whereupon suddenly a miraculous whirlwind came, and overthrew that chest and cast it far off, all other things remaining still in their former places ; by which all did plainly perceive of what worth and merit that man was, whose body lay there buried.

To this must I also add another thing, which I heard of venerable Fortunatus, a man that doth much please me for his years, life, and simplicity. At such time as the Lombards came into the province of Valeria, the monks of the monastery of the reverent man Equitius fled from thence into the oratory, to the holy man's sepulchre, into which place the cruel men entering, they began by violence to pull the monks forth, either to torment them, or else with their swords to kill them. Amongst whom one sighed, and for very bitter grief cried out : "Alas, alas, holy Equitius, is it thy pleasure, and art thou content, that we should be thus miserably haled and violently drawn forth, and dost not thou vouchsafe to defend us ?" Which words were no sooner spoken, but a wicked spirit possessed those savage soldiers in such sort that, falling down upon the ground, they were there so long tormented, until all the rest of the Lombards which were without understood of the matter, to the end that none should be so hardy as to presume to violate that holy place. And thus, as the holy man at that time defended his own monks, so did he likewise afterward succour and preserve many more that fled unto the same place.

Chapter Five: of Constantius, Clerk of the Church of St. Stephen. ¶ That which I intend now to tell you, I learned by the relation of one of my fellow Bishops, who lived in a monk's weed many years in the city of Ancona, and led there a good and religious life. Many also of mine own friends, who be now of good years and live in the same parts, affirm it to be most true. Near to the foresaid city of Ancona there is a church of the blessed martyr St. Stephen, in which one called Constantius, a man of venerable life, did serve there for clerk, who for his virtue and holiness was famous far and near, being one that utterly despised all worldly things, and with the whole power of his soul thirsted after the joys of heaven. Upon a certain day, it fell so out that there wanted oil in the church, by reason whereof the foresaid servant of God had not wherewith to light the lamps : whereupon he filled them all with water, and, as the manner is, put a piece of paper in the midst, and then set them on fire, and the water did so burn in the lamps as though it had been very oil ; by which you may gather, Peter, of what merit this man was, who, enforced by necessity, did change the nature of the element.

Peter. Very strange it is that you say, but desirous I am to know what humility he had inwardly in his soul, who outwardly was so wonderful in the eyes of the world.

Gregory. Among miracles very fitly do you enquire the inward state of the mind ; for it is almost incredible how miracles, wrought in the sight of men, do with their temptation inwardly assault the soul. But after you have heard only one thing, which this venerable Constantius did, you will quickly perceive what an humble man he was.

Peter. Having now told me one of his miracles, it remaineth that you do edify me also with the humility of his soul.

Gregory. Because the report of his holy life was very much spread abroad, many from divers countries travelled

to Ancona, being very desirous to see him ; and amongst
others a certain country fellow was come far off, for that
very purpose : at which time it so chanced that the holy
man was standing upon a pair of wooden stairs, busying
himself there in mending of lamps.   A very little person
he was of stature, with a thin face, and to the outward
view contemptible.   This fellow that came to see him
enquired earnestly which was the man for whose sake he
had travelled so long a journey.   Those that knew him
forthwith told him, pointing to Constantius.   But as
foolish souls do measure the merits of men by the quality
of their bodies, so he, beholding him so little and contemptible, by no means could be persuaded that they
told him truth ; for in the country fellow's mind there
fell out, as it were, a great contention betwixt that which
he had heard, and that which he saw ; and he verily persuaded himself that he could not be so little in his eyes,
who was so great in his former conceit ; and therefore,
when very many did constantly affirm that he was the
man, the simple soul despised him, and in scoffing manner
said · " I verily believed that he had been a goodly great
man, but this fellow hath not any thing at all in him
that is like a man."   Which words of his the servant of
God, Constantius, hearing, forthwith left his lamps which
he was in hand with, and in great haste came merrily
down the stairs, embraced the country clown, and of
exceeding love held him fast in his arms, kissed him,
gave him great thanks for having that opinion, and spake
thus unto him : " Thou only," quoth he, " hast thine
eyes open, and dost truly behold what I am."   By which
fact we may easily gather what an humble man he was,
that loved the country fellow the more for contemning
him ; for injurious words and contumelious usage try
what a man is inwardly in his soul : for as proud men
are glad of honour, so those that be humble for the most
part rejoice in contempt and disgrace, and when they

behold themselves to be of no account in the opinion of others, glad they are, because they see that to be confirmed by the judgment of others which inwardly in their own souls they had of themselves.

Peter. This man, as I perceive, was outwardly great in miracles, but yet greater by his inward humility of soul.

Chapter Six: of Marcellinus, Bishop of Ancona.

¶ Gregory. Marcellinus, also a man of holy life, was Bishop of the same city of Ancona ; who was so sore troubled with the gout, that being not able to go, his servants were enforced to carry him in their hands. Upon a day, by negligence, the city was set on fire, and though many laboured by throwing on of water to quench it, yet did it so increase and go forward that the whole city was in great danger ; for it had laid hold of all the houses that were next it, and consumed already a great part of the town, none being able to help or withstand it. In so pitiful a necessity and great danger, the Bishop, carried by his servants, came thither, and commanded himself to be set down right against those furious flames, and in that very place whither the force of the fire did seem most to bend : which being done, the fire marvellous strangely turned back into itself, and as it were cried out, that it could not pass the Bishop ; and by this means was it stopped from going forward, [and] went out of itself, not being able to touch any other buildings. By which, Peter, you see what an argument of great holiness it was, for a sick man to sit still, and by his prayers to quench those raging flames.

Peter. I do both see it and much wonder at so notable a miracle.

Chapter Seven: of Nonnosus, Prior of the Abbey in Mount Soracte. ¶ Gregory. Now I intend to let

you understand somewhat of a place not far distant, which I heard of the reverent Bishop Maximianus, and of the old monk Laurio, one whom you know : both which are yet living ; and as for Laurio, he was brought up under that holy man Anastasius, in the Abbey which is hard by the city of Nepi ; and Anastasius, both by reason of the nearness of the place, equal love of virtue, and like profession of life, was daily in the company of holy Nonnosus, Prior of the Abbey which is in mount Soracte. This Nonnosus had for his Abbot a very sharp man, whose rough conditions notwithstanding he did always bear with wonderful patience, and did in such sweet sort govern the monks, that oftentimes by his humility he appeased the Abbot's anger. The Abbey, standing in the top of an hill, had never an even and plain place fit for a garden ; one only little plot of ground there was, in the side of the mountain, but that was taken up of a great stone which did naturally grow there, so that by no means it could serve for a garden. Yet venerable Nonnosus, upon a day, began to think with himself that at least that piece of ground would serve very well to set worts, if by any means that huge stone could be taken away ; but then he likewise thought that five hundred yoke of oxen would not be able to stir it ; whereupon, despairing of all human help, he betook himself to God's goodness, and in that very place gave himself to prayer in the quiet time of the night, and behold, on the morning, when the monks came thither, they found that huge stone removed far off, and a very fit plot of ground left to make them a garden.

At another time, the same holy man being washing of lamps made of glass, one of them by chance fell out of his hands, and brake into many pieces ; who, fearing the great fury of the Abbot, did forthwith gather up all the fragments, laid them before the altar, and therewith great sighing fell to his prayers ; and afterward, lifting up his head, he found the lamp entire and whole. And thus, in these two miracles, did he imitate two notable fathers, to wit, Gregory and Donatus ; the first of which removed a mountain, and the other made a broken chalice safe and sound.

Peter. We have, as I perceive now, miracles after the imitation of old saints.

Gregory. How say you ? are you content also in the conversation of Nonnosus, to hear how he did imitate the fact of the prophet Heliseus ?

Peter. Content I am, and most earnestly desire it.

Gregory. Upon a certain day, when the old oil was spent, and the time to gather olives was now at hand, the Abbot, because their own trees took not, thought it best to send the monks abroad to help strangers in the gathering of theirs, that for the recompense of their labour they might bring home some oil for the necessities of their own house. This determination the man of God, Nonnosus, in great humility did hinder, lest the monks, going abroad from their cloister to get oil, might lose somewhat in the devotion of their souls. And therefore, because he saw that their own trees had yet a few olives, he willed those to be gathered and put into the press, and that oil which came forth to be brought unto him, though it were never so little ; which being done, he set the little vessel before the altar, and after their departure he offered his prayers to God, which being ended, he called for the monks, commanding them to take away the oil which they brought, and to pour a little thereof into all the vessels which they had, that each of them might have some of the benediction of that oil : which being done, he caused the vessels, empty as they were, to be close stopped, and the next day they found them all full.

Peter. We find daily the words of our Saviour to be verified, who saith : *My Father even to this time doth work, and I do work.*[1]

[1] John 5, 17.

Chapter Eight: of Anastasius, Abbot of the Monastery called Suppentonia. ¶ Gregory.

At the same time the reverent man Anastasius, of whom I spake before, was notary to the church of Rome, whereof by God's providence I have now the charge ; who desirous only to serve God, gave over his office, and made choice of a monastical life : and in that Abbey which is called Suppentonia, he lived many years virtuously, and governed that place with great care and diligence. Over the Abbey there hangeth an huge rock, and beneath it there is a steep downfall. Upon a certain night, when God had determined to reward the labours of venerable Anastasius, a voice was heard from the top of that rock, which very leisurely did cry out : " Come away, Anastasius " ; who being so called, straight after, seven other monks were severally called by their names. And then the voice stayed for a little time, and then called again the eighth monk. Which strange voice the Convent hearing very plainly, made no doubt but that the death of them that were so called was not far off ; wherefore not many days after, before the rest, Anastasius himself, and then the others in order, departed this mortal life, as they were before called from the top of the rock. And that monk who was called after some pausing did a little while survive the rest, and then he also ended his life : whereby it was plain that the staying of the voice did signify that he should live a little longer than the other. But a strange thing happened, for when holy Anastasius lay upon his death-bed, a certain monk there was in the Abbey, that would needs die with him, and therefore fell down at his feet, and there began with tears to beg of him in this manner : " For his love to whom you are now going, I beseech and adjure you, that I may not remain in this world seven days after your departure "; and indeed it so fell out, that before the seventh day was come, that he left this mortal life, and yet was not he that night named by that voice amongst the rest, so that it appeareth plainly that it was only the intercession of Anastasius which obtained that his departure.

Peter. Seeing that monk was not called amongst the other, and yet by the intercession of that holy man was taken out of this life : what other thing can we gather hereof, but that such as be of great merit, and in favour with God, can sometime obtain those things which be not predestinate ?

Gregory. Such things as be not predestinate by God, cannot by any means be obtained at his hands ; but those things which holy men do by their prayers effect, were from all eternity predestinate to be obtained by prayers. For very predestination itself to life everlasting, is so by almighty God disposed, that God's elect servants do through their labour come unto it, in that by their prayers they do merit to receive that which almighty God determined before all worlds to bestow upon them.

Peter. Desirous I am to have this point more plainly proved : to wit, that predestination may by prayers be holpen.

Gregory. That which I inferred, Peter, may quickly be proved ; for ignorant you are not that our Lord said to Abraham : *In Isaac shall seed be called to thee ;*[1] to whom also he said : *I have appointed thee to be a father of many nations ;*[2] and again he promised him, saying : *I will bless thee, and multiply thy seed as the stars of the heaven, and as the sand of the sea.*[3] Out of which place it is plain that almighty God had predestinate to multiply the seed of Abraham by Isaac, and yet the scripture saith : *Isaac did pray unto our Lord for his wife because she was barren, who did hear him, and Rebecca conceived.*[1] If, then, the increase of Abraham's posterity was predestinate by Isaac, how came it to pass that his wife was barren ? by which most

[1] Gen. 21, 12.   [2] Gen. 27, 29.
[3] Gen. 22, 17.   [4] Gen. 25, 21.

certain it is, that predestination is fulfilled by prayers, when as we see that he by whom God had predestinate to increase Abraham's seed obtained by prayer to have children.

Peter. Seeing reason hath made that plain, which before I knew not, I have not herein any further doubt.

Gregory. Shall I now tell you somewhat of such holy men as have been in Tuscania; that you may be informed what notable persons have flourished in those parts, and how greatly they were in the favour of almighty God?

Peter. Willing I am to give you the hearing; and therefore beseech you to proceed forward.

Chapter Nine: of Bonifacius, Bishop of Ferenti. ¶ Gregory. A man of holy life there was, called Bonifacius, Bishop of the city of Ferenti, one that with his virtuous conversation did well discharge his duty. Many miracles he did, which Gaudentius the Priest, who yet liveth, doth still report: and seeing he was brought up under him, no question but by reason of that his presence he is able to tell all things the more truly.

His Bishopric was passing poor (a thing which to good men is the preserver of humility), for he had nothing else for his revenues, but only one vineyard, which was also at one time so spoiled with a tempest of hail, that very few grapes did remain. Bonifacius coming in, and seeing what was happened, gave God great thanks, for that he had sent him further poverty to his former necessity. And when the time came that those few grapes which remained were ripe, he appointed one, according to the custom, to keep his vineyard, commanding him carefully to look well unto it. And upon a certain day, he willed Constantius, who both was a Priest and his nephew, to make ready, as before they were wont to do, all the barrels and wine-vessels they had: which thing when his nephew the Priest understood, he marvelled much to hear him command so mad a thing, as to make ready the vessels for wine, himself having no wine at all to put in : yet durst he not enquire the reason why he gave that charge, but did as he commanded, and made all the vessels and other things ready, as before they had always used to do. Then the man of God caused the poor remnant of grapes to be gathered and carried to the wine-press, and dispatching all others away, himself tarried there still with a little boy whom he commanded to tread those grapes, and when he perceived that a little wine began to run forth, the man of God took it, and put it into a little vessel, and poured somewhat thereof into all the other barrels and vessels which were made ready, as it were to bless them with that little quantity : when he had so done, he called straightways for the Priest, commanding him to send for the poor, upon whose coming the wine in the press began to increase and run out so plentifully, that it did fill all the pots and other vessels which they brought. When they were all served, he bade the boy to leave treading, and come down ; then, locking up the storehouse, into which he had put his own vessels, and setting his own seal upon the door, to the church he went, and three days after he called for Constantius, and having said a few prayers, he opened the door, where he found all the vessels into which he had before poured but a very little liquor working so plentifully, that, if he had not then come, they had all run over into the floor. Then he straightly commanded the Priest his kinsman, not to reveal this miracle to any, so long as he lived, fearing lest, by means thereof, the outward opinion of men might through vain glory inwardly have hurt his soul : following therein the example of our master Christ, who, to teach us to walk in the path of humility, commanded his disciples concerning himself, not to tell any what they had seen, until the Son of Man was risen again from death.

Peter. Because fit occasion is now offered, desirous I am to know what the reason was, that when our Saviour restored sight unto two blind men, and commanded them to tell nobody; yet they, after their departure, made him known throughout all that country. For had the only-begotten Son of God, who is co-eternal to his Father and the Holy Ghost, a desire herein to do that which he could not perform: to wit, that the miracle which he would have kept secret, could not yet be concealed?

Gregory. All that which our blessed Saviour wrought in his mortal body, he did it for our example and instruction, to the end that, following his steps, according to our poor ability, we might without offence pass over this present life: and therefore, when he did that miracle, he both commanded them to conceal it, and yet it could not be kept in, and all this to teach his elect servants to follow his doctrine; to wit, that when they do any notable thing whereof glory may arise to themselves, that they should have a desire not to be spoken of, and yet for the good of others, contrary to their own mind, they should be laid open and known: so that it proceed of their great humility to desire that their works may be buried with silence, and yet, for the profit of others, it should fall so out, that they can not be concealed. Wherefore our Lord would not have any thing done which he could not effect: but what his servants ought to desire, and what also, contrary to their minds, was convenient to be done, like a good master he taught us by his own example.

Peter. I am very well satisfied with this your answer.

Gregory. For as much as we have now made mention of Bonifacius, let us prosecute a few more of his acts, not yet spoken of. At another time, upon the feast-day of St. Proculus the martyr, one Fortunatus, a noble man that dwelt in that town, did heartily entreat the Bishop that, after he had done the solemnity of mass, he would vouchsafe to come unto his house, to bless his meat and dine with him. The man of God was content to satisfy his request, so charitably was he invited : and therefore, when mass was done, he went thither : but before the table was yet blessed, suddenly (as some men by such means get their living) one came to the gate with an ape, who began to play upon an instrument, which the holy man hearing, was discontented, and said · "Alas, alas, this wretched man is dead, this wretched man is dead. Behold, I am come hither to dinner, and have not yet opened my lips to praise God, and he is here with his ape, playing upon his instrument." Then he desired them to give him some meat and drink : "Yet I would have you know," quoth he, "that he is a dead man." When the unhappy wretch had filled himself and was going out at the gate, a great stone fell from the house, and brake his head. Of which blow he fell down, and was taken up half dead, and being carried away the next day, as the man of God had before said, he departed this life ; wherein, Peter, we have to consider how holy men are with fear to be reverenced : for they no question be the temples of God, and when an holy man is enforced to anger, who is then moved but he that dwelleth in that temple ? wherefore we have so much the more cause to fear how we provoke such kind of persons to wrath, seeing we know that he is present in their souls, who hath power and might sufficient to inflict what punishment himself best pleaseth.

At another time, the aforesaid Priest Constantius, his nephew, had sold his horse for twelve crowns, which money he laid up in his chest ; and being abroad about other business, it so happened, that certain poor people pitifully begged of the holy Bishop, that he would vouchsafe to bestow something upon them for the relief of their necessity. The man of God, not having anything

34

to give them, was much grieved to send them away empty : whiles he was thus troubled, suddenly it came to his mind how his nephew had sold his horse, and that the money was in his chest ; whereupon, in his absence, by virtuous violence, he brake open the lock, took away the twelve crowns, and bestowed them as best pleased himself upon the poor people. Constantius, returning home and finding his chest open, looked for his money, and finding it not, he began to exclaim, and with great noise and fury to cry out against his uncle, saying "All other can live here in quiet, only I can not." The Bishop, hearing him crying out in that manner, came unto him, as also the rest of his family ; and when he began with sweet speech to mitigate his fury, in great anger he replied, saying : "All other can live with you, only I can not be suffered to be in quiet : give me my money, which you have taken out of my chest." The Bishop, moved at his words, departed away, and went into the church of the blessed virgin Mary, where, lifting up his hands with his vestment upon them, he began standing to pray, that she would help him to so much money, that he might quiet the fury of the mad Priest : and casting suddenly his eyes upon the garment that lay between his arms stretched out, he found twelve crowns lying there, so fair and bright, as though they had then newly come from the mint ; who forthwith going out of the church, cast them to the raging Priest with these words : "Lo, there is your money which you have kept such a stir for ; but know you that after my death you shall never be Bishop of this place, and that for your covetous mind." By which true censure of his we gather that the Priest provided that money for the getting of the Bishopric. But the words of the man of God did prevail : for the same Constantius ended his life without any further promotion than to the dignity of Priesthood.

At another time, two Goths came unto him for

hospitality, saying that they were travelling to Ravenna ;
unto whom he gave with his own hands a little
wooden bottle full of wine, enough, haply, for their
dinner ; of which, notwithstanding, they drank until
they came to Ravenna, and though they stayed some
days in that city, yet they had no other wine than that
which the holy man bestowed upon them : and so likewise they continued until they returned back again to
the same venerable Bishop, drinking daily of the same,
and yet never lacking wine to serve their necessity : as
though, in that wooden bottle which he gave them, wine
had grown, and not there increased.

Not long sithence, there came from the same country
a certain old man that is a clerk, who reporteth divers
notable things of him, which must not be passed over
with silence. For he saith that going upon a day into
his garden, he found it all full of caterpillars, and seeing
all his worts spoiled, turning himself to them, he spake
thus : "I adjure you, in the name of our Lord Jesus
Christ, to depart from hence, and not to eat any more
of these worts" : after which words, those worms did
forthwith so vanish away, that there was not one to be
found in all the whole garden. But what great marvel
is it, to hear such things reported of him that was now
a Bishop, being then, both by reason of his orders, and
also holy conversation of life, grown into favour with
almighty God, seeing those are more to be admired
which this old clergyman said that he did, being yet but
a little boy ? For he affirmeth, that at such time as
Bonifacius dwelt with his mother, and went abroad, that
sometime he came home without his shirt, and oftentimes without his coat : for no sooner did he see a
naked man, but he gave away his clothes, and put them
upon him, to the end that himself might be clothed with
a reward in the sight of God. His mother rebuked him
often for doing so, and told him that it was no reason

that, being poor himself, he should give away his apparel to other. Upon another day, going into the barn, she found almost all her wheat, which she had provided for the whole year, given away by her son to the poor : and as she was, for very grief thereof, beating and tearing of herself, the child of God, Bonifacius, came, and with the best words he could began to comfort his afflicted mother ; but when by no means she would be quieted, he entreated her to go out of the barn where the little wheat that remained was. When she was departed, the virtuous youth fell straightway to his prayers ; and after a little while, going out, he brought his mother back again, where she found it as full of wheat as before it was : at the sight of which miracle, she, being touched in soul, exhorted him to give as he pleased, seeing he could so soon obtain at God's hands what he asked. His mother also kept hens before her door, which a fox, that had his berry not far off, used to carry away : and upon a certain day, as the youth Bonifacius was standing in the entry, the fox, after his old manner, came and took away one of the hens ; whereupon in all haste he ran to the church, and prostrate there in prayer, with loud voice he spake thus : " Is it thy pleasure, O Lord, that I shall not eat of my mother's hens ? for behold, the fox doth devour them up " : and rising from his prayers, he went out of the church, and straightways the fox came back again with the hen in his mouth, leaving it where he found it, and forthwith fell down dead in the presence of Bonifacius.

Peter. It seemeth strange unto me, that God vouch-safeth in such small things to hear the prayers of them that put their trust in him.

Gregory. This falleth out, Peter, by the great provi-dence of our Creator, to the end that by little things which we receive at his hands, we should hope for greater : for the holy and simple lad was heard in praying for small matters, that by them he should learn how much he ought to trust in God, when he prayed for things of greater importance.

Peter. What you say pleaseth me very well.

Chapter Ten : of Fortunatus, Bishop of the City of Tuderti. ¶ Gregory. Another man also there was in the same parts, called Fortunatus, Bishop of Tuderti, who had a most singular grace in casting out of devils, in so much that sometime he did cast out of possessed bodies whole legions ; and by the continual exercise of prayer, he overcame all their temptations. Julianus, who had an office here in our church, and not long since died in this city, was familiarly acquainted with him, by whose relation I learned that which I will now tell you : for by reason of his great and inward familiarity, often was he present at such miracles as he wrought, and did divers times talk of him to our instruction and his own comfort.

A certain noble matron there was, dwelling in the hither parts of Tuscania, that had a daughter-in-law, which, not long after the marriage of her son, was, together with her mother-in-law, invited to the dedication of the oratory of the blessed martyr, St. Sebastian : and the night before this solemnity, overcome with carnal pleasure, she could not abstain from her husband ; and though in the morning her former delight troubled her conscience, yet shame drave her forth to the procession, being more ashamed of men than fearing the judgment of God, and therefore thither she went together with her mother-in-law. And behold, straight upon the bringing of the relics of St. Sebastian the martyr into the oratory, a wicked spirit possessed the foresaid matron's daughter-in-law, and pitifully tormented her before all the people. The Priest of the oratory, beholding her so terribly vexed and lifted up, took a white linen cloth and cast upon her ; and forthwith the devil also entered into him, and because he presumed above his strength, enforced also he was by his own vexation, to know what himself was. Those that were present took up the young gentlewoman in their hands, and carried her home to her own house. And for as much as she was by the enemy continually and cruelly tormented, her kinsfolk that carnally loved her, and with their love did persecute her, cause her to be carried for help to certain witches; so utterly to cast away her soul, whose body they went about by sorcery for a time to relieve. Coming into their hands, she was by them brought to a river, and there washed in the water, the sorcerers labouring a long time by their enchantments to cast out the devil, that had possessed her body : but by the wonderful judgment of almighty God, it fell out that whiles one by unlawful art was expelled, suddenly a whole legion did enter in. And from that time forward, she began to be tossed with so many varieties of motions, to shriek out in so many sundry tunes, as there were devils in her body. Then her parents, consulting together, and confessing their own wickedness, carried her to the venerable Bishop Fortunatus, and with him they left her : who, having taken her to his charge, fell to his prayers many days and nights, and he prayed so much the more earnestly, because he had against him, in one body, an whole army of devils : and many days passed not, before he made her so safe and sound, as though the devil had never had any power or interest in her body.

At another time, the same servant of almighty God cast forth a devil out of one that was possessed : which wicked spirit, when it was now night and saw few men stirring in the streets, taking upon him the shape of a stranger, began to go up and down the city, crying out · " O holy Bishop Fortunatus, behold what he hath done; he hath turned a stranger out of his lodging, and now

I seek for a place to rest in, and in his whole city can find none." A certain man, sitting in his house by the fire, with his wife and his little son, hearing one to cry out in that manner, went forth, and enquired what the Bishop had done, and withal invited him to his house, where he caused him to sit with them by the fire : and as they were among themselves discoursing of divers matters, the same wicked spirit on a sudden entered into his little child, cast him into the fire, and forthwith killed him : then the wretched father, by the loss of his son in this manner, knew full well whom he had entertained, and the Bishop turned out of his lodging.

Peter. What was the cause, that the old enemy presumed to kill his son in his own house : who, thinking him to be a stranger, vouchsafed him of lodging and entertainment ?

Gregory. Many things, Peter, seem to be good and yet are not, because they be not done with a good mind and intention ; and therefore our Saviour saith in the gospel : *If thy eye be naught, all thy body shall be dark.*[1] For when the intention is wicked, all the work that followeth is naught, although it seem to be never so good ; and therefore this man who lost his child, though he seemed to give hospitality, yet I think that he took not any pleasure in that work of mercy, but rather in the detraction and infamy of the Bishop : for the punishment which followed did declare that his entertainment going before, was not void of sin. For some there be, which are careful to do good works, to the end they may obscure the virtue of another man's life ; neither take they pleasure in the good thing which they do, but in the conceit of that hurt which thereby they imagine redoundeth to others ; and therefore I verily suppose that this man, which gave entertainment to the devil, was more desirous to seem to do a good work than to do

[1] Matt. 6, 23.

it indeed ; to the end that he might seem more charitable than the Bishop, in that he entertained him whom the man of God, Fortunatus, had thrust out of his house.

Peter. It is verily so, as you say : for the end of the work declared that the intent of the doer was not good.

Gregory. At another time, likewise, one that had lost his eyesight was brought unto him, who craved his intercession and obtained it : for so soon as the man of God had prayed for him, and made the sign of the cross upon his eyes, straightways he received his sight. Beside this, a certain soldier's horse became so mad, that he could scant be holden by many, and so cruel he was, that he rent and tare the flesh of all such as he could reach with his teeth. At length, as well as they could, they tied him with ropes, and so brought him to the man of God ; who putting forth his hand, made upon his head the sign of the cross, and forthwith all his madness departed, in such sort that he became more gentle than ever he was before. Then the soldier, seeing his horse so miraculously cured, determined to bestow him upon the Bishop : which because he refused, and yet the other instantly entreated that he would not reject his poor gift, the holy man took the middle way, and yielded so to the soldier's request, that yet he would not take any reward for the doing of that miracle ; for he gave him first so much money as the horse was worth, and then received him ; for perceiving that the soldier would have been grieved, if he had refused his courteous offer, upon charity he bought that whereof he had then no need.

Neither must I pass over with silence that which I heard almost twelve days since : for a certain poor old man was brought unto me (because I loved always to talk with such kind of men), of whom I enquired his country ; and understanding that he was of the city of

Tuderti, I asked him whether he knew the good old father, Bishop Fortunatus ; to which he answered that he knew him, and that very well. "Then I beseech you," quoth I, "tell me whether you know of any miracles which he did, and because I am very desirous, let me understand what manner of man he was." "This man," quoth he, "was far different from all those which live in our days ; for he obtained at God's hands whatsoever he requested. One of his miracles which cometh to my mind, I will now tell you.

"Certain Goths, upon a day, travelling not far from the city of Tuderti, as they were in their journey to Ravenna, carried away with them two little boys from a place which belonged to the said city. News hereof being brought to the holy Bishop Fortunatus, he sent straightways, desiring those Goths to come unto him : to whom he spake very courteously, being willing by fair speech to pacify their fierce and cruel natures ; and afterward told them that they should have what money they desired, so they would make restitution of the children : 'and therefore, I beseech you,' quoth he, 'gratify my request in this one thing.' Then he which seemed to be the chief of them two told him, that whatsoever else he commanded they were ready to perform, but as for the boys, by no means they would let them go. To whom the venerable man (threatening in sweet sort) spake unto him in this manner : 'You grieve me, good son, to see that you will not be ruled by your father ; but give me not any such cause of grief, for it is not good that you do.' But for all this the Goth, continuing still hard-hearted, denied his request, and so went his way, yet coming again the next day, the holy man renewed his former suit concerning the children ; but when he saw that by no means he could persuade him, in sorrowful manner he spake thus : 'Well I know that it is not good for you to depart in this manner, and leave me thus afflicted.' But the Goth, not esteeming his words, returned to his inn, set those children on horseback, and sent them before with his servants, and straightways himself took horse and followed after; and as he was riding in the same city by the church of St. Peter the Apostle, his horse stumbling, fell down, and brake his thigh in such sort that the bone was quite asunder: up was he taken, and carried back again to his inn; who in all haste sent after his servants, and caused the boys to be brought back again. Then he sent one to venerable Fortunatus with this message: 'I beseech you, father, to send unto me your deacon'; who when he was come unto him lying in his bed, he made those boys, which before upon no entreaty he would restore, to be brought forth, and delivered them to him, saying: 'Go and tell my Lord the Bishop: Behold you have cursed me, and I am punished, but I have now sent you those children which before you required, take them, and I beseech you to pray for me.' The deacon received the children, and carried them to the Bishop; whereupon the holy man forthwith gave his deacon some holy water, saying: 'Go quickly and cast it upon him where he lieth'; who went his way, and coming to the Goth, he sprinkled all his body with holy water: and O strange and admirable thing! the holy water no sooner touched his thigh but all the rupture was so healed, and himself so perfectly restored to his former health, that he forsook his bed that very hour, took his horse, and went on his journey, as though he had never been hurt at all: and thus it fell out, that he which refused for money and upon obedience to restore the children, was by punishment enforced to do it for nothing." When the old man had told me this strange story, ready he was to proceed unto other; but because I was at that time to make an exhortation to some that expected me, and the day was well spent, I could not at that time hear any more of the notable acts of venerable Fortunatus ; and yet if I might, never would I do any thing else, than give ear to such excellent stories.

The next day, the same old man reported a thing far more wonderful : for he said that in the same city of Tuderti, there dwelt a good virtuous man called Marcellus, together with two of his sisters, who, falling sick, somewhat late upon Easter even departed this life : and because he was to be carried far off, he could not be buried that day. His sisters having now longer respite for his burial, with heavy hearts ran weeping unto the Bishop ; where they began to cry out aloud in this manner : " We know that thou leadest an Apostolical life, that thou dost heal lepers, restore sight to the blind : come, therefore, we beseech you, and raise up our dead brother." The venerable man, hearing of their brother's death, began himself likewise to weep, desired them to depart, and not to make any such petition unto him "for it is our Lord's pleasure," quoth he, " which no man can resist." When they were gone, the Bishop continued still sad and sorrowful for the good man's death ; and the next day being the solemn feast of Easter, very early in the morning he went with two of his deacons to Marcellus' house, and coming to the place where his dead body lay, he fell to his prayers ; and when he had made an end, he rose up and sat down by the corpse, and with a low voice called the dead man by his name, saying : " Brother Marcellus " ; whereat, as though he had been lightly asleep, and awaked with that voice, he rose up, opened his eyes, and looking upon the Bishop, said : " O what have you done ? O what have you done ? " To whom the Bishop answered, saying : " What have I done ? " " Marry," quoth he, " yesterday there came two unto me, and discharged my soul out of my body, and carried me away to a good place, and this day one was sent, who bade them carry me back again, because Bishop Fortunatus was gone to mine house." And when he had spoken these words, straightways he recovered of his sickness, and lived long after. And yet for all this we must not think that he lost that place which he had, because there is no doubt, but that he might, by the prayers of his intercessor, live yet more virtuously after his death, who had a care before he died to please almighty God.

But why do I spend so many words in discoursing of his wonderful life, when as we have so many miracles, even at these days, wrought at his body ? for, as he was wont to do when he lived upon earth, so doth he now continually at his dead bones dispossess devils, and heal such as be sick, so often as men pray for such graces with faith and devotion. But I mean now to return to the province of Valeria, of which I have heard most notable miracles from the mouth of venerable Fortunatus, of whom long before I have made mention, who, coming often to visit me, whiles he reporteth old stories, continually he bringeth me new delight.

Chapter Eleven : of Martirius, a Monk in the Province of Valeria.

¶ A certain man lived in that province, called Martirius, who was a very devout servant of almighty God, and gave this testimony of his virtuous life. For, upon a certain day, the other monks, his brethren, made a hearth-cake, forgetting to make upon it the sign of the cross : for in that country they use to make a cross upon their loaves, dividing them so into four parts : when the servant of God came, they told him that it was not marked : who, seeing it covered with ashes and coals, asked why they did not sign it, and speaking so, he made the sign of the cross with his hand against the coals : which thing whiles he was in doing, the cake gave a great crack, as though the pan had been broken with the fire : after it was baked and taken out, they found it marked with the sign of the cross, which yet not any corporal touching, but the faith of Martirius had imprinted.

Chapter Twelve: of Severus, a Priest in the same Province.

¶ In the same country there is a valley, which is called of the plain people Interocrina; in which there lived a certain man of a rare life, called Severus, who was a parish priest of the church of our blessed Lady the mother of God and perpetual virgin. One that lay at the point of death sent for him in great haste, desiring him to come with all speed, and by his prayers to make intercession for him, that doing penance for his wickedness, and loosed from his sins, he might depart this life. So it chanced, that the Priest at that time was busy in pruning of his vines; and therefore he bade them that came for him to go on before: "and I will," quoth he, "come after by and by." For seeing he had but a little to do, he stayed a pretty while to make an end of that, and when it was dispatched, away he went to visit the sick man; but as he was going, the former messengers met with him, saying: "Father, why have you stayed so long? go not now any further, for the man is dead." At which news the good man fell a trembling, and cried out aloud that he had killed him; whereupon he fell a weeping, and in that manner came to the dead corpse, where before the bed he fell prostrate upon the earth, pouring out of tears. Lying there weeping very pitifully, beating his head against the ground, and crying out that he was guilty of his death, suddenly the dead man returned to life: which many that were present beholding cried out, and began to weep more plentifully for joy, demanding of him where he had been, and by what means he came back again; to whom he said: "Certain cruel men," quoth he, "did carry me away; out of whose mouth and nostrils fire came forth, which I could not endure; and as they were leading me through dark places, suddenly a beautiful young man with others met us, who said unto them that were drawing me forward : 'Carry him back again ; for Severus the Priest lamenteth his death, and our Lord, for his tears, hath given him longer life.' " Then Severus rose up from the earth, and by his intercession did assist him in doing of penance. And when the sick man that revived had done penance for his sins by the space of seven days, upon the eighth with a cheerful countenance he departed this life. Consider, Peter, I pray you, how dearly our Lord loved this Severus, that would not suffer him to be grieved for a little time.

Peter. They be marvellous strange things which you report, and which before this time I never heard of : but what is the reason that in these days there be not any such men now living ?

Gregory. I make no doubt, Peter, but that there be many such holy men now living ; for though they work not the like miracles, yet for all that, may they be as virtuous and as holy. For true judgment of one's life is to be taken from his virtuous conversation, and not from the working of miracles, for many there be who, although they do not any such strange things, yet are they not in virtue inferior to them that do them.

Peter. How, I beseech you, can it be maintained for true, that there be some that work not any miracles, and yet be as virtuous as they which work them ?

Gregory. Sure I am that you know very well that the Apostle St. Paul is brother to St. Peter, chief of the Apostles in Apostolical principality.

Peter. I know that indeed, for no doubt can be made thereof : for though he were the least of the Apostles, yet did he labour more than all they.

Gregory. Peter, as you well remember, walked with his feet upon the sea ; Paul in the sea suffered shipwrack. And in one and the same element, where Paul could not pass with a ship, Peter went upon his feet; by which apparent it is, that though their virtue in working of miracles was not alike, yet their merit is alike in the kingdom of heaven.

Peter. I confess that I am well pleased with that you say, for I know most assuredly that the life, and not the miracles, are to be considered ; but yet, seeing such miracles as be wrought do give testimony of a good life, I beseech you, if any more be yet remaining, that you would, with the examples and virtuous lives of holy men, feed mine hungry soul.

Gregory. Desirous I am, to the honour of our blessed Saviour, to tell you some things now concerning the miracles of the man of God, venerable St. Bennet : but to do it as it ought, this day is not sufficient ; wherefore we will here make a pause, and to handle this matter more plentifully, take another beginning.

The End of the First Book

Perugino

Alinari

ST BENEDICT
(Vatican Gallery, Rome)

The Second Book
Of the Life and Miracles of St. Bennet

The Second Book
Of the Life and Miracles of St. Bennet

There was a man of venerable life, blessed by grace, and blessed in name, for he was called *Benedictus* or Bennet : who, from his younger years, carried always the mind of an old man ; for his age was inferior to his virtue : all vain pleasure he contemned, and though he were in the world, and might freely have enjoyed such commodities as it yieldeth, yet did he nothing esteem it, nor the vanities thereof. He was born in the province of Nursia, of honourable parentage, and brought up at Rome in the study of humanity. But for as much as he saw many by reason of such learning to fall to dissolute and lewd life, he drew back his foot, which he had as it were now set forth into the world, lest, entering too far in acquaintance therewith, he likewise might have fallen into that dangerous and godless gulf : wherefore, giving over his book, and forsaking his father's house and wealth, with a resolute mind only to serve God, he sought for some place, where he might attain to the desire of his holy purpose : and in this sort he departed, instructed with learned ignorance, and furnished with unlearned wisdom. All the notable things and acts of his life I could not learn ; but those few, which I mind now to report, I had by the relation of four of his disciples : to wit, of

51

Constantinus, a most rare and reverent man, who was next Abbot after him ; of Valentinianus, who many years had the charge of the Lateran Abbey; of Simplicius, who was the third General of his order ; and lastly of Honoratus, who is now Abbot of that monastery in which he first began his holy life.

Chapter One : how he made a broken sieve whole and sound.

Bennet having now given over the school, with a resolute mind to lead his life in the wilderness : his nurse alone, which did tenderly love him, would not by any means give him over. Coming, therefore, to a place called Enside and remaining there in the church of St. Peter, in the company of other virtuous men, which for charity lived in that place, it fell so out that his nurse borrowed of the neighbours a sieve to make clean wheat, which being left negligently upon the table, by chance it was broken in two pieces : whereupon she fell pitifully a weeping, because she had borrowed it. The devout and religious youth Bennet, seeing his nurse so lamenting, moved with compassion, took away with him both the pieces of the sieve, and with tears fell to his prayers ; and after he had done, rising up he found it so whole, that the place could not be seen where before it was broken ; and coming straight to his nurse, and comforting her with good words, he delivered her the sieve safe and sound : which miracle was known to all the inhabitants thereabout, and so much admired, that the townsmen, for a perpetual memory, did hang it up at the church door, to the end that not only men then living, but also their posterity might understand, how greatly God's grace did work with him upon his first renouncing of the world. The sieve continued there many years after, even to these very troubles of the Lombards, where it did hang over the church door.

But Bennet, desiring rather the miseries of the world than the praises of men : rather to be wearied with labour

for God's sake, than to be exalted with transitory commendation: fled privily from his nurse, and went into a desert place called Sublacum, distant almost forty miles from Rome: in which there was a fountain springing forth cool and clear water; the abundance whereof doth first in a broad place make a lake, and afterward running forward, cometh to be a river. As he was travelling to this place, a certain monk called Romanus met him, and demanded whither he went, and understanding his purpose, he both kept it close, furthered him what he might, vested him with the habit of holy conversation, and as he could, did minister and serve him.

The man of God, Bennet, coming to this foresaid place, lived there in a strait cave, where he continued three years unknown to all men, except to Romanus, who lived not far off, under the rule of Abbot Theodacus, and very virtuously did steal certain hours, and likewise sometime a loaf given for his own provision, which he did carry to Bennet. And because from Romanus' cell to that cave there was not any way, by reason of an high rock which did hang over it, Romanus, from the top thereof, upon a long rope, did let down the loaf, upon which also with a band he tied a little bell, that by the ringing thereof the man of God might know when he came with his bread, and so be ready to take it. But the old enemy of mankind, envying at the charity of the one and the refection of the other, seeing a loaf upon a certain day let down, threw a stone and brake the bell; but yet, for all that, Romanus gave not over to serve him by all the possible means he could.

At length when almighty God was determined to ease Romanus of his pains, and to have Bennet's life for an example known to the world, that such a candle, set upon a candlestick, might shine and give light to the Church of God, our Lord vouchsafed to appear unto a certain Priest dwelling a good way off, who had made ready his dinner for Easter day, and spake thus unto him : "Thou hast provided good cheer for thyself, and my servant in such a place is afflicted with hunger" : who hearing this forthwith rose up, and upon Easter day itself, with such meat as he had prepared, went to the place, where he sought for the man of God amongst the steep hills, the low valleys and hollow pits, and at length found him in his cave : where, after they had prayed together, and sitting down had given God thanks, and had much spiritual talk, then the Priest said unto him : "Rise up, brother, and let us dine, because to-day is the feast of Easter." To whom the man of God answered, and said : "I know that it is Easter with me and a great feast, having found so much favour at God's hands as this day to enjoy your company" (for by reason of his long absence from men, he knew not that it was the great solemnity of Easter). But the reverent Priest again did assure him, saying : "Verily, to-day is the feast of our Lord's Resurrection, and therefore meet it is not that you should keep abstinence, and besides I am sent to that end, that we might eat together of such provision as God's goodness hath sent us." Whereupon they said grace, and fell to their meat, and after they had dined, and bestowed some time in talking, the Priest returned to his church.

About the same time likewise, certain shepherds found him in that same cave : and at the first, when they espied him through the bushes, and saw his apparel made of skins, they verily thought that it had been some beast : but after they were acquainted with the servant of God, many of them were by his means converted from their beastly life to grace, piety, and devotion. And thus his name in the country there about became famous, and many after this went to visit him, and for corporal meat which they brought him, they carried away spiritual food for their souls.

The Life and Miracles of St. Bennet

Chapter Two : how he overcame a great temptation of the flesh.

¶ Upon a certain day being alone, the tempter was at hand : for a little black bird, commonly called a merle or an ousel, began to fly about his face, and that so near as the holy man, if he would, might have taken it with his hand : but after he had blessed himself with the sign of the cross, the bird flew away · and forthwith the holy man was assaulted with such a terrible temptation of the flesh, as he never felt the like in all his life. A certain woman there was which some time he had seen, the memory of which the wicked spirit put into his mind, and by the representation of her did so mightily inflame with concupiscence the soul of God's servant, which did so increase that, almost overcome with pleasure, he was of mind to have forsaken the wilderness. But, suddenly assisted with God's grace, he came to himself; and seeing many thick briers and nettle-bushes to grow hard by, off he cast his apparel, and threw himself into the midst of them, and there wallowed so long that, when he rose up, all his flesh was pitifully torn : and so by the wounds of his body, he cured the wounds of his soul, in that he turned pleasure into pain, and by the outward burning of extreme smart, quenched that fire which, being nourished before with the fuel of carnal cogitations, did inwardly burn in his soul : and by this means he overcame the sin, because he made a change of the fire. From which time forward, as himself did afterward report unto his disciples, he found all temptation of pleasure so subdued, that he never felt any such thing. Many after this began to abandon the world, and to become his scholars. For being now freed from the vice of temptation, worthily and with great reason is he made a master of virtue : for which cause, in *Exodus*, commandment is given by Moses, that the Levites from five-and-twenty years and upward should serve, but, after they came to fifty, that they should be ordained keepers of the holy vessels.[1]

Peter. Somewhat I understand of this testimony alleged : but yet I beseech you to tell me the meaning thereof more fully.

Gregory. It is plain, Peter, that in youth the temptation of the flesh is hot : but after fifty years the heat of the body waxeth cold, and the souls of faithful people become holy vessels. Wherefore necessary it is that God's elect servants, whiles they are yet in the heat of temptation, should live in obedience, serve, and be wearied with labour and pains. But when, by reason of age, the heat of temptation is past, they become keepers of holy vessels ; because they then are made the doctors of men's souls.

Peter. I cannot deny, but that your words have given me full satisfaction : wherefore, seeing you have now expounded the meaning of the former text alleged, prosecute, I pray, as you have begun, the rest of the holy man's life.

Chapter Three : how Bennet, by the sign of the holy cross, brake a drinking-glass in pieces.

¶ **Gregory.** When this great temptation was thus overcome, the man of God, like unto a piece of ground well tilled and weeded, of the seed of virtue brought forth plentiful store of fruit : and by reason of the great report of his wonderful holy life, his name became very famous. Not far from the place where he remained there was a monastery, the Abbot whereof was dead : whereupon the whole Convent came unto the venerable man Bennet, entreating him very earnestly that he would vouchsafe to take upon him the charge and government of their Abbey : long time he denied them, saying that their manners were divers from his, and therefore that they should never agree together : yet

[1] Numbers 8, 24–26.

at length, overcome with their entreaty, he gave his consent. Having now taken upon him the charge of the Abbey, he took order that regular life should be observed, so that none of them could, as before they used, through unlawful acts decline from the path of holy conversation, either on the one side or on the other : which the monks perceiving, they fell into a great rage, accusing themselves that ever they desired him to be their Abbot, seeing their crooked conditions could not endure his virtuous kind of government : and therefore when they saw that under him they could not live in unlawful sort, and were loath to leave their former conversation, and found it hard to be enforced with old minds to meditate and think upon new things : and because the life of virtuous men is always grievous to those that be of wicked conditions, some of them began to devise, how they might rid him out of the way : and therefore, taking counsel together, they agreed to poison his wine : which being done, and the glass wherein that wine was, according to the custom, offered to the Abbot to bless, he, putting forth his hand, made the sign of the cross, and straightway the glass, that was holden far off, brake in pieces, as though the sign of the cross had been a stone thrown against it : upon which accident the man of God by and by perceived that the glass had in it the drink of death, which could not endure the sign of life : and therefore rising up, with a mild countenance and quiet mind, he called the monks together, and spake thus unto them : "Almighty God have mercy upon you, and forgive you : why have you used me in this manner ? Did not I tell you before hand, that our manner of living could never agree together ? Go your ways, and seek ye out some other father suitable to your own conditions, for I intend not now to stay any longer amongst you." When he had thus discharged himself, he returned back to the wilderness which so much he loved, and dwelt alone with himself, in the sight of his Creator, who beholdeth the hearts of all men.

Peter. I understand not very well what you mean, when you say that he dwelt with himself.

Gregory. If the holy man had longer, contrary to his own mind, continued his government over those monks, who had all conspired against him, and were far unlike to him in life and conversation : perhaps he should have diminished his own devotion, and somewhat withdrawn the eyes of his soul from the light of contemplation ; and being wearied daily with correcting of their faults, he should have had the less care of himself, and so haply it might have fallen out, that he should both have lost himself, and yet not found them : for so often as by infectious motion we are carried too far from ourselves, we remain the same men that we were before, and yet be not with ourselves as we were before : because we are wandering about other men's affairs, little considering and looking into the state of our own soul. For shall we say that he was with himself, who went into a far country, and after he had, as we read in the Gospel,[1] prodigally spent that portion which he received of his father, was glad to serve a citizen, to keep his hogs, and would willingly have filled his hungry belly with the husks which they did eat : who notwithstanding afterward, when he thought with himself of those goods which he had lost, it is written of him that, returning into himself, he said : *How many hired men in my father's house do abound with bread?* If then, before he were with himself, from whence did he return home unto himself? and therefore I said that this venerable man did dwell with himself, because carrying himself circumspectly and carefully in the sight of his Creator, always considering his own actions, always examining

[1] Luke 15.

58

himself, never did he turn the eyes of his soul from himself, to behold aught else whatsoever.

Peter. Why, then, is it written of the Apostle, St. Peter, after he was by the Angel delivered out of prison, that, returning to himself, he said : *Now I know verily, that our Lord hath sent his Angel, and hath delivered me from the hand of Herod, and from all the expectation of the people of the Jews.*[1]

Gregory. We are two manner of ways, Peter, carried out of ourselves : for either we fall under ourselves by sinful cogitation, or else we are, by the grace of contemplation, lifted above ourselves : for he that kept hogs, through wandering of his mind and unclean thoughts, fell under himself : but he whom the Angel delivered out of prison, being also rapt by the Angel into an ecstasy, was in truth out of himself, but yet above himself. Both of them, therefore, did return unto themselves ; the one when he recollected himself, and forsook his lewd kind of life ; and the other from the top of contemplation, to have that usual judgment and understanding, which before he had : wherefore venerable Bennet in that solitary wilderness dwelt with himself, because he kept himself, and retired his cogitations within the closet of his own soul : for when the greatness of contemplation rapt him up aloft, out of all question he did then leave himself under himself.

Peter. Your discourse doth very well content me : yet I beseech you to answer me this question, whether he could in conscience give over those monks, whose government he had now taken upon him ?

Gregory. In mine opinion, Peter, evil men may with good conscience be tolerated in that community, where there be some good that may be holpen and reap commodity. But where there be none good at all, that may receive spiritual profit, often times all labour is lost, that

---

[1] Acts 12, 11.

is bestowed in bringing of such to good order, especially
if other occasions be offered of doing God presently
better service elsewhere : for whose good, then, should
the holy man have expected, seeing them all to persecute him with one consent ? and (that which is not to
be passed over with silence) those that be perfect carry
always this mind, that when they perceive their labour
to be fruitless in one place, to remove straight to another,
where more good may be done. And for this cause,
that notable preacher of the world, who was desirous to
be dissolved, and to be with Christ, *unto whom to live
is Christ, and to die is gain* :[1] and who not only desired
himself to suffer persecution, but did also animate and
encourage others to suffer the same ; yet being himself
in persecution at Damascus, got a rope and a basket to
pass over the wall, and was privily let down. What
then ? shall we say that Paul was afraid of death, when
as himself said, that he desired it for Christ's sake ? not
so : but when he perceived that in that place little good
was to be done by great labour, he reserved himself to
further labour, where more fruit and better success
might be expected : and therefore the valiant soldier of
Christ would not be kept within walls, but sought for
a larger field where he might more freely labour for his
master. And so, in like manner, you shall quickly
perceive, if you mark well, that venerable Bennet forsook not so many in one place, that were unwilling to
be taught, as he did in sundry other places raise up from
the death of soul many more, that were willing to be
instructed.

Peter. It is so as you say, and plain reason teacheth
it, and the example of St. Paul alleged doth confirm it.
But I beseech you to return unto your former purpose,
and to prosecute the life of the holy man.

Gregory. When as God's servant daily increased in

[1] Phil. 1, 21.

ST. MAURUS
(San Pietro, Perugia)

virtue, and became continually more famous for miracles, many were by him in the same place drawn to the service of almighty God, so that by Christ's assistance he built there twelve Abbeys; over which he appointed governors, and in each of them placed twelve monks, and a few he kept with himself, namely, such as he thought would more profit, and be better instructed by his own presence. At that time also many noble and religious men of Rome came unto him, and committed their children to be brought up under him, for the service of God. Then also Evitius delivered him Maurus, and Tertullius the Senator brought Placidus, being their sons of great hope and towardness: of which two, Maurus, growing to great virtue, began to be his master's co-adjutor; but Placidus, as yet, was but a boy of tender years.

Chapter Four: how Bennet reformed a monk that would not stay at his prayers.

¶ In one of the monasteries which he had built in those parts, a monk there was, which could not continue at prayers; for when the other monks knelt down to serve God, his manner was to go forth, and there with wandering mind to busy himself about some earthly and transitory things. And when he had been often by his Abbot admonished of this fault without any amendment, at length he was sent to the man of God, who did likewise very much rebuke him for his folly; yet notwithstanding, returning back again, he did scarce two days follow the holy man's admonition; for, upon the third day, he fell again to his old custom, and would not abide within at the time of prayer: word whereof being once more sent to the man of God, by the father of the Abbey whom he had there appointed, he returned him answer that he would come himself, and reform what was amiss, which he did accordingly: and it fell so out, that when the singing of psalms was ended, and the hour come in which the monks betook themselves to prayer, the holy man perceived that the monk, which used at that time to go forth, was by a little black boy drawn out by the skirt of his garment; upon which sight, he spake secretly to Pompeianus, father of the Abbey, and also to Maurus, saying: "Do you not see who it is, that draweth this monk from his prayers?" and they answered him, that they did not. "Then let us pray," quoth he, "unto God, that you also may behold whom this monk doth follow": and after two days Maurus did see him, but Pompeianus could not. Upon another day, when the man of God had ended his devotions, he went out of the oratory, where he found the foresaid monk standing idle, whom for the blindness of his heart he strake with a little wand, and from that day forward he was so freed from all allurement of the little black boy, that he remained quietly at his prayers, as other of the monks did: for the old enemy was so terrified, that he durst not any more suggest any such cogitations: as though by that blow, not the monk, but himself had been strooken.

Chapter Five: of a fountain that sprung forth in the top of a mountain, by the prayers of the man of God. ¶ Amongst the monasteries which he had built in those parts, three of them were situated upon the rocks of a mountain, so that very painful it was for the monks to go down and fetch water, especially because the side of the hill was so steep that there was great fear of danger: and therefore the monks of those Abbeys with one consent came unto the servant of God, Bennet, giving him to understand, how laborious it was for them daily to go down unto the lake for water: and therefore they added, that it was very necessary to have them removed to some other places. The man of God, comforting them with sweet words, caused them to return back again; and the next night, having with him only the little boy Placidus (of whom we spake before), he ascended up to the rock of that mountain, and continued there a long time in prayer; and when he had done, he took three stones, and laid them in the same place for a mark, and so, none of them being privy to that he had done, he returned back to his own Abbey. And the next day, when the foresaid monks came again about their former business, he said thus unto them: "Go your way to the rock, and in the place where you find three stones laid one upon another, dig a little hole, for almighty God is able to bring forth water in the top of that mountain, and so to ease you of that great labour which you take in fetching it so far." Away they went, and came to the rock of the mountain according to his direction, which they found as it were sweating drops of water, and after they had with a spade made an hollow place, it was straightways filled, and water flowed out so abundantly, that it doth plentifully, even to this day, spring out and run down from the top to the very bottom of that hill.

Chapter Six: how the iron head of a bill, from the bottom of the water, returned to the handle again. ¶ At another time, a certain Goth, poor of spirit, that gave over the world, was received by the man of God; whom on a day he commanded to take a bill, and to cleanse a certain plot of ground from briers, for the making of a garden, which ground was by the side of a lake. The Goth as he was there labouring, by chance the head of the bill slipped off, and fell into the water, which was so deep, that there was no hope ever to get it again. The poor Goth, in great fear, ran unto Maurus and told him what he had lost, confessing his own fault and negligence: Maurus forthwith went to the servant of God, giving him to understand thereof, who came straightways to the lake: and took the handle out of the Goth's hand, and put it into the water, and the iron head by and by ascended from the bottom, and

63

entered again into the handle of the bill, which he delivered to the Goth, saying : "Behold here is thy bill again, work on, and be sad no more."

Chapter Seven : how Maurus walked upon the water. ¶ On a certain day, as venerable Bennet was in his cell, the foresaid young Placidus, the holy man's monk, went out to take up water at the lake, and putting down his pail carelessly, fell in himself after it, whom the water forthwith carried away from the land so far as one may shoot an arrow. The man of God, being in his cell, by and by knew this, and called in haste for Maurus, saying : " Brother Maurus, run as fast as you can, for Placidus, that went to the lake to fetch water, is fallen in, and is carried a good way off." A strange thing, and since the time of Peter the Apostle never heard of ! Maurus, craving his father's blessing, and departing in all haste at his commandment, ran to that place upon the water, to which the young lad was carried by force thereof, thinking that he had all that while gone upon the land : and taking fast hold of him by the hair of his head, in all haste he returned back again : and so soon as he was at land, coming to himself he looked behind him, and then knew very well that he had before run upon the water : and that which before he durst not have presumed, being now done and past, he both marvelled, and was afraid at that which he had done. Coming back to the father, and telling him what had happened, the venerable man did not attribute this to his own merits, but to the obedience of Maurus : but Maurus on the contrary, said that it was done only upon his commandment, and that he had nothing to do in that miracle, not knowing at that time what he did. But the friendly contention proceeding of mutual humility, the young youth himself that was saved from drowning did determine : for he said that he saw when he was drawn out of the water, the Abbot's garment upon his

IAURUS SAVING PLACID IS FROM DROWNING

head, affirming that it was he that had delivered him from that great danger.

Peter. Certainly they be wonderful things which you report, and such as may serve for the edification of many : for mine own part, the more that I hear of his miracles, the more do I still desire.

Chapter Eight : how a loaf was poisoned, and carried far off by a crow. ¶ Gregory. When as the foresaid monasteries were zealous in the love of our Lord Jesus Christ, and their fame dispersed far and near, and many gave over the secular life, and subdued the passions of their soul under the light yoke of our Saviour : then (as the manner of wicked people is, to envy at that virtue which themselves desire not to follow) one Florentius, Priest of a church hard by, and grandfather to Florentius our sub-deacon, possessed with diabolical malice, began to envy the holy man's virtues, to backbite his manner of living, and to withdraw as many as he could from going to visit him : and when he saw that he could not hinder his virtuous proceedings, but that, on the contrary, the fame of his holy life increased, and many daily, upon the very report of his sanctity, did betake themselves to a better state of life : burning more and more with the coals of envy, he became far worse ; and though he desired not to imitate his commendable life, yet fain he would have had the reputation of his virtuous conversation.   In conclusion so much did malicious envy blind him, and so far did he wade in that sin, that he poisoned a loaf, and sent it to the servant of almighty God, as it were for an holy present. The man of God received it with great thanks, yet not ignorant of that which was hidden within.   At dinner time, a crow daily used to come unto him from the next wood, which took bread at his hands ; coming that day after his manner, the man of God threw him the loaf which the Priest had sent him, giving him this charge :

"In the name of Jesus Christ our Lord, take up that loaf, and leave it in some such place where no man may find it." Then the crow, opening his mouth, and lifting up his wings, began to hop up and down about the loaf, and after his manner to cry out, as though he would have said that he was willing to obey, and yet could not do what he was commanded. The man of God again and again bade him, saying: "Take it up without fear, and throw it where no man may find it." At length, with much ado, the crow took it up, and flew away, and after three hours, having dispatched the loaf, he returned back again, and received his usual allowance from the man of God.

But the venerable father, perceiving the Priest so wickedly bent against his life, was far more sorry for him than grieved for himself. And Florentius, seeing that he could not kill the body of the master, laboureth now what he can, to destroy the souls of his disciples; and for that purpose he sent into the yard of the Abbey before their eyes seven naked young women, which did there take hands together, play and dance a long time before them, to the end that, by this means, they might inflame their minds to sinful lust: which damnable sight the holy man beholding out of his cell, and fearing the danger which thereby might ensue to his younger monks, and considering that all this was done only for the persecuting of himself, he gave place to envy; and therefore, after he had for those abbeys and oratories which he had there built appointed governors, and left some under their charge, himself, in the company of a few monks, removed to another place. And thus the man of God, upon humility, gave place to the other's malice; but yet almighty God of justice did severely punish his wickedness. For when the foresaid Priest, being in his chamber, understood of the departure of holy Bennet, and was very glad of that news, behold (the whole house besides continuing safe and sound) that chamber alone in which he was, fell down, and so killed him : which strange accident the holy man's disciple Maurus understanding, straightways sent him word, he being as yet scarce ten miles off, desiring him to return again, because the Priest that did persecute him was slain ; which thing when Bennet heard, he was passing sorrowful, and lamented much : both because his enemy died in such sort, and also for that one of his monks rejoiced thereat ; and therefore he gave him penance, for that, sending such news, he presumed to rejoice at his enemy's death.

Peter. The things you report be strange, and much to be wondered at : for in making the rock to yield forth water, I see Moses ; and in the iron, which came from the bottom of the lake, I behold Heliseus ; in the walking of Maurus upon the water, I perceive Peter ; in the obedience of the crow, I contemplate Helias ; and in lamenting the death of his enemy, I acknowledge David : and therefore, in mine opinion, this one man was full of the spirit of all good men.

Gregory. The man of God, Bennet, had the spirit of the one true God, who, by the grace of our redemption, hath filled the hearts of his elect servants ; of whom St. John saith : *He was the true light, which doth lighten every man coming into this world.*[1]   Of whom, again, we find it written : *Of his fulness we have all received.*[2]   For God's holy servants might receive virtues of our Lord, but to bestow them upon others they could not ; and therefore it was he that gave the signs of miracles to his servants, who promised to give the sign of Jonas to his enemies :[3] so that he vouchsafed to die in the sight of the proud, and to rise again before the eyes of the humble : to the end, that they might behold what they contemned, and those see that which they ought to worship and love : by reason of which mystery it cometh to pass that, whereas

---

[1] John 1, 9.   [2] Ibid. 1, 16.   [3] Matt. 12, 40.

the proud cast their eyes upon the contempt of his death, the humble contrariwise, against death, lay hold of the glory of his power and might.

Peter. To what places, I pray you, after this, did the holy man go : and whether did he afterward in them work any miracles, or no ?

Gregory. The holy man, changing his place, did not for all that change his enemy. For afterward he endured so much the more grievous battles, by how much he had now the master of all wickedness fighting openly against him. For the town, which is called Cassino, standeth upon the side of an high mountain, which containeth, as it were in the lap thereof, the foresaid town, and afterward so riseth in height the space of three miles, that the top thereof seemeth to touch the very heavens : in this place there was an ancient chapel in which the foolish and simple country people, according to the custom of the old gentiles, worshipped the god Apollo. Round about it likewise upon all sides, there were woods for the service of the devils, in which, even to that very time, the mad multitude of infidels did offer most wicked sacrifice. The man of God coming thither, beat in pieces the idol, overthrew the altar, set fire on the woods, and in the temple of Apollo, he built the oratory of St. Martin, and where the altar of the same Apollo was, he made an oratory of St. John : and by his continual preaching, he brought the people dwelling in those parts to embrace the faith of Christ. The old enemy of mankind, not taking this in good part, did not now privily or in a dream, but in open sight present himself to the eyes of that holy father, and with great outcries complained that he had offered him violence. The noise which he made, the monks did hear, but himself they could not see : but, as the venerable father told them, he appeared visibly unto him most fell and cruel, and as though, with his fiery mouth and flaming eyes, he would have torn him in pieces : what the devil

THE WOMEN SENT BY FLORENTIUS

Razzi

said unto him, all the monks did hear ; for first he would call him by his name, and because the man of God vouchsafed him not any answer, then would he fall a reviling and railing at him : for when he cried out, calling him " Blessed Bennet," and yet found that he gave him no answer, straightways he would turn his tune, and say : " Cursed Bennet, and not blessed : what hast thou to do with me ? and why dost thou thus persecute me ? " Wherefore new battles of the old enemy against the servant of God are to be looked for, against whom willingly did he make war, but, against his will, did he give him occasion of many notable victories.

Chapter Nine : how venerable Bennet, by his prayer, removed an huge stone. ¶ Upon a certain day, when the monks were building up the cells of the same Abbey, there lay a stone which they meant to employ about that business : and when two or three were not able to remove it, they called for more company, but all in vain, for it remained so immovable as though it had grown to the very earth : whereby they plainly perceived that the devil himself did sit upon it, seeing so many men's hands could not so much as once move it : wherefore, finding that their own labours could do nothing, they sent for the man of God, to help them with his prayers against the devil, who hindered the removing of that stone. The holy man came, and after some praying, he gave it his blessing, and then they carried it away so quickly, as though it had been of no weight at all.

Chapter Ten : of the fantastical fire, which burnt the kitchen. ¶ Then the man of God thought good that they should presently before his departure dig up the ground in the same place ; which being done, and a deep hole made, the monks found there an idol of brass, which being for a little while by chance cast into the kitchen, they beheld fire suddenly to come from it, which to all their sight seemed to set the whole kitchen on fire ; for the quenching whereof, the monks by casting on of water made such a noise, that the man of God, hearing it, came to see what the matter was : and himself beholding not any fire at all, which they said that they did, he bowed down his head forthwith to his prayers, and then he perceived that they were deluded with fantastical fire, and therefore bad them bless their eyes, that they might behold the kitchen safe and sound, and not those fantastical flames, which the devil had falsely devised.

Chapter Eleven: how venerable Bennet revived a boy, crushed to death with the ruin of a wall.

❡ Again, as the monks were making of a certain wall somewhat higher, because that was requsite, the man of God in the meantime was in his cell at his prayers. To whom the old enemy appeared in an insulting manner, telling him, that he was now going to his monks, that were a working : whereof the man of God, in all haste, gave them warning, wishing them to look unto themselves, because the devil was at that time coming amongst them. The message was scarce delivered, when as the wicked spirit overthrew the new wall which they were a building, and with the fall slew a little young child, a monk, who was the son of a certain courtier. At which pitiful chance all were passing sorry and exceedingly grieved, not so much for the loss of the wall, as for the death of their brother : and in all haste they sent this heavy news to the venerable man Bennet ; who commanded them to bring unto him the young boy, mangled and maimed as he was, which they did, but yet they could not carry him any otherwise than in a sack : for the stones of the wall had not only broken his limbs, but also his very bones. Being in that manner brought unto the man of God, he bad them to lay him in his cell, and in that place upon which he used to pray ; and then, putting them all forth, he shut

70

the door, and fell more instantly to his prayers than he used at other times. And O strange miracle! for the very same hour he made him sound, and as lively as ever he was before; and sent him again to his former work, that he also might help the monks to make an end of that wall, of whose death the old serpent thought he should have insulted over Bennet, and greatly triumphed.

Chapter Twelve: how by revelation venerable Bennet knew that his Monks had eaten out of the Monastery. ¶ Among other miracles which the man of God did, he began also to be famous for the spirit of prophecy: as to foretell what was to happen, and to relate unto them that were present, such things as were done in absence. The order of his Abbey was, that when the monks went abroad (to deliver any message) never to eat or drink anything out of their cloister: and this being diligently observed, according to the prescription of their rule, upon a certain day some of the monks went forth upon such business: and being enforced about the dispatch thereof to tarry somewhat long abroad, it fell so out that they stayed at the house of a religious woman, where they did eat and refresh themselves. And being late before they came back to the Abbey, they went as the manner was, and asked their father's blessing: of whom he demanded where they had eaten: and they said nowhere. "Why do you," quoth he, "tell an untruth? for did you not go into such a woman's house? and eat such and such kind of meat, and drink so many cups?" When they heard him recount so in particular, both where they had stayed, what kind of meat they had eaten, and how often they had drunk, and perceived well that he knew all whatsoever they had done, they fell down trembling at his feet, and confessed that they had done wickedly: who straightways pardoned them for that fault, persuading himself

that they would not any more in his absence presume
to do any such thing, seeing they now perceived that
he was present with them in spirit.

**Chapter Thirteen : of the brother of Valentinian
the Monk, whom the man of God blamed for eating
in his journey.** ¶ A brother also of Valentinian the
monk, of whom I made mention before, was a layman,
but devout and religious : who used every year, as well
to desire the prayers of God's servant, as also to visit
his natural brother, to travel from his own house to the
Abbey : and his manner was, not to eat anything all that
day before he came thither. Being therefore upon a time
in his journey, he lighted into the company of another,
that carried meat about him to eat by the way : who,
after the day was well spent, spake unto him in this
manner : "Come, brother," quoth he, "let us refresh
ourselves, that we faint not in our journey" : to whom
he answered : "God forbid : for eat I will not by any
means, seeing I am now going to the venerable father
Bennet, and my custom is to fast until I see him." The
other, upon this answer, said no more for the space of
an hour. But afterward, having travelled a little further,
again he was in hand with him to eat something : yet
then likewise he utterly refused, because he meant to go
through fasting as he was. His companion was content,
and so went forward with him, without taking anything
himself. But when they had now gone very far, and
were well wearied with long travelling, at length they
came unto a meadow, where there was a fountain, and all
such other pleasant things as use to refresh men's bodies.
Then his companion said to him again : "Behold here is
water, a green meadow, and a very sweet place, in which
we may refresh ourselves and rest a little, that we may
be the better able to dispatch the rest of our journey."
Which kind words bewitching his ears, and the pleasant
place flattering his eyes, content he was to yield unto

the motion, and so they fell to their meat together : and coming afterward in the evening to the Abbey, they brought him to the venerable father Bennet, of whom he desired his blessing. Then the holy man objected against him what he had done in the way, speaking to him in this manner : "How fell it out, brother," quoth he, "that the devil talking to you, by means of your companion, could not at the first nor second time persuade you : but yet he did at the third, and made you do what best pleased him ?" The good man, hearing these words, fell down at his feet, confessing the fault of his frailty ; was grieved, and so much the more ashamed of his sin, because he perceived that though he were absent, that yet he did offend in the sight of that venerable father.

Peter. I see well that the holy man had in his soul the spirit of Heliseus, who was present with his servant Giezi, being then absent from him.

Chapter Fourteen : how the dissimulation of king Totilas was discovered and found out by venerable Bennet. ¶ Gregory. You must, good Peter, for a little while be silent, that you may know matters yet far more important. For in the time of the Goths, when Totilas, their king, understood that the holy man had the spirit of prophecy, as he was going towards his monastery, he remained in a place somewhat far off, and beforehand sent the father word of his coming : to whom answer was returned, that he might come at his pleasure. The king, as he was a man wickedly disposed, thought he would try whether the man of God were a prophet, as it was reported, or no. A certain man of his guard he had, called Riggo, upon whom he caused his own shoes to be put, and to be apparelled with his other princely robes, commanding him to go as it were himself to the man of God ; and to give the better colour to this device, he sent three to attend upon him, who especially were

always about the king : to wit, Vultericus, Rudericus, and
Blindinus ; charging them that in the presence of the servant of God, they should be next about him, and behave
themselves in such sort as though he had been king
Totilas indeed : and that diligently they should do unto
him all other services, to the end that both by such dutiful kind of behaviour, as also by his purple robes, he
might verily be taken for the king himself. Riggo, furnished with that brave apparel, and accompanied with
many courtiers, came unto the Abbey : at which time the
man of God sat a little way off, and when Riggo was come
so near that he might well understand what the man of
God said, then, in the hearing of them all, he spake thus :
"Put off, my good son, put off that apparel, for that
which thou hast on, is none of thine." Riggo, hearing
this, fell straightways down to the ground, and was very
much afraid, for presuming to go about to mock so
worthy a man, and all his attendants and servitors fell
down likewise to the earth, and after they were up again,
they durst not approach any nearer to his presence : but
returned back to their king, telling him with fear, how
quickly they were discovered.

**Chapter Fifteen : how venerable Bennet prophesied to king Totilas, and also to the Bishop of
Camisina, such things as were afterward to fall
out.** ¶ Then Totilas himself in person went unto the
man of God ; and seeing him sitting afar off, he durst not
come near, but fell down to the ground : whom the holy
man (speaking to him twice or thrice) desired to rise up,
and at length came unto him, and with his own hands
lifted him up from the earth, where he lay prostrate :
and then, entering into talk, he reprehended him for his
wicked deeds, and in few words told him all that which
should befall him, saying : "Much wickedness do you
daily commit, and many great sins have you done : now
at length give over your sinful life. Into the city of

Speckle Aretino

THE MEETING OF ST. BENEDICT AND KING TOTILA

Alinari

Rome shall you enter, and over the sea shall you pass: nine years shall you reign, and in the tenth shall you leave this mortal life." The king, hearing these things, was wonderfully afraid, and desiring the holy man to commend him to God in his prayers, he departed: and from that time forward he was nothing so cruel as before he had been. Not long after he went to Rome, sailed over into Sicily, and, in the tenth year of his reign, he lost his kingdom together with his life.

The Bishop also of Camisina used to visit the servant of God, whom the holy man dearly loved for his virtuous life. The Bishop, therefore, talking with him of king Totilas, of his taking of Rome, and the destruction of that city, said: "This city will be so spoiled and ruined by him, that it will never be more inhabited." To whom the man of God answered: "Rome," quoth he, "shall not be utterly destroyed by strangers: but shall be so shaken with tempests, lightnings, whirlwinds, and earthquakes, that it will fall to decay of itself." The mysteries of which prophecy we now behold as clear as the day: for we see before our eyes in this very city, by a strange whirlwind the world shaken, houses ruined, and churches overthrown, and buildings rotten with old age we behold daily to fall down. True it is that Honoratus, by whose relation I had this, saith not that he received it from his own mouth, but that he had it of other monks, which did hear it themselves.

Chapter Sixteen: of a certain clergyman, whom venerable Bennet for a time delivered from a devil.
¶ At the same time a certain clergyman, that served in the church of Aquinum, was possessed: whom the venerable man Constantius, Bishop of the same city, sent unto many places of holy martyrs for help: but God's holy martyrs would not deliver him, to the end that the world might know what great grace was in the servant of God, Bennet: wherefore at length he was brought unto him,

who, praying for help to Jesus Christ our Lord, did forthwith cast the old enemy out of the possessed man's body, giving him this charge : "Go your way, and hereafter abstain from eating of flesh, and presume not to enter into holy orders, for whensoever you shall attempt any such thing, the devil again will have power over you." The man departed safe and sound, and because punishment fresh in memory useth to terrify the mind, he observed for a time what the man of God had given him in commandment. But after many years, when all his seniors were dead, and he saw his juniors preferred before him to holy orders, he neglected the words of the man of God, as though forgotten through length of time, and took upon him holy orders : whereupon straightways the devil that before had left him entered again, and never gave over to torment him, until he had separated his soul from his body.

Peter. This holy man, as I perceive, did know the secret counsel of God : for he saw that this clergyman was delivered to the power of the devil, to the end he should not presume to enter into holy orders.

Gregory. Why should he not know the secrets of God, who kept the commandments of God : when as the scripture saith : *He that cleaveth unto our Lord, is one spirit with him ?*[1]

Peter. If he that cleaveth unto our Lord, be one spirit with our Lord, what is the meaning of that which the Apostle saith : *Who knoweth the sense of our Lord, or who hath been his counsellor ?*[2] for it seemeth very inconvenient to be ignorant of his sense, to whom being so united he is made one thing.

Gregory. Holy men, in that they be one with our Lord, are not ignorant of his sense : for the same Apostle saith[3] : *For what man knoweth those things which belong to man, but the spirit of man which is in him ? Even so, the*

---

[1] Cor. 6.   [2] Rom. 11, 34.   [3] 1 Cor. 2, 9–11.

things which belong to God, no man knoweth, but the spirit of God. And to show also that he knew such things as belong to God, he addeth straight after : *But we have not received the spirit of this world, but the spirit which is of God.* And for this cause, again he saith : *that eye hath not seen, nor ear heard, nor it hath ascended into the heart of man, those things which God hath prepared for them that love him, but God hath revealed to us by his spirit."*

Peter. If, then, the mysteries of God were revealed to the same Apostle by the spirit of God, why did he then, entreating of this question, set down these words beforehand, saying : *O the depth of the riches of the wisdom and knowledge of God : how incomprehensible be his judgments, and his ways investigable ?* And again, whiles I am thus speaking of this matter, another question cometh to my mind : for the prophet David said to our Lord : *With my lips have I uttered all the judgments of thy mouth.* Wherefore, seeing it is less to know, than to utter : what is the reason that St. Paul affirmeth the judgments of God to be incomprehensible ; and yet David saith that he did not know only them, but also with his lips pronounce them ?

Gregory. To both these questions I have already briefly answered, when I said that holy men, in that they be one with our Lord, are not ignorant of the sense of our Lord. For all such, as do devoutly follow our Lord, be also by devotion one with our Lord ; and yet for all this, in that they are laden with the burthen of their corruptible flesh, they be not with God : and so in that they be joined with him, they know the secret judgments of God, and in that they be separated from God, they know them not : for seeing they do not as yet perfectly penetrate his secret mysteries, they give testimony that his judgments be incomprehensible. But those that do with their soul adhere unto him, and cleaving unto the sayings of the holy scripture, or to secret revelations, acknowledge what they receive : such persons both know these things and do utter them : for those judgments which God doth conceal they know not, and those which he doth utter they know : and therefore the prophet David, when he had said : *I have with my lips uttered all the judgments;*[1] he addeth immediately, *of thy mouth:* as though he should plainly say : Those judgments I may both know and utter, which I knew thou didst speak, for those things which thou dost not speak, without all question, thou dost conceal from our knowledge. Wherefore the saying of David and St. Paul agree together : for the judgments of God are incomprehensible ; and yet those which himself with his own mouth vouchsafeth to speak, are uttered with men's tongues : because men may come to the knowledge of them, and being revealed, they may be uttered, and by no means can be kept secret. **Peter.** Now I see the answer to my question. But I pray you to proceed, if anything yet remaineth to be told of his virtue and miracles.

Chapter Seventeen : how the man of God, Bennet, did foretell the suppression of one of his own Abbeys. ¶ Gregory. A certain noble man called Theoprobus was by the good counsel of holy Bennet converted : who, for his virtue and merit of life, was very intrinsical and familiar with him. This man upon a day, coming into his cell, found him weeping very bitterly. And having expected a good while, and yet not seeing him to make an end (for the man of God used not in his prayers to weep, but rather to be sad), he demanded the cause of that his so great heaviness, to whom he answered straightway, saying : "All this Abbey which I have built, and all such things as I have made ready for my brethren, are by the judgment of almighty God delivered to the gentiles, to be spoiled and overthrown : and scarce could I obtain of God to have their lives spared, that should then live in it " His words Theoprobus then heard,

[1] Ps. 119, 13.

but we see them to be proved most true, who know that very Abbey to be now suppressed by the Lombards. For not long since, in the night time, when the monks were asleep, they entered in, and spoiled all things, but yet not one man could they retain there, and so almighty God fulfilled what he promised to his faithful servant: for though he gave them the house and all the goods, yet did he preserve their lives. In which thing I see that Bennet imitated St. Paul: whose ship [1] though it lost all the goods, yet, for his comfort, he had the lives of all that were in his company bestowed upon him, so that no one man was cast away.

Chapter Eighteen: how blessed Bennet knew the hiding away of a flagon of wine. ¶ Upon a certain time, Exhilaratus our monk, a lay-brother, whom you know, was sent by his master to the monastery of the man of God, to carry him two wooden bottles, commonly called flagons, full of wine: who in the way, as he was going, hid one of them in a bush for himself, and presented the other to venerable Bennet: who took it very thankfully, and, when the man was going away, he gave him this warning: "Take heed, my son," quoth he, "that thou drinkest not of that flagon which thou hast hidden in the bush: but first be careful to bow it down, and thou shalt find what is within it." The poor man, thus pitifully confounded by the man of God, went his way, and coming back to the place where the flagon was hidden, and desirous to try the truth of that was told him, as he was bowing it down, a snake straightways leaped forth. Then Exhilaratus perceiving what was gotten into the wine, began to be afraid of that wickedness which he had committed.

Chapter Nineteen: how the man of God knew that one of his Monks had received certain handkerchiefs. ¶ Not far from his Abbey, there was a

[1] Acts 27, 22-44.

village, in which very many men had, by the sermons
of Bennet, been converted from idolatry to the true
faith of Christ. Certain Nuns also there were in the
same town, to whom he did often send some of his
monks to preach unto them, for the good of their souls.
Upon a day, one that was sent, after he had made an
end of his exhortation, by the entreaty of the Nuns took
certain small napkins, and hid them for his own use in
his bosom : whom, upon his return to the Abbey, the
man of God very sharply rebuked, saying : "How
cometh it to pass, brother, that sin is entered into your
bosom ?" At which words the monk was much amazed :
for he had quite forgotten what he had put there ; and
therefore knew not any cause why he should deserve
that reprehension : whereupon the holy man spake to
him in plain terms, and said : " Was not I present when
you took the handkerchiefs of the Nuns, and put them
up in your bosom for your own private use ? " The
monk, hearing this, fell down at his feet, and was sorry
that he had behaved himself so indiscreetly : forth he
drew those napkins from his bosom, and threw them all
away.

Chapter Twenty : how holy Bennet knew the proud thought of one of his Monks.

¶ Upon a
time, whiles the venerable Father was at supper, one of
his monks, who was the son of a great man, held the
candle : and as he was standing there, and the other at
his meat, he began to entertain a proud cogitation in his
mind, and to speak thus within himself : "Who is he,
that I thus wait upon at supper, and hold him the
candle ? and who am I, that I should do him any such
service ? " Upon which thought straightways the holy
man turned himself, and with severe reprehension spake
thus unto him : " Sign your heart, brother, for what is
it that you say ? Sign your heart " : and forthwith he
called another of the monks, and bad him take the

ST. PLACIDUS
(Vatican Gallery, Rome)

candle out of his hands, and commanded him to give over his waiting, and to repose himself: who being demanded of the monks, what it was that he thought, told them, how inwardly he swelled with pride, and what he spake against the man of God, secretly in his own heart. Then they all saw very well that nothing could be hidden from venerable Bennet, seeing the very sound of men's inward thoughts came unto his ears.

Chapter Twenty-one: of two hundred bushels of meal, found before the man of God's cell.

¶ At another time, there was a great dearth in the same country of Campania: so that all kind of people tasted of the misery: and all the wheat of Bennet's monastery was spent, and likewise all the bread, so that there remained no more than five loaves for dinner. The venerable man, beholding the monks sad, both rebuked them modestly for their pusillanimity, and again did comfort them with this promise: "Why," quoth he, "are you so grieved in your minds for lack of bread? Indeed, to-day some want there is, but to-morrow you shall have plenty": and so it fell out, for the next day two hundred bushels of meal was found in sacks before his cell door, which almighty God sent them: but by whom, or what means, that is unknown to this very day: which miracle when the monks saw, they gave God thanks, and by this learned in want, not to make any doubt of plenty.

Peter. Tell me, I pray you, whether this servant of God had always the spirit of prophecy, when himself pleased, or only at certain times?

Gregory. The spirit of prophecy doth not always illuminate the minds of the prophets; because, as it is written of the Holy Ghost that *he breatheth where he will*,[1] so we are also to know that he doth breathe likewise for what cause, and when he pleaseth. And

[1] John 3, 8.

hereof it cometh, that when king David demanded of Nathan[1] whether he might build a temple for the honour of God, the prophet Nathan gave his consent ; and yet afterward utterly forbad it. From hence likewise it proceedeth that, when Heliseus saw the woman weeping, and knew not the cause, he said to his servant that did trouble her : *Let her alone, for her soul is in grief, and God hath concealed it from me, and hath not told me.*[2] Which thing almighty God of great piety so disposeth : for giving at some times the spirit of prophecy, and at other times withdrawing it, he doth both lift up the prophets minds on high, and yet doth preserve them in humility that by the gift of the Spirit, they may know what they are by God's grace : and at other times, destitute of the same Spirit, may understand what they are of themselves.

Peter. There is very great reason for that you say. But, I pray you, let me hear more of the venerable man Bennet, if there be anything else that cometh to your remembrance.

Chapter Twenty-two : how, by vision, venerable Bennet disposed the building of the Abbey of Taracina. ¶ Gregory. At another time he was desired by a certain virtuous man, to build an Abbey for his monks upon his ground, not far from the city of Taracina. The holy man was content, and appointed an Abbot and Prior, with divers monks under them : and when they were departing, he promised that, upon such a day, he would come and shew them in what place the oratory should be made, and where the refectory should stand, and all the other necessary rooms : and so they, taking his blessing, went their way ; and against the day appointed, which they greatly expected, they made all such things ready as were necessary to entertain him, and those that should come in his company. But the very night before, the man of God in sleep appeared to

---

[1] I Chr. 17, 2-4. [2] 4 Kings 4, 27.

the Abbot and the Prior, and particularly described unto them where each place and office was to be builded. And when they were both risen, they conferred together what either of them had seen in their sleep : but yet not giving full credit to that vision, they expected the man of God himself in person, according to his promise. But when they saw that he came not, they returned back unto him very sorrowfully, saying: "We expected, father, that you should have come according to promise, and told us where each place should have been built, which yet you did not." To whom he answered : "Why say you so, good brethren ? Did not I come as I promised you ?" And when they asked at what time it was : "Why," quoth he, "did not I appear to either of you in your sleep, and appointed how and where every place was to be builded ? Go your way, and according to that platform which you then saw, build up the abbey." At which word they much marvelled, and returning back, they caused it to be builded in such sort as they had been taught of him by revelation.

Peter. Gladly would I learn, by what means that could be done : to wit, that he should go so far to tell them that thing in their sleep, which they should both hear and know by vision.

Gregory. Why do you, Peter, seek out and doubt, in what manner this thing was done ? For certain it is, that the soul is of a more noble nature than the body. And by authority of scripture we know that the prophet Abacuck was carried from Judea with that dinner which he had, and was suddenly set in Chaldea ;[1] by which meat the prophet Daniel was relieved : and presently after was brought back again to Judea. If, then, Abacuck could in a moment with his body go so far, and carry provision for another man's dinner : what marvel is it, if the holy father Bennet obtained grace to go in spirit

[1] Daniel 14, 32–38 (Vulgate).

and to inform the souls of his brethren that were asleep, concerning such things as were necessary : and that as Abacuck about corporal meat went corporally, so Bennet should go spiritually about the dispatch of spiritual business ?

Peter. I confess that your words have satisfied my doubtful mind. But I would know what manner of man he was in his ordinary talk and conversation.

Chapter Twenty-three : of certain Nuns absolved after their death. ¶ Gregory. His common talk, Peter, was usually full of virtue : for his heart conversed so above in heaven, that no words could in vain proceed from his mouth. And if at any time he spake aught, yet not as one that determined what was best to be done, but only in a threatening manner, his speech in that case was so effectual and forcible, as though he had not doubtfully or uncertainly, but assuredly pronounced and given sentence. For not far from his Abbey, there lived two Nuns in a place by themselves, born of worshipful parentage : whom a religious good man did serve for the dispatch of their outward business. But as nobility of family doth in some breed ignobility of mind, and maketh them in conversation to show less humility, because they remember still what superiority they had above others : even so was it with these Nuns : for they had not yet learned to temper their tongues, and keep them under with the bridle of their habit : for often did they by their indiscreet speech provoke the foresaid religious man to anger ; who having borne with them a long time, at length he complained to the man of God, and told him with what reproachful words they entreated him : whereupon he sent them by and by this message, saying : "Amend your tongues, otherwise I do excommunicate you" ; which sentence of excommunication notwithstanding, he did not then presently pronounce against them, but only threatened if they amended not

84

themselves. But they, for all this, changed their conditions nothing at all: both which not long after departed this life, and were buried in the church: and when solemn mass was celebrated in the same church, and the Deacon, according to custom, said with loud voice: "If any there be that do not communicate, let them depart": the nurse, which used to give unto our Lord an offering for them, beheld them at that time to rise out of their graves, and to depart the church. Having often times, at those words of the Deacon, seen them leave the church, and that they could not tarry within, she remembered what message the man of God sent them whiles they were yet alive. For he told them that he did deprive them of the communion, unless they did amend their tongues and conditions. Then with great sorrow, the whole matter was signified to the man of God, who straightways with his own hands gave an oblation, saying: "Go your ways, and cause this to be offered unto our Lord for them, and they shall not remain any longer excommunicate": which oblation being offered for them, and the Deacon, as he used, crying out, that such as did not communicate should depart, they were not seen any more to go out of the church: whereby it was certain that, seeing they did not depart with them which did not communicate, that they had received the communion of our Lord by the hands of his servant.

Peter. It is very strange that you report: for how could he, though a venerable and most holy man, yet living in mortal body, loose those souls which stood now before the invisible judgment of God?

Gregory. Was he not yet, Peter, mortal, that heard from our Saviour: *Whatsoever thou shalt bind upon earth, it shall be bound also in the heavens: and whatsoever thou shalt loose in earth, shall be loosed also in the heavens?*[1] whose place of binding and loosing those have at this time,

[1] Matt. 16, 19.

which by faith and virtuous life possess the place of holy government : and to bestow such power upon earthly men, the Creator of heaven and earth descended from heaven to earth : and that flesh might judge of spiritual things, God, who for man's sake was made flesh, vouchsafed to bestow upon him : for from thence our weakness did rise up above itself, from whence the strength of God was weakened under itself.

Peter. For the virtue of his miracles, your words do yield a very good reason.

Chapter Twenty-four: of a boy that after his burial was cast out of his grave.

¶ Gregory. Upon a certain day, a young boy that was a monk, loving his parents more than reason would, went from the Abbey to their house, not craving the father's blessing beforehand : and the same day that he came home unto them, he departed this life. And being buried, his body, the next day after, was found cast out of the grave ; which they caused again to be put in, and again, the day following, they found it as before. Then in great haste they went to the man of God, fell down at his feet, and with many tears beseeched him that he would vouchsafe him that was dead of his favour. To whom the man of God with his own hands delivered the holy communion of our Lord's body, saying : " Go, and lay with great reverence this our Lord's body upon his breast, and so bury him " : which when they had done, the dead corpse after that remained quietly in the grave. By which you perceive, Peter, of what merit he was with our Lord Jesus Christ, seeing the earth would not give entertainment to his body, who departed this world out of Bennet's favour.

Peter. I perceive it very well, and do wonderfully admire it.

Chapter Twenty-five: how a Monk, forsaking the Abbey, met with a dragon in the way.

¶ Gregory. A certain monk there was so inconstant and fickle of mind, that he would needs give over the Abbey; for which fault of his, the man of God did daily rebuke him, and often times gave him good admonitions: but yet, for all this, by no means would he tarry amongst them, and therefore continual suit he made that he might be discharged. The venerable man upon a time, wearied with his importunity, in anger bad him depart; who was no sooner out of the Abbey gate, but he found a dragon in the way expecting him with open mouth, which being about to devour him, he began in great fear and trembling to cry out aloud, saying: "Help, help! for this dragon will eat me up." At which noise the monks running out, dragon they saw none, but finding him there shaking and trembling, they brought him back again to the Abbey, who forthwith promised that he would never more forsake the monastery, and so ever after he continued in his profession: for by the prayers of the holy man, he saw the dragon coming against him, whom before, when he saw not, he did willingly follow.

Chapter Twenty-six: how holy Bennet cured a boy of the leprosy.

¶ But I must not here pass over with silence that which I had by relation of the honourable man, Anthony, who said that his father's boy was so pitifully punished with a leprosy, that all his hair fell off, his body swelled, and filthy corruption did openly come forth. Who being sent by his father to the man of God, he was by him quickly restored to his former health.

Chapter Twenty-seven: how Bennet found money miraculously to relieve a poor man.

¶ Neither is that to be omitted, which one of his disciples called Peregrinus used to tell: for he said that, upon a certain day, an honest man, who was in debt, found no other means to help himself, but thought it his best way to acquaint the man of God with his necessity: whereupon he came to the Abbey, and finding the servant of almighty God, gave him to understand, how he was troubled by his creditor for twelve shillings which he did owe him. To whom the venerable man said that himself had not so much money, yet giving him comfortable words, he said : " Go your ways, and after two days come to me again, for I can not presently help you ": in which two days, after his manner, he bestowed himself in prayer : and when upon the third day the poor man came back, there were found suddenly upon the chest of the Abbey, which was full of corn, thirteen shillings : which the man of God caused to be given to him that required but twelve, both to discharge his debt, and also to defray his own charges. But now will I return to speak of such things as I had from the mouth of his own scholars, mentioned before in the beginning of this book. A certain man there was who had an enemy that did notably spite and malign him, whose damnable hatred proceeded so far, that he poisoned his drink, which, although it killed him not, yet did it change his skin in such sort that it was of many colours, as though he had been infected with a leprosy : but the man of God restored him to his former health : for so soon as he touched him, forthwith all that variety of colours departed from his body.

Chapter Twenty-eight: how a cruet of glass was thrown upon the stones, and not broken. ¶ At such time as there was a great dearth in Campania, the man of God had given away all the wealth of the Abbey to poor people, so that in the cellar there was nothing left but a little oil in a glass. A certain sub-deacon called Agapitus came unto him, instantly craving that he would bestow a little oil upon him. Our Lord's servant, that was resolved to give away all upon earth, that he might find all in heaven, commanded that oil to be given him : but the monk that kept the cellar heard what the father commanded, yet did he not perform it : who inquiring not long after whether he had given that which he willed, the monk told him that he had not,

adding that if he had given it away, that there was
not any left for the Convent. Then in an anger he
commanded others to take that glass with the oil, and
to throw it out at the window, to the end that nothing
might remain in the Abbey contrary to obedience. The
monks did so, and threw it out at a window, under which
there was an huge downfall, full of rough and craggy
stones upon which the glass did light, but yet continued
for all that so sound as though it had never been thrown
out at all, for neither the glass was broken nor any of
the oil shed. Then the man of God did command it
to be taken up again, and, whole as it was, to be given
unto him that desired it, and in the presence of the
other brethren he reprehended the disobedient monk,
both for his infidelity, and also for his proud mind.

**Chapter Twenty-nine: how an empty barrel was
filled with oil.** ¶ After which reprehension, with the
rest of his brethren he fell to praying, and in the place
where they were, there stood an empty barrel with a
cover upon it: and as the holy man continued in his
prayers, the oil within did so increase, that the cover
began to be lifted up, and at length fell down, and the
oil, that was now higher than the mouth of the barrel,
began to run over upon the pavement, which so soon as
the servant of God, Bennet, beheld, forthwith he gave
over his prayers, and the oil likewise ceased to overflow
the barrel. Then he did more at large admonish that
mistrusting and disobedient monk, that he would learn
to have faith and humility, who upon so wholesome an
admonition was ashamed, because the venerable father
had by miracle shown the power of almighty God, as
before he told him when he did first rebuke him: and
so no cause there was why any should afterward doubt
of his promise, seeing at one and the same time, for a
small glass almost empty which he gave away, he bestowed
upon them an whole barrel full of oil.

Chapter Thirty: how Bennet delivered a Monk from a Devil. ¶ Upon a certain time, as he was going to the oratory of St. John, which is in the top of the mountain, the old enemy of mankind upon a mule, like a physician, met him, carrying in his hand an horn and a mortar. And when he demanded whither he was going: "To your monks," quoth he, "to give them a drench." The venerable father went forward to his prayers, and when he had done, he returned in all haste, but the wicked spirit found an old monk drawing of water, into whom he entered, and straightways cast him upon the ground, and grievously tormented him. The man of God coming from his prayers, and seeing him in such pitiful case, gave him only a little blow with his hand, and at the same instant he cast out that cruel devil, so that he durst not any more presume to enter in.

Peter. I would gladly know, whether he obtained always by prayer, to work such notable miracles; or else sometimes did them only at his will and pleasure.

Gregory. Such as be the devout servants of God, when necessity requireth, use to work miracles both manner of ways: so that sometime they effect wonderful things by their prayers, and sometime only by their power and authority: for St. John saith: *So many as received him, he gave them power to be made the sons of God.*[1] They, then, - that by power be the sons of God, what marvel is it, if by power they be able to do wonderful things? And that both ways they work miracles, we learn of St. Peter: who by his prayers did raise up Tabitha; and by his sharp reprehension did sentence Ananias and Sapphira to death for their lying.[2] For we read not, that in the death of them he prayed at all, but only rebuked them for that sin which they had committed. Certain therefore it is, that sometimes they do these things by power, and sometimes by prayer: for Ananias and Sapphira by a severe

[1] John I, 12.   [2] Acts 9 and 5.

rebuke, St. Peter deprived of life : and by prayer restored Tabitha to life. And for proof of this, I will now tell you of two miracles, which the faithful servant of God, Bennet, did, in which it shall appear most plainly that he wrought the one by that power which God gave him, and obtained the other by virtue of his prayers.

Chapter Thirty-one : of a country fellow, that, with the only sight of the man of God, was loosed from his bands. ¶ A certain Goth there was called Galla, an Arian heretic, who, in the time of King Totilas, did with such monstrous cruelty persecute religious men of the Catholic church, that what priest or monk soever came in his presence, he never departed alive. This man on a certain day, set upon rapine and pillage, pitifully tormented a poor country man, to make him confess where his money and wealth was : who, overcome with extremity of pain, said that he had committed all his substance to the custody of Bennet, the servant of God : and this he did, to the end that his tormentor, giving credit to his words, might at least for a while surcease from his horrible cruelty. Galla hearing this tormented him no longer : but binding his arms fast with strong cords, drave him before his horse, to bring him unto this Bennet, who, as he said, had his wealth in keeping. The country fellow, thus pinioned and running before him, carried him to the holy man's Abbey, where he found him sitting before the gate, reading upon a book. Then turning back to Galla that came raging after, he said : " This is father Bennet, of whom I told you " : who looking upon him, in a great fury, thinking to deal as terribly with him as he had with others, cried out aloud to him, saying : " Rise up, sirrah, rise up, and deliver me quickly such wealth as thou hast of this man's in keeping." The man of God, hearing such a noise, straightways lifted up his eyes from reading, and beheld both him and the country

fellow; and turning his eyes to his bands, very strangely
they fell from his arms, and that so quickly as no man
with any haste could have undone them. Galla, seeing
him so wonderfully and quickly loosed, fell straight a
trembling, and prostrating himself upon the earth,
bowed down his cruel and stiff neck to the holy man's
feet, and with humility did commend himself to his
prayers. But the venerable man for all this rose not
up from his reading, but calling for some of his monks,
commanded them to have him in, and to give him some
meat. And when he was brought back again, he gave
him a good lesson, admonishing him not to use any
more such rigour and cruel dealing. His proud mind
thus taken down, away he went, but durst not demand
after that anything of the country fellow, whom the man
of God, not with hands, but only with his eyes, had
loosed from his bands. And this is that, Peter, which
I told you, that those which in a more familiar sort serve
God, do sometime, by certain power and authority bestowed upon them, work miracles. For he that sitting
still did appease the fury of that cruel Goth, and un-
loose with his eyes those knots and cords which did
pinion the innocent man's arms, did plainly shew by
the quickness of the miracle, that he had received power
to work all that which he did. And now will I likewise
tell you of another miracle, which by prayer he obtained
at God's hands.

**Chapter Thirty-two: how by prayer venerable
Bennet raised up a dead child.** ¶ Being upon a day
gone out with his monks to work in the field, a country
man carrying the corpse of his dead son, came to the
gate of the Abbey, lamenting the loss of his child: and
inquiring for holy Bennet, they told him that he was
abroad with his monks in the field. Down at the gate
he laid the dead body, and with great sorrow of soul
ran in haste to seek out the venerable father. At the

same time, the man of God was returning homeward from work with his monks : whom so soon as he saw, he began to cry out : " Give me my son, give me my son ! " The man of God, amazed at these words, stood still, and said : " What, have I taken away your son ? " " No, no," quoth the sorrowful father, "but he is dead : come for Christ Jesus' sake and restore him to life." The servant of God, hearing him speak in that manner, and seeing his monks upon compassion to solicit the poor man's suit, with great sorrow of mind he said : " Away, my good brethren, away : such miracles are not for us to work, but for the blessed Apostles : why will you lay such a burthen upon me, as my weakness cannot bear ? " But the poor man, whom excessive grief enforced, would not give over his petition, but swore that he would never depart, except he did raise up his son. " Where is he, then ? " quoth God's servant. He answered that his body lay at the gate of the Abbey : to which place when the man of God came with his monks, he kneeled down and lay upon the body of the little child, and rising, he held up his hands towards heaven, and said · " Behold not, O Lord, my sins, but the faith of this man, that desireth to have his son raised to life, and restore that soul to the body, which thou hast taken away." He had scarce spoken these words, and behold the soul returned back again, and therewith the child's body began to tremble in such sort that all which were present did behold it in strange manner to pant and shake. Then he took it by the hand and gave it to his father, but alive and in health. Certain it is, Peter, that this miracle was not in his own power, for which prostrate upon the ground he prayed so earnestly.

Peter. All is most true that before you said, for what you affirmed in words, you have now verified by examples and works. But tell me, I beseech you, whether holy

men can do all such things as they please, and obtain
at God's hands whatsoever they desire.

**Chapter Thirty-three : of a miracle wrought by his
sister Scholastica. ¶ Gregory.** What man is there,
Peter, in this world, that is in greater favour with God
than St. Paul was : who yet three times desired our
Lord to be delivered from the prick of the flesh, and
obtained not his petition ?[1] Concerning which point
also I must needs tell you, how there was one thing
which the venerable father Bennet would have done,
and yet he could not. For his sister called Scholastica,
dedicated from her infancy to our Lord, used once a
year to come and visit her brother. To whom the man
of God went not far from the gate, to a place that did
belong to the Abbey, there to give her entertainment.
And she coming thither on a time according to her
custom, her venerable brother with his monks went to
meet her, where they spent the whole day in the praises
of God and spiritual talk : and when it was almost night
they supped together, and as they were yet sitting at
the table, talking of devout matters, and darkness came
on, the holy Nun his sister entreated him to stay there
all night, that they might spend it in discoursing of the
joys of heaven. But by no persuasion would he agree
unto that, saying that he might not by any means tarry
all night out of his Abbey. At that time, the sky was
so clear that no cloud was to be seen. The Nun, receiving this denial of her brother, joining her hands
together, laid them upon the table : and so, bowing
down her head upon them, she made her prayers to
almighty God : and lifting her head from the table,
there fell suddenly such a tempest of lightning and
thundering, and such abundance of rain, that neither
venerable Bennet, nor his monks that were with him,
could put their head out of door : for the holy Nun,

[1] 2 Cor. 12, 8.

94

resting her head upon her hands, poured forth such a flood of tears upon the table, that she drew the clear air to a watery sky, so that after the end of her devotions, that storm of rain followed : and her prayer and the rain did so meet together, that as she lifted up her head from the table, the thunder began, so that in one and the very same instant, she lifted up her head and brought down the rain. The man of God, seeing that he could not by reason of such thunder and lightning and great abundance of rain, return back to his Abbey, began to be heavy and to complain of his sister, saying : "God forgive you, what have you done ?" to whom she answered : " I desired you to stay, and you would not hear me, I have desired our good Lord, and he hath vouchsafed to grant my petition : wherefore if you can now depart, a God's name return to your monastery, and leave me here alone." But the good father, being not able to go forth, tarried there against his will, where willingly before he would not stay. And so by that means they watched all night, and with spiritual and heavenly talk did mutually comfort one another : and therefore by this we see, as I said before, that he would have had that thing, which yet he could not : for if we respect the venerable man's mind, no question but he would have had the same fair weather to have continued as it was, when he set forth, but he found that a miracle did prevent his desire, which, by the power of almighty God, a woman's prayers had wrought. And it is not a thing to be marvelled at, that a woman which of long time had not seen her brother, might do more at that time than he could, seeing, according to the saying of St. John, *God is charity*,[1] and therefore of right she did more which loved more.

Peter. I confess that I am wonderfully pleased with that which you tell me.

[1] 1 John 4, 8.

95

Chapter Thirty-four: how Bennet saw the soul of his Sister ascend into Heaven. ¶ Gregory.

The next day the venerable woman returned to her Nunnery, and the man of God to his Abbey: who three days after, standing in his cell, and lifting up his eyes to heaven, beheld the soul of his sister (which was departed from her body), in the likeness of a dove to ascend into heaven: who rejoicing much to see her great glory, with hymns and lauds gave thanks to almighty God, and did impart the news of this her death to his monks, whom also he sent presently to bring her corpse to his Abbey, to have it buried in that grave which he had provided for himself: by means whereof it fell out that, as their souls were always one in God whiles they lived, so their bodies continued together after their death.

Chapter Thirty-five: how he saw the whole world represented before his eyes: and also the soul of Germanus, Bishop of Capua, ascending to heaven. ¶ At another time, Servandus, the Deacon,

and Abbot of that monastery, which in times past was founded by the noble man Liberius in the country of Campania, used ordinarily to come and visit the man of God: and the reason why he came so often was, because himself also was a man full of heavenly doctrine: and so they two had often together spiritual conference, to the end that, albeit they could not perfectly feed upon the celestial food of heaven, yet, by means of such sweet discourses, they might at least, with longing and fervent desire, taste of those joys and divine delights. When it was time to go to rest, the venerable father Bennet reposed himself in the top of a tower, at the foot whereof Servandus the Deacon was lodged, so that one pair of stairs went to them both: before the tower there was a certain large room in which both their disciples did lie. The man of God, Bennet,

Perugino

ST. SCHOLASTICA

(San Pietro, Perugia)

being diligent in watching, rose early up before the time of matins (his monks being yet at rest) and came to the window of his chamber, where he offered up his prayers to almighty God. Standing there, all on a sudden in the dead of the night, as he looked forth, he saw a light, which banished away the darkness of the night, and glittered with such brightness, that the light which did shine in the midst of darkness was far more clear than the light of the day. Upon this sight a marvellous strange thing followed, for, as himself did afterward report, the whole world, gathered as it were together under one beam of the sun, was presented before his eyes, and whiles the venerable father stood attentively beholding the brightness of that glittering light, he saw the soul of Germanus, Bishop of Capua, in a fiery globe to be carried up by Angels into heaven. Then, desirous to have some witness of this so notable a miracle, he called with a very loud voice Servandus the Deacon twice or thrice by his name, who, troubled at such an unusual crying out of the man of God, went up in all haste, and looking forth saw not anything else, but a little remnant of the light, but wondering at so great a miracle, the man of God told him all in order what he had seen, and sending by and by to the town of Cassino, he commanded the religious man Theoprobus to dispatch one that night to the city of Capua, to learn what was become of Germanus their Bishop : which being done, the messenger found that reverent Prelate departed this life, and enquiring curiously the time, he understood that he died at that very instant, in which the man of God beheld him ascending up to heaven.

Peter. A strange thing and very much to be admired. But whereas you say that the whole world, as it were under one sunbeam, was presented before his eyes, as I must needs confess that in myself I never had experience of any such thing, so neither can I conceive by what means the whole world can be seen of any one man.

Gregory. Assure yourself, Peter, of that which I speak : to wit, that all creatures be as it were nothing to that soul which beholdeth the Creator : for though it see but a glimpse of that light which is in the Creator, yet very small do all things seem that be created : for by means of that supernatural light, the capacity of the inward soul is enlarged, and is in God so extended, that it is far above the world : yea and the soul of him that seeth in this manner, is also above itself; for being rapt up in the light of God, it is inwardly in itself enlarged above itself, and when it is so exalted and looketh downward, then doth it comprehend how little all that is, which before in former baseness it could not comprehend. The man of God, therefore, who saw the fiery globe, and the Angels returning to heaven, out of all doubt could not see those things but in the light of God : what marvel, then, is it, if he saw the world gathered together before him, who, rapt up in the light of his soul, was at that time out of the world ? But albeit we say that the world was gathered together before his eyes, yet were not heaven and earth drawn into any lesser room than they be of themselves, but the soul of the beholder was more enlarged, which, rapt in God, might without difficulty see that which is under God, and therefore in that light which appeared to his outward eyes, the inward light which was in his soul ravished the mind of the beholder to supernal things, and shewed him how small all earthly things were.

Peter. I perceive now that it was to my more profit that I understood you not before : seeing, by reason of my slow capacity, you have delivered so notable an exposition. But now, because you have made me thrughly to understand these things, I beseech you to continue on your former narration.

Chapter Thirty-six: how holy Bennet wrote a rule for his monks. ¶ Gregory.

Desirous I am, Peter, to tell you many things of this venerable father, but some of purpose I let pass, because I make haste to entreat also of the acts of other holy men : yet I would not have you to be ignorant, but that the man of God amongst so many miracles, for which he was so famous in the world, was also sufficiently learned in divinity : for he wrote a rule for his monks, both excellent for discretion and also eloquent for the style. Of whose life and conversation, if any be curious to know further, he may in the institution of that rule understand all his manner of life and discipline : for the holy man could not otherwise teach, than himself lived.

Chapter Thirty-seven: how venerable Bennet did prophesy to his monks, the time of his own death. ¶

The same year in which he departed this life, he told the day of his holy death to his monks, some of which did live daily with him, and some dwelt far off, willing those that were present to keep it secret, and telling them that were absent by what token they should know that he was dead. Six days before he left this world, he gave order to have his sepulchre opened, and forthwith falling into an ague, he began with burning heat to wax faint, and when as the sickness daily increased, upon the sixth day he commanded his monks to carry him into the oratory, where he did arm himself with receiving the body and blood of our Saviour Christ ; and having his weak body holden up betwixt the hands of his disciples, he stood with his own lifted up to heaven, and as he was in that manner praying, he gave up the ghost. Upon which day two monks, one being in his cell, and the other far distant, had concerning him one and the self-same vision : for they saw all the way from the holy man's cell, towards the east even up to heaven, hung and adorned with tapestry, and shining with an infinite number of lamps, at the top whereof a man, reverently attired, stood and demanded if they knew who passed that way, to whom they answered saying, that they knew not. Then he spake thus unto them : "This is the way," quoth he, "by which the beloved servant of God, Bennet, is ascended up to heaven." And by this means, as his monks that were present knew of the death of the holy man, so likewise they which were absent, by the token which he foretold them, had intelligence of the same thing. Buried he was in the oratory of St. John Baptist which himself built, when he overthrew the altar of Apollo ; who also in that cave in which he first dwelled, even to this very time, worketh miracles, if the faith of them that pray requireth the same.

Chapter Thirty-eight : how a mad woman was cured in his cave. ¶ For the thing which I mean now to rehearse fell out lately. A certain woman falling mad, lost the use of reason so far, that she walked up and down, day and night, in mountains and valleys, in woods and fields, and rested only in that place where extreme weariness enforced her to stay. Upon a day it so fell out, that albeit she wandered at random, yet she missed not the right way: for she came to the cave of the blessed man Bennet : and not knowing anything, in she went, and reposed herself there that night, and rising up in the morning, she departed as sound in sense and well in her wits, as though she had never been distracted in her whole life, and so continued always after, even to her dying day.

Peter. What is the reason that in the patronage of martyrs we often times find, that they do not afford so great benefits by their bodies, as they do by other of their relics : and do there work greater miracles, where themselves be not present ?

Gregory. Where the holy martyrs lie in their bodies, there is no doubt, Peter, but that they are able to work

number of lamps, at the top whereof a man, reverently
attired, stood and demanded if they knew who passed that
way, to whom they answered saying, that they knew not.
Then he spake thus unto them : "This is the way," quoth
he, "by which the beloved servant of God, Bennet, is
ascended up to heaven." And by this means, as his
monks that were present knew of the death of the holy
man, so likewise they which were absent, by the token
which he foretold them, had intelligence of the same
thing. Buried he was in the oratory of St. John Baptist
which himself built, when he overthrew the altar of
Apollo ; who also in that cave in which he first dwelled,
even to this very time, worketh miracles, if the faith of
them that pray requireth the same.

**Chapter Thirty-eight : how a mad woman was
cured in his cave.** ¶ For the thing which I mean now
to rehearse fell out lately. A certain woman falling mad,
lost the use of reason so far, that she walked up and down,
day and night, in mountains and valleys, in woods and
fields, and rested only in that place where extreme
weariness enforced her to stay. Upon a day it so fell
out, that albeit she wandered at random, yet she missed
not the right way : for she came to the cave of the
blessed man Bennet : and not knowing anything, in she
went, and reposed herself there that night, and rising up
in the morning, she departed as sound in sense and well
in her wits, as though she had never been distracted in
her whole life, and so continued always after, even to her
dying day.

Peter. What is the reason that in the patronage of
martyrs we often times find, that they do not afford so
great benefits by their bodies, as they do by other of
their relics : and do there work greater miracles, where
themselves be not present ?

Gregory. Where the holy martyrs lie in their bodies,
there is no doubt, Peter, but that they are able to work

many miracles, yea and also do work infinite, to such as seek them with a pure mind. But for as much as simple people might have some doubt whether they be present, and do in those places hear their prayers where their bodies be not, necessary it is that they should in those places shew greater miracles, where weak souls may most doubt of their presence. But he whose mind is fixed in God, hath so much the greater merit of his faith, in that he both knoweth that they rest not there in body, and yet be there present to hear our prayers. And therefore our Saviour himself, to increase the faith of his disciples, said : *If I do not depart, the Comforter will not come unto you :*[1] for, seeing certain it is that the comforting Spirit doth always proceed from the Father and the Son, why doth the Son say that he will depart that the Comforter may come, who never is absent from the Son ? But because the disciples, beholding our Lord in flesh, did always desire to see him with their corporal eyes, very well did he say unto them : *Unless I do go away, the Comforter will not come :* as though he had plainly told them : If I do not withdraw my body, I cannot let you understand what the love of the spirit is : and except you give over to love my carnal presence, never will you learn to affect me with true spiritual love.

Peter. That you say pleaseth me very well.

Gregory. Let us now for a while give over our discourse, to the end that if we mean to prosecute the miracles of other Saints, we may through silence be the more able to perform it.

[1] John 16, 7.

The end of the Second Book

The Dialogues of St. Gregory
The Third Book

St. Gregory's Dialogues
The Third Book

Being careful to entreat of such fathers as lived not long since, I passed over the worthy acts of those that were in former times : so that I had almost forgot the miracle of Paulinus, Bishop of Nola, who both for time was more ancient, and for virtue more notable, than many of those which I have spoken of : wherefore I will now speak of him, but as briefly as I can. For as the life and actions of good men are soonest known to such as be like them, so the famous name of venerable Paulinus became known to mine holy elders, and his admirable fact served for their instruction : who, for their gravity and old years, are as well to be credited, as if that which they reported they had seen with their own eyes.

Chapter One : of St. Paulinus, Bishop of the City of Nola. ¶ When as in the time of the cruel Vandals, that part of Italy which is called Campania was overrun and sacked, and many were from thence carried captive into Africk : then the servant of God, Paulinus, bestowed all the wealth of his Bishopric upon prisoners and poor people. And not having now anything more left, a certain widow came unto him, lamenting how her son was taken prisoner by one that was son-in-law to the king of the Vandals, and by him carried away to be his slave : and therefore she besought him, that he would vouchsafe to help her with a ransom for the redeeming of her son. But the man of God, seeking what he had to give the poor woman, found nothing left but himself alone, and therefore he answered her in this manner: "Good woman, nothing have I to help thee withal but myself, and therefore take me, and a God's name say that I am your servant, and see whether he will receive me for his slave, and so set your son at liberty": which words she hearing from the mouth of so notable a man, took them rather for a mock, than to proceed indeed from true compassion. But as he was an eloquent man, and passing well learned in humanity, so did he quickly persuade the doubtful woman to give credit to his words, and not to be afraid to offer a Bishop for the ransom of her son; whereupon away they travelled both into Africk. And when the king's son-in-law came abroad, the widow put up her petition concerning her son, humbly beseeching him that he would vouchsafe to set him now at liberty, and bestow him upon his mother. But the barbarous man, swelling with pride and puffed up with the joy of transitory prosperity, refused not only to do it, but disdained also to give any ear to her petition. This way therefore taking no success, the desolate widow tried the next, and said unto him: "Behold, I give you here this man instead of him, only take compassion on me, and restore to me mine only son." At which words he, casting his eyes upon Paulinus, and seeing him to have an honest and good face, asked him of what occupation he was: to whom the man of God answered: "Trade or occupation I can none, but some skill I have in keeping of a garden." This pleased the Pagan very well, whereupon he admitted him for his servant, and restored the widow her son, with whom she departed out of **Africk**, and Paulinus took charge of the garden. The king's son-in-law coming often into the garden, demanded certain questions of his new man, and perceiving him to be very wise and of good judgment, he began to give over the company of his old familiar friends, and conversed much with his gardener, taking great pleasure in his talk. Every day Paulinus brought him to his table divers sorts of green herbs, and after dinner returned to his garden. After he had used this a long time, upon a day, as his master and he were in secret talk together, Paulinus spake unto him in this manner : "Consider, my Lord, what is your best course, and how the kingdom of the Vandals shall be disposed of, for the king is to die shortly ": which news, because he was in special grace with the king, he gave him to understand, adding that his gardener, who was a passing wise man, had told him so much. The king, hearing this, was desirous to see the man he spake of : "Your Majesty," quoth he, "shall see him, for his manner is to bring me in daily fresh herbs for my dinner, and I will give orders that he shall do it in your presence ": which direction being given, as the king sat at dinner, Paulinus came in, bringing with him divers sallettes and fresh herbs : whom so soon as the king beheld, he fell a trembling, and sending for Paulinus' master (who by the marriage of his daughter was so near allied unto him), acquainted him with that secret which before he had concealed, saying : "It is very true that which you have heard, for the last night, in a dream, I saw certain judges in their seats sitting upon me, amongst whom this man also sat for one : and by their sentence that whip was taken from me, which for the punishment of others some time I had. But inquire, I pray you, what he is, for I do not think one of so great merit to be an ordinary man, as he outwardly seemeth." Then the king's son-in-law took Paulinus in secret, and asked him what he was : to whom the man of God answered : "Your servant I am," quoth he, "whom you took for the ransom of the widow's son "; but when he would not be satisfied with that answer, but did instantly press him to tell, not what he was now, but what he had been in his own country, and did urge him very often to answer to this point : the man of God, adjured so strictly, not being able any longer to deny his request, told him that he was a Bishop ; which his master and lord hearing became wonderfully afraid, and humbly offered him, saying : " Demand what you will, that you may be well rewarded of me, and so return home to your country." To whom the man of God, Paulinus, said : " One thing there is wherein you may much pleasure me, and that is, to set at liberty all those that be of my city " : which suit he obtained, for straightways throughout Africk all were sought out, their ships laden with wheat, and to give venerable Paulinus satisfaction, they were all discharged, and in his company sent home : and not long after the king of the Vandals died, and so he lost that whip and severe government, which to his own destruction and the punishment of Christians by God's providence he had before received. And thus it came to pass that Paulinus, the servant of almighty God, told truth, and he that voluntarily alone made himself a bondman, returned not back alone, but with many from captivity : imitating him who took upon him the form of a servant, that we should not be servants to sin : for Paulinus, following his example, became himself for a time a servant alone, that afterward he might be made free with many.

Peter. When I hear that which I cannot imitate, I desire rather to weep than to say anything.

Gregory. Concerning this holy man's death, it remaineth yet in the records of his own church, how that he was with a pain of his side brought to the last cast : and that, whiles all the rest of the house stood sound, the chamber only in which he lay sick was shaken with an earthquake, and so his soul was loosed from his body : and by this means it fell out, that they were all strooken with a great fear that might have seen Paulinus departing this life. But because his virtue by that which I spoke of before is sufficiently handled, now, if you please, we will come to other miracles, which are both known to many, and which I have heard by the relation of such persons, that I can make no doubt but that they be most true.

Chapter Two: of St. John, the Pope. ¶ In the time of the Goths, when the most blessed man John, Bishop of this church of Rome, travelled to the Emperor Justinian the elder, he came into the country of Corinth, where he lacked an horse to ride upon : which a certain noble man understanding, lent him that horse which, because he was gentle, his wife used for her own saddle, with order that when he came where he could provide himself of another, his wife's horse should be sent back again. And so the Bishop rode upon him, until he came to a certain place where he got another, and then he returned that which he had borrowed. But afterward, when his wife came to take his back, as before she used, by no means could she do it, because the horse, having carried so great a Bishop, would not suffer a woman to come any more upon his back, and therefore he began with monstrous snorting, neighing, and continual stirring, as it were in scorn, to shew that he could not bear any woman, upon whom the Pope himself had ridden : which thing her husband wisely considering, straightways sent him again to the holy man, beseeching him to accept of that horse, which by riding he had dedicated to his own service. Of the same man, another miracle is also reported by our ancestors : to wit, that in Constantinople, when he came to the gate called Aurea, where he was met with great numbers of people, in the presence of them all, he restored sight to a blind man that did instantly crave it : for laying his hand upon him, he banished away that darkness which possessed his eyes.

Chapter Three: of St. Agapitus, the Pope. ¶ Not long after, about business concerning the Goths, the most blessed man Agapitus, Bishop of this holy church of Rome (in which by God's providence I do now serve), went to the Emperor Justinian. And, as he was travelling through Greece, a dumb and lame man was brought unto him for help. The holy man carefully demanded of his kinsfolk, that brought him thither and stood there weeping, whether they did believe that it was in his power to cure him : who answered, that they did firmly hope that he might help him in the virtue of God by the authority of St. Peter : upon which words forthwith the venerable man fell to his prayers, and beginning solemn mass, he offered sacrifice in the sight of almighty God : which being ended, he came from the altar, took the lame man by the hand, and straightways, in the presence and sight of all the people, he restored him to the use of his legs : and after he had put our Lord's body into his mouth, that tongue, which long time before had not spoken, was loosed. At which miracle all did wonder, and began to weep for joy : and forthwith both fear and reverence possessed their minds, beholding what Agapitus could do in the power of our Lord, by the help of St. Peter.

Chapter Four : of Datius, Bishop of Milan. ¶ In the time of the same Emperor, Datius, Bishop of Milan, about matters of religion, travelled to Constantinople. And coming to Corinth, he sought for a large house to receive him and his company, and could scarce find any · at length he saw afar off a fair great house, which he commanded to be provided for him : and when the inhabitants of that place told him that it was for many years haunted by the devil, and therefore stood empty : "so much the sooner," quoth the venerable man, "ought we to lodge in it, if the wicked spirit hath taken possession thereof, and will not suffer men to dwell in it." Whereupon he gave order to have it made ready : which being done, he went without all fear to combat with the old enemy. In the dead of the night, when the man of God was asleep, the devil began, with an huge noise and great outcry, to imitate the roaring of lions, the bleating of sheep, the braying of asses, the hissing of serpents, the grunting of hogs, and the screeching of rats. Datius, suddenly awaked with the noise of so many beasts, rose up, and in great anger spake aloud to the old serpent, and said : "Thou art served well, thou wretched creature : thou art he that diddest say : *I will place my seat in the north, and I will be like to the highest:*[1] and now through thy pride, see how thou art become like unto hogs and rats ; and thou that wouldest needs unworthily be like unto God, behold how thou dost now, according to thy deserts, imitate brute beasts." At these words the wicked serpent was, as I may well term it, ashamed, that he was so disgraciously and basely put down, for well may I say that he was ashamed, who never after troubled that house with any such terrible and monstrous shapes as before he did : for ever after that time, Christian men did inhabit the same ; for so soon as one man that was a true and faithful Christian took possession thereof, the lying and faithless spirit straightways did forsake it. But I will now surcease from speaking of things done in former times, and come to such miracles as have happened in our own days.

Chapter Five : of Sabinus, Bishop of Camisina.

¶ Certain religious men, well known in the province of Apulia, do report that which many both far and near know to be most true, and that is of Sabinus, Bishop of Camisina : who, by reason of his great age, was become so blind that he saw nothing at all. And for as much as Totilas, King of the Goths, hearing that he had the gift of prophecy, and would not believe it, but was desirous to prove whether it were so or no, it fell so out, that coming into those parts, the man of God did invite him to dinner. And when the meat was brought in, the King would not sit at the table, but sat beside at the right hand of venerable Sabinus : and when

[1] Isai. 14, 13, 14.

the Bishop's man brought him, as he used to do, a cup of wine, the King softly put forth his hand, took the cup, and gave it himself to the Bishop, to try whether he could tell who he was that gave him the wine. Then the man of God taking the cup, but not seeing him that did deliver it, said : "Blessed be that hand." At which words the King very merrily blushed, because, albeit he was taken, yet did he find that gift in the man of God which before he desired to know. The same reverent man, to give good example of life to others, lived until he was passing old : which nothing pleased his Archdeacon, that desired his Bishopric : and therefore upon ambition he sought how to dispatch him with poison, and for that purpose corrupted his cup-bearer, who, overcome with money, offered the Bishop at dinner that poison in his wine which he had received of the Archdeacon. The holy man, knowing what he brought, willed himself to drink that which he offered him. The wretch trembled at those words, and perceiving his villany to be detected, thought better to drink it, and so quickly dispatch himself, than with shame to suffer torments for the sin of so horrible a murder : but as he was putting the cup to his mouth, the man of God hindered him, saying : "Do not take it, but give it me, and I will drink it myself, but go thy way, and tell him that gave it thee, that I will drink the poison, but yet shall he never live to be Bishop" : and so blessing the cup with the sign of the cross, he drunk it without any harm at all ; at which very time the Archdeacon, being in another place, departed this life ; as though that poison had by the Bishop's mouth passed to his Archdeacon's bowels : for although he had no corporal poison to kill him, yet the venom of his own malice did destroy him in the sight of the everlasting Judge.

Peter. These be strange things, and much in our days to be wondered at : yet the life of the man is such, that he which knoweth his holy conversation hath no such cause to marvel at the miracle.

Chapter Six: of Cassius, Bishop of Narni.

¶ **Gregory.** Neither can I, Peter, pass over with silence that thing, which many of the city of Narni, which be here present, affirm to be most true. For in the time of the same Goths, the foresaid King Totilas coming to Narni, Cassius, a man of venerable life, Bishop of the same city, went forth to meet him, whom the king utterly contemned, because his face was high-coloured, thinking that it proceeded not from any other cause than drinking. But almighty God, to show how worthy a man was despised, permitted a wicked spirit before his whole army, in the fields of Narni, where the king also himself was, to possess one of his guard, and cruelly to torment him. Straightways was he brought to the venerable man Cassius, in the presence of the king : who praying to God for him, and making the sign of the cross, forthwith he cast out the devil, so that never after he durst presume any more to enter into his body. And by this means it fell out that the barbarous king, from that day forward, did with his heart much reverence the servant of God, whom before by his face he judged to be a man of no account : for seeing him now to be one of such power and virtue, he gave over those proud thoughts which before he had conceived.

Chapter Seven: of Andrew, Bishop of Funda.

¶ But as I am thus busied in telling the acts of holy men, there cometh to my mind what God of his great mercy did for Andrew, Bishop of the city of Funda : which notable story I wish all so to read, that they which have dedicated themselves to continency, presume not in any wise to dwell amongst women : lest in time of temptation their soul perish the sooner, by having that at hand which is unlawfully desired.

Neither is the story which I report either doubtful or uncertain : for so many witnesses to justify the truth thereof may be produced, as there be almost inhabitants in that city. When, therefore, this venerable man Andrew lived virtuously, and with diligent care, answerable to his priestly function, led a continent and chaste life : he kept in his house a certain Nun, which also had remained with him before he was preferred to that dignity ; for assuring himself of his own continency, and nothing doubting of hers, content he was to let her remain still in his house : which thing the devil took as an occasion to assault him with temptation : and so he began to present before the eyes of his mind the form of that woman, that by such allurements he might have his heart wholly possessed with ungodly thoughts. In the meantime it so fell out, that a Jew was travelling from Campania to Rome, who drawing nigh to the city of Funda, was so overtaken with night, that he knew not where to lodge, and therefore, not finding any better commodity, he retired himself into a temple of the god Apollo, which was not far off, meaning there to repose himself : but much afraid he was, to lie in so wicked and sacrilegious a place : for which cause, though he believed not what we teach of the cross, yet he thought good to arm himself with that sign. About midnight, as he lay waking for very fear of that forlorn and desert temple, and looked suddenly about him, he espied a troop of wicked spirits walking before another of greater authority : who coming in took up his place, and sat down in the body of the temple : where he began diligently to inquire of those his servants, how they had bestowed their time, and what villany they had done in the world. And when each one told what he had done against God's servants, out stepped a companion, and made solemn relation, with a notable temptation of carnality he had put into the mind of

Bishop Andrew, concerning that Nun which he kept in his palace : whereunto whiles the master devil gave attentive ear, considering with himself what a notable gain it would be, to undo the soul of so holy a man ; the former devil went on with his tale, and said that the very evening before he assaulted him so mightily, that he drew him so far forth, that he did merrily strike the said Nun upon the back. The wicked serpent and old enemy of mankind hearing this joyful news, exhorted his agent with very fair words, diligently to labour about the effecting of that thing which he had already so well begun, that for so notable a piece of service, as the contriving the spiritual ruin of that virtuous Prelate, he might have a singular reward above all his fellows. The Jew who all this while lay waking, and heard all that which they said, was wonderfully afraid : at length the master devil sent some of his followers to see who he was, and how he durst presume to lodge in their temple. When they were come, and had narrowly viewed him, they found that he was marked with the mystical sign of the cross : whereat they marvelled and said : "Alas, alas, here is an empty vessel, but yet it is signed" : which news the rest of those hell-hounds hearing, suddenly vanished away. The Jew, who had seen all that which then passed among them, presently rose up, and in all haste sped himself to the Bishop, whom he found in the church : and taking him aside, he demanded with what temptation he was troubled : but shame so prevailed, that by no means he would confess the truth. Then the Jew replied and told him, that he had cast his eyes wickedly upon such a one of God's servants ; but the Bishop would not acknowledge that there was any such thing. "Why do you deny it," quoth the Jew, " for is it not so true that yesternight you were brought so far by sinful temptation, that you did strike her on the back?" When the Bishop, by these particulars, perceived that the matter was broken forth, he humbly confessed what before he obstinately denied. Then the Jew, moved with compassion to his soul, and tendering his credit, told him by what means he came to the knowledge thereof, and what he heard of him in that assembly of wicked spirits. The Bishop, hearing this, fell prostrate upon the earth, and betook himself to his prayers : and straight after he discharged out of his house, not only that Nun, but all other women that attended upon her. And not long after, he converted the temple of Apollo into an oratory of the blessed Apostle, St. Andrew : and never after was he troubled with that carnal temptation : and the Jew, by whose means he was so mercifully preserved, he brought to everlasting salvation : for he baptized him, and made him a member of holy Church. And thus, by God's providence, the Jew having care of the spiritual health of another, attained also himself the singular benefit of the same : and almighty God by the same means brought one to embrace piety and virtue, by which he preserved another in an holy and godly life.

Peter. This history which I have heard worketh in me fear, and yet withal giveth me cause of hope.

Gregory. That is not amiss, Peter, for necessary it is that we should both trust upon the mercy of God, and yet, considering our own frailty, be afraid : for we have now heard how one of the cedars of Paradise was shaken, and yet not blown down, to the end that, knowing our own infirmity, we should both tremble at his shaking, and yet conceive hope, in that he was not overthrown, but kept his standing still.

Chapter Eight : of Constantius, Bishop of Aquinum. ¶ Constantius, likewise a man of holy life, was Bishop of Aquinum, who not long since died, in the time of Pope John of blessed memory, my predecessor : many that knew him familiarly, say that he had

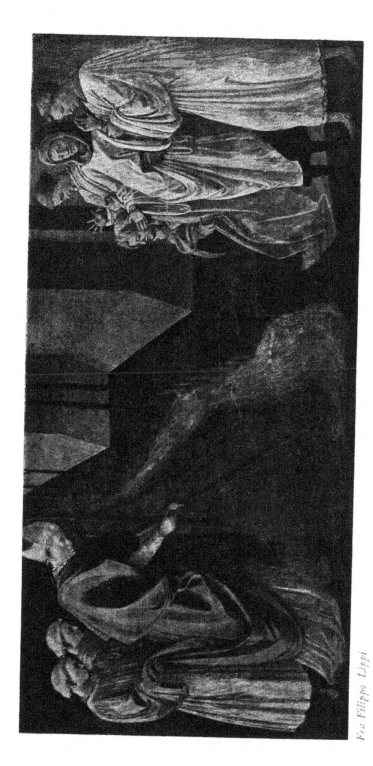

Fra Filippo Lippi

ST. FRIGIDIANUS TURNING THE COURSE OF THE SERCHIO

(Accademia, Florence)

the gift of prophecy. And amongst divers other things which he did, religious and honest men then present report that, lying upon his deathbed, the citizens that stood about him wept bitterly, and asked him with tears, who should be their father and Bishop after him. To whom by the spirit of prophecy he answered, saying "After Constantius, you shall have a muleteer, and after a muleteer, a fuller of cloth: and these men," quoth he, "be now in the city of Aquinum" · and having spoken these prophetical words, he gave up the ghost. After whose departure one Andrew, his Deacon, was made Bishop: who in times past had kept mules and post horses. And when he died, one Jovinus was preferred to that dignity, who in former times had been a fuller in the same city: in whose days all the citizens were so wasted, some by the sword of barbarous people, and some by a terrible plague, that after his death neither could any be found to be made Bishop, nor yet any people for whose sake he should be created. And so the saying of the man of God was fulfilled, in that his church, after the death of two that followed him, had no Bishop at all.

Chapter Nine: of Frigidianus, Bishop of Lucca.

¶ But I must not forget to tell you what I heard of the reverent man Venantius, Bishop of Luna, some two days ago: who said that there was, nigh unto him, a man of rare virtue called Frigidianus, Bishop of Lucca, who wrought a strange miracle, which, as he saith, all the inhabitants of that place do speak of, and it was this. Hard by the walls of the city, there runneth a river called Anser, which divers times doth so swell and overflow the banks, that it drowneth many acres of ground, and spoileth much corn and fruit. The inhabitants, enforced by necessity, seeing that this did often happen, went about by all means possible to turn the stream another way: but when they had bestowed much labour, yet could they not cause it to leave the old channel. Whereupon the man of God, Frigidianus, made a little rake, and came to the river, where all alone he bestowed some time in prayer; and then he commanded the river to follow him, and going before, he drew his rake over such places as he thought good, and the whole river, forsaking the old channel, did follow him, and kept possession of that which the holy man by that sign of his rake had appointed: and so never afterward did it hurt any more either corn or other things planted for the maintenance of men.

Chapter Ten: of Sabinus, Bishop of Placentia.

¶ The same Venantius told me likewise another miracle, done as he said in the city of Placentia, which one John, the servant of God, and a man of credit living now here amongst us, and who was born and brought up in that city, affirmeth also to be most true. For in that town of Placentia, they say that there was a Bishop of wonderful virtue, called Sabinus: who understanding by one of his Deacons, that the great river of Po was broken forth, and had overflowed the land which belonged to the church, and done much harm, he bad him go unto the river, and deliver it this message from him: "The Bishop commandeth you to retire, and keep yourself within your own bounds." His Deacon, hearing these words, scornfully contemned to be employed in any such business. Then the man of God, Sabinus, sent for a notary, and willed him to write these words: "Sabinus, the servant of our Lord Jesus Christ, sendeth admonition to Po. I command thee, in the name of our Lord Jesus Christ, that thou come not out of thy channel, nor presume any more to hurt the lands of the church." This short letter he bad the notary write, and when he had so done, to go and cast it into the river. The notary did as he bad him, and the river obeyed the precept of the holy man, for straightways it withdrew

itself from the church-lands, returned to his own channel, and never presumed any more to overflow those
grounds. By which fact, Peter, the pride of disobedient
men is confounded, seeing that the very senseless element, in the name of Jesus, obeyed the holy man's
commandment.

Chapter Eleven : of Cerbonius, Bishop of Populonium. ❡ Cerbonius, also a man of holy life, Bishop of
Populonium, hath made great proof in our time of his
rare virtue. For being much given to hospitality, upon
a certain day he gave entertainment to divers soldiers,
which, for fear of the Goths (that passed likewise by his
house), he conveyed out of the way, and so saved their
lives from those wicked men. Totilas, their impious
king, having intelligence thereof, in great rage and
cruelty commanded him to be brought unto a place
called Merulis (eight miles from Populonium), where
he remained with his whole army, and in the sight of
the people to be cast unto wild bears to be devoured.
And because the wicked king would needs be present
himself, to behold the Bishop torn in pieces, great store
of people were likewise assembled, to see that pitiful
pageant. The Bishop was brought forth, and a terrible
bear provided, that might in cruel manner tear his body
in pieces, so to satisfy the mind of that bloody king.
Out of his den was the beast let loose, who in great
fury and haste set upon the Bishop : but suddenly, forgetting all cruelty, with bowed neck and humbled head,
he began to lick his feet : to give them all to understand
that men carried towards the man of God the hearts of
beasts, and the beasts as it were the heart of a man. At
this sight the people, with great shouting and outcries,
declared how highly they did admire the holy man : and
the king himself was moved to have him in great reverence : and so by God's providence it fell out, that he
which before refused to obey and follow God by saving

the Bishop's life, was brought to do it by the miraculous meekness of a cruel bear. Many of them which were then present, and saw it, be yet living, who do all affirm this to be most true.

Another miracle concerning the same man I heard of Venantius, Bishop of Luna, and it was this. Cerbonius had in the church of Populonium a tomb provided for himself; but when the Lombards invaded Italy, and spoiled all that country, he retired himself into the island of Helba. Where falling sore sick, before his death he commanded his chaplains to bury his body in the foresaid tomb at Populonium: and when they told him how hard a thing it was by reason of the Lombards, which were lords of the country, and did range up and down in all places: "Carry me thither," quoth he, "securely, and fear nothing, but bury me in all haste, and that being done, come away as fast as you can." For performing of this his will they provided a ship, and away they went with his body towards Populonium: in which journey there fell great store of rain, but that the world might know whose body was transported in that ship, in that twelve miles' space which is betwixt the island and Populonium, a great storm of rain fell upon both sides of the ship, but not one drop within. When they were come to the place, they buried his body, and, according to his commandment, returned to their ship with all speed: and they were no sooner aboard, than there entered into the church, where the Bishop was buried, a most cruel captain of the Lombards called Gunmar. By whose sudden coming to that place, it appeared plainly that the man of God had the spirit of prophecy, when he willed them in all haste to depart from the place of his burial.

Chapter Twelve : of Fulgentius, Bishop of Otricoli.

The very same miracle, which I told you concerning the division of the rain, happened likewise to the great veneration of another Bishop. For a certain old Priest, who yet liveth, was then present when it happened, and saith that Fulgentius, Bishop of Otricoli, was in disgrace with that cruel tyrant Totilas : and therefore, as he was passing that way with his army, the Bishop did carefully beforehand by his chaplains send him certain presents, by that means, if it were possible, to mitigate his furious mind. But the tyrant contemned them, and in great rage commanded his soldiers hardly to bind the Bishop, and to keep him safe until he had heard his examination. The merciless Goths executed his cruel commandment : and setting him upon a piece of ground, they made a circle round about him, out of which they commanded him not to stir his foot. Whiles the man of God stood there in great extremity of heat, environed round about with those Goths, suddenly there fell such thunder and lightning, and such plenty of rain, that his keepers could not endure that terrible storm : and yet for all that, not one drop fell within the circle, where the man of God, Fulgentius, stood. Which strange news being told to that tyrannical king, his barbarous mind was brought to have him in great reverence, whose torment before he desired and so cruelly thirsted after his blood. Thus almighty God, to bring down the lofty minds of carnal men, doth work miracles by such as they most contemn : that truth, proceeding from the mouths of his humble servants, may subdue those, which of pride do extol and advance themselves against the doctrine of truth.

Chapter Thirteen : of Herculanus, Bishop of Perusium.

¶ Not long since, the virtuous Bishop Floridus told me a notable miracle, which was this. "The great holy man," quoth he, "Herculanus, who brought me up, was Bishop of Perusium, exalted to that dignity from the state of a monk : in whose time the perfidious king Totilas besieged it for seven years together, and the famine within was so great that many of the townsmen forsook the place : and before the seventh year was ended, the army of the Goths took the city. The commander of his camp dispatched messengers to Totilas, to know his pleasure what he should do with the Bishop, and the rest of the citizens : to whom he returned answer, that he should, from the top of the Bishop's head to his very foot, cut off a thong of his skin, and that done, to strike off his head : and as for the rest of the people, to put them all to the sword. When he had received this order, he commanded the reverent Bishop Herculanus to be carried to the walls, and there to have his head strooken off, and when he was dead, that his skin should be cut from the very crown down to the very foot, as though indeed a thong had been taken from his body ; after which barbarous fact they threw his dead corpse over the wall. Then some upon pity, joining the head to the body, did bury him, together with an infant that was there found dead. Forty days after, Totilas making proclamation that the inhabitants, which were gone, should without all fear come back again : those, which upon extremity of hunger departed, returned home to their houses, and calling to mind the holy life of their Bishop, they sought for his body, that it might, as he deserved, be buried in the church of St. Peter. And when they came to the place where it lay, they digged, and found the body of the infant that was buried together with him, putrefied and full of worms : but the Bishop's body was so sound as though it had been newly put into the earth, and that which is more to be admired, and deserveth greater reverence, his head was so fast joined to his body as though it had never been cut off, neither did any sign of his beheading appear at all. Then they viewed likewise his back, whether that were also whole and sound, and they found it so perfect and well, as though never any knife had touched the same."

Peter. Who would not wonder at such miracles of them

Benedetto Bonfigli

Alinari

THE TRANSLATION OF ST. HERCOLANUS
(Accademia, Perugia)

that be dead : wrought, no question, for the spiritual good of the living ?

Chapter Fourteen : of the servant of God, Isaac.

¶ **Gregory.** At such time as the Goths first invaded Italy, there was, near to the city of Spoleto, a virtuous and holy man called Isaac : who lived almost to the last days of the Goths, whom many did know, and especially the holy virgin Gregoria, which now dwelleth in this city, hard by the church of the blessed and perpetual Virgin Mary : which woman, in her younger years, desiring to live a nun's life, fled to the church from marriage, already agreed upon by her friends, and was by this man defended : and so, through God's providence, obtained to have that habit which so much she desired, and so, leaving her spouse upon earth, she merited a spouse in heaven. Many things also I had by the relation of the reverent man Eleutherius, who was familiarly acquainted with him ; and his virtuous life doth give credit to his words. This holy man Isaac was not born in Italy ; and therefore I will only speak of such miracles as he did living here in our country. At his first coming out of Syria to the city of Spoleto, he went to the church, and desired the keepers that he might have free leave to pray there, and not to be enforced to depart when night came. And so he began his devotions, and spent all that day in prayer, and likewise the night following. The second day and night he bestowed in the same manner, and remained there also the third day : which when one of the keepers of the church perceived, who was a man of a proud spirit, he took scandal by that, whereof he ought to have reaped great profit. For he began to say that he was an hypocrite and cozening companion, who in the sight of the world remained at his prayers three days and three nights together : and forthwith running upon the man of God, he strook him, to make him by that means with shame to depart the church as an hypocrite, and one that desired to be reputed an holy man. But to revenge this injury, a wicked spirit did presently possess his body, who cast him down at the feet of the man of God, and began by his mouth to cry out: "Isaac doth cast me forth, Isaac doth cast me forth." For what name the strange man had, none at that time did know, but the wicked spirit told it, when he cried out that he had power to cast him out. Straightways the man of God laid himself upon his body, and the cursed devil that was entered in, departed in all haste. News of this was by and by blown over the whole city, and men and women, rich and poor, came running, every one striving to bring him home to their own house: some for the building of an Abbey, did humbly offer him lands, others money, and some such other helps as they could. But the servant of almighty God, refusing to accept any of their offers, departed out of the city, and not far off he found a desert place, where he built a little cottage for himself: to whom many repairing began by his example to be inflamed with the love of everlasting life, and so, under his discipline and government, gave themselves to the service of almighty God. And when his disciples would often humbly insinuate, that it were good for the necessity of the Abbey to take such livings as were offered, he, very careful to keep poverty, told them constantly, saying: "A monk that seeketh for livings upon earth is no monk": for so fearful he was to lose the secure state of his poverty, as covetous rich men are careful to preserve their corruptible wealth.

In that place, therefore, he became famous for the spirit of prophecy: and his life was renowned far and near, for the notable miracles which he wrought. For upon a day, towards evening, he caused his monks to lay a certain number of spades in the garden. The night following, when according to custom they rose up to their prayers, he commanded them, saying: "Go your ways, and make pottage for our workmen, that it may be ready very early in the morning." And when it was day, he bad them bring the pottage which they had provided ; and going with his monks into the garden, he found there so many men working as he had commanded them to lay spades for it fell so out, that certain thieves were entered in to spoil and rob it ; but God changing their minds, they took the spades which they found there, and so wrought from the time of their first entrance, until the man of God came unto them : and all such parts of the ground as before were not manured, they had digged up and made ready. When the man of God was come, he saluted them in this wise : " God save you, good brethren : you have laboured long, wherefore now rest yourselves ": then he caused such provision as he had brought to be set before them, and so after their labour and pains refreshed them. When they had eaten that was sufficient, he spake thus unto them : "Do not hereafter any more harm : but when you desire anything that is in the garden, come to the gate, quietly ask it, and take it a God's blessing, but steal no more ": and so bestowing upon them good store of worts, he sent them away. And by this means it fell out that they which came into the garden to do harm, departed thence not doing any damage at all, and besides had the reward of their pains, and somewhat also of charity bestowed upon them.

At another time, there came unto him certain strange men a begging, so torn and tattered, that they had scant any rags to cover them, humbly beseeching him to help them with some clothes. The man of God, hearing their demand, gave them no answer : but secretly calling for one of his monks, bad him go into such a wood, and in such a place of the wood to seek for an hollow tree, and to bring unto him that apparel which he found there. The monk went his way, and brought closely to his master that which he had found. Then the man of God called for those poor naked men, and gave them that apparel,

The Dialogues of St. Gregory

saying : "Put on these clothes to cover your naked bodies withal." They, seeing their own garments, were wonderfully confounded : for thinking by cunning to have gotten other men's apparel, with shame they received only their own.

Again, at another time, one there was that commended himself to his prayers, and sent him by his servant two baskets full of meat : one of the which, as he was in his journey, he took away, and hid in a bush till his return back again ; and the other he presented to the man of God, telling him how his master had sent him that, heartily commending himself to his prayers. The holy man took that which was sent very kindly, giving the messenger this good lesson : "I pray thee, my friend, to thank thy master, and take heed how thou dost lay hand upon the basket, for a snake is crept in, and therefore be careful, lest otherwise it doth sting thee." At these words the messenger was pitifully confounded, and though glad he was that by this means he escaped death, yet somewhat grieved that he was put to that shame. Coming back to the basket, very diligent and careful he was in touching it ; for as the man of God had told him, a snake in very deed was got in. This holy man, therefore, albeit he were incomparably adorned with the virtue of abstinence, contempt of worldly wealth, the spirit of prophecy, and perseverance in prayer : yet one thing there was in him which seemed reprehensible, to wit, that sometime he would so exceed in mirth, that if men had not known him to have been so full of virtue, none would ever have thought it.

Peter. What, I beseech you, shall we say to that ? for did he willingly give himself sometime to such recreation or else excelling in virtue, was he, contrary to his own mind, drawn sometime to present mirth ?

Gregory. God's providence, Peter, in bestowing of his gifts, is wonderful: for often it falleth out, that upon

126

whom he vouchsafeth the greater, he giveth not the less : to the end that always they may have somewhat to mislike in themselves : so that desiring to arrive unto perfection and yet can not : and labouring about that which they have not obtained, and can not prevail : by this means they become not proud of those gifts which they have received, but do thereby learn that they have not those greater graces of themselves, who of themselves cannot overcome small faults. And this was the cause that, when God had brought his people into the land of promise, and destroyed all their mighty and potent enemies, yet did he long time after reserve the Philisteans and Chananites, that, as it is written, *He might in them try Israel.*[1] For sometime as hath been said, upon whom he bestoweth great gifts, he leaveth some small things that be blameworthy, that always they may have somewhat to fight against, and not to be proud, though their great enemies be vanquished, seeing other adversaries in very small things do put them to great trouble : and therefore it falleth out strangely, that one and the self same man is excellent for virtue, and yet of infirmity sometime doth offend, so that he may behold himself on the one side strong and well furnished, and on another open and not defended : that by the good thing which he seeketh for, and is not able to procure, he may with humility preserve that virtue which already he hath in possession. But what wonder is it that we speak this concerning man, when as heaven itself lost some of his citizens, and other some continued sound in God's grace : that the elect Angels of God, seeing others through pride to fall from heaven, might stand so much the more steadfast, by how much with humility they preserved God's grace received? They, therefore, took profit by that loss which heaven then had, and were thereby made to persevere more constantly in God's service for all eternity. In like manner

[1] Judges 3, 1.

127

it fareth with each man's soul, which sometime for preserving of humility, by a little loss it attaineth to great
spiritual perfection.

Peter. I am very well pleased with that you say.

Chapter Fifteen : of the servants of God Euthicius and Florentius.

¶ **Gregory.** Neither will
I pass over that with silence, which I heard from the
mouth of that reverent Priest, Sanctulus, one of the same
country : and of whose report I am sure you make no
doubt, for you know very well his life and fidelity.

At the same time, in the province of Nursia there
dwelt two men, observing the life and habit of holy conversation : the one was called Euthicius and the other
Florentius ; of which Euthicius bestowed his time in
spiritual zeal and fervour of virtue, and laboured much
by his exhortations, to gain souls to God ; but Florentius
led his life in simplicity and devotion.   Not far from
the place where they remained, there was an Abbey, the
governor whereof was dead, and therefore the monks
made choice of Euthicius, to take the charge thereof :
who, condescending to their petition, governed the Abbey
many years.   And not to have his former oratory utterly
destitute, he left the reverent man Florentius to keep the
same ; who dwelt there all alone, and upon a day, being
at his prayers, he besought almighty God to vouchsafe
him of some comfort in that place ; and having ended
his devotions, he went forth, where he found a bear
standing before the door, which by the bowing down of
his head to the ground, and shewing in the gesture of his
body no sign of cruelty, gave the man of God to understand that he was come thither to do him service, and
himself likewise did forthwith perceive it.   And because
he had in the house four or five sheep which had no
keeper, he commanded the bear to take charge of them,
saying : "Go and lead these sheep to the field, and at
twelve of the clock come back again" : which charge he

took upon him, and did daily come home at that hour: and so he performed the office of a good shepherd, and those sheep, which before time he used to devour, now fasting himself, he took care to have them safely kept. And when God's servant determined to fast until three of the clock, then he commanded the bear to return with his sheep at the same hour; but when he would not fast so long, to come at twelve. And whatsoever he commanded his bear, that he did, so that bidden to return at three of the clock, he would not come at twelve; and commanded to return at twelve, he would not tarry till three. And when this had continued a good while, he began to be famous far and near for his virtue and holy life. But the old enemy of mankind by that means which he seeth the good to come unto glory, by the same doth he draw the wicked through hatred to procure their own misery; for four of Euthicius' monks, swelling with envy that their master wrought not any miracles, and that he who was left alone by him was famous for so notable a one, upon very spite went and killed his bear. And therefore, when the poor beast came not at his appointed hour, Florentius began to suspect the matter: but expecting yet until the evening, very much grieved he was that the bear, whom in great simplicity he called his brother, came not home. The next day, he went to the field, to seek for his sheep and his shepherd, whom he found there slain; and making diligent inquisition, he learned quickly who they were that had committed that uncharitable fact. Then was he very sorry, bewailing yet more the malice of the monks than the death of his bear; whom the reverent man Euthicius sent for, and did comfort him what he might: but the holy man Florentius, wonderfully grieved in mind, did in his presence curse them, saying: "I trust in almighty God, that they shall in this life, and in the sight of the world, receive the reward of their malice, that have thus killed my bear which did them no harm"; whose words God's vengeance did straight follow, for the four monks that killed the poor beast were straight so strooken with a leprosy, that their limbs did rot away, and so they died miserably : whereat the man of God, Florentius, was greatly afraid, and much grieved, that he had so cursed the monks ; and all his life after he wept, for that his prayer was heard, crying out that himself was cruel, and that he had murdered those men. Which thing I suppose almighty God did, to the end that he should not, being a man of great simplicity, upon any grief whatsoever, afterward presume to curse any.

Peter. What ? is it any great sin, if in our anger we curse others ?

Gregory. Why do you ask me whether it be a great sin, when as St. Paul saith : *Neither cursers shall possess the kingdom of God ?* [1] Think, then, how great the sin is, which doth exclude a man out of heaven.

Peter. What if a man, haply not of malice, but of negligence in keeping his tongue, doth curse his neighbour ?

Gregory. If before the severe judge idle speech is reprehended, how much more that which is hurtful. Consider, then, how damnable those words be, which proceed of malice, when that talk shall be punished which proceedeth only from idleness.

Peter. I grant it be most true.

Gregory. The same man of God did another thing which I must not forget. For, the report of his virtue reaching far and near, a certain Deacon, that dwelt many miles off, travelled unto him, to commend himself to his prayers. And coming to his cell, he found it round about full of innumerable snakes ; at which sight being wonderfully afraid, he cried out, desiring Florentius to pray : who came forth, the sky being then very clear,

[1] I Cor. 6, 10.

and lifted up his eyes and his hands to heaven, desiring God to take them away in such sort as he best knew. Upon whose prayers, suddenly it thundered, and that thunder killed all those snakes. Florentius, seeing them all dead, said unto God : "Behold, O Lord, thou hast destroyed them all, but who shall now carry them away ?" And straight as he had thus spoken, so many birds came as there were snakes killed, which took them all up, and carried them far off, discharging his habitation from those venomous creatures.

Peter. Certainly he was a man of great virtue and merit, whose prayers God did so quickly hear.

Gregory. Purity of heart and simplicity, Peter, is of great force with almighty God, who is in purity most singular, and of nature most simple. For those servants of his, which do retire themselves from worldly affairs, avoid idle words, labour not to lose their devotion, nor to defile their soul with talking, do especially obtain to be heard of him, to whom, after a certain manner, and as they may, they be like in purity and simplicity of heart. But we that live in the world, and speak oftentimes idle words, and that which is worse, sometime those that be hurtful : our words and prayers are so much the farther off from God, as they be near unto the world : for we are drawn too much down towards the earth, by continual talking of secular business : which thing the prophet Esaye did very well reprehend in himself, after he had beheld the King and Lord of armies, and was penitent, crying out : *Woe be to me for being silent, because I am a man that have defiled lips :* and he sheweth straight after the reason why his lips were defiled, when he saith : *I dwell in the midst of a people that hath defiled lips.*[1] For sorry he was that his lips were defiled, yet concealeth not from whence he had them, when he saith, that he dwelt in the midst of a people

[1] Isai. 6, 5.

that had defiled lips. For very hard it is that the tongues of secular men should not defile their souls, with whom they talk; for when we do sometime condescend to speak with them of certain things, by little and little we get such a custom, that we hear that spoken with pleasure which is not meet to be heard at all, so that afterward we are loath to give that over, to which at the first, to gratify others, we were brought against our wills. And by this means we fall from idle words to hurtful speeches, and from talk of small moment to words of great importance: and so it cometh to pass that our tongue is so much the less respected of God when we pray, by how much we are more defiled with foolish speech, because, as it is written: *He that turneth away his ear that he hear not the law, his prayer shall be execrable.*[1] What marvel, then, is it, if, when we pray, God doth slowly hear us, when as we hear God's commandments, either slowly or not at all? And what marvel if Florentius, when he prayed, was quickly heard, who obeyed God in observing his commandments?

Peter. The reason alleged is so plain, that nothing with reason can be said against it.

Gregory. But Euthicius, who was companion to Florentius in serving of God, was famous also for miracles after his death. For the inhabitants of that city do speak of many: but the principal is that which, even to these times of the Lombards, almighty God hath vouchsafed to work by his coat: for when they had any great drougth the citizens, gathering themselves together, did carry that, and together with their prayers offer it in the sight of our Lord. And when they went with that through the fields, praying to God, forthwith they had such plenty of rain as the dryness of the ground required: whereby it was apparent, what virtue

[1] Prov. 28, 9.

and merits were in his soul, whose garment shewed outwardly did pacify the anger of almighty God.

Chapter Sixteen: of Marcius, the Monk of Mount Marsico.

¶ Not long since, there was a reverent man in Campania, called Marcius, who lived a solitary life in the mountain of Marsico : and many years together did he continue in a narrow and straight cave : whom many of our acquaintance knew very well, and were present at such miracles as he did, and many things concerning him have I heard from the mouth of Pope Pelagius of blessed memory, my predecessor, and also of others, who be very religious men. His first miracle was that, so soon as he made choice of that cave for his habitation, there sprung water out of the hollow rock, which was neither more nor less than served for his necessity : by which almighty God did shew what great care he had of his servant, seeing miraculously, as in ancient time he had before done to the children of Israel, he caused the hard rock to yield forth water. But the old enemy of mankind, envying at his virtues, went about by his ancient slight to drive him from that place : for he entered into a serpent, his old friend, and so thought to have terrified him from thence. For the serpent alone would come into the cave where he lived also alone, and when he was at his prayers, it would cast itself before him, and when he took his rest, it would lie down by his side. The holy man was nothing at all dismayed at this : for sometime he would put his hand or leg to his mouth, saying : "If thou hast leave to sting me, I hinder thee not" : and when he had lived thus continually the space of three years, upon a day the old enemy, overcome with his heavenly courage, made a great hissing, and tumbling himself down by the side of the mountain, he consumed all the bushes and shrubs with fire : in which fact by the power of God he was enforced to shew of what force he was, that departed with loss of the victory. Consider, I pray you then, in the top of what mountain this man of God stood, that continued three years together with a serpent, without taking any harm at all.

Peter. I do consider it, and do tremble at the very hearing of the story.

Gregory. This reverent man, when he first shut himself up, was determined never to behold women any more : not because he contemned them, but for that he feared lest their sight might be the occasion of sinful temptation : which resolution of his a certain woman understanding, up she went boldly to the mountain, and forgetting all modesty, impudently approached to his cave. He seeing her a good way off, and perceiving by the apparel that it was a woman, he fell straight to his prayers, with his face upon the earth, and there he lay prostrate, until the shameless creature, wearied with staying at his window, departed : and that very day after she was descended the mountain, she ended her life ; to give all the world to understand how highly she displeased almighty God, in offending his servant with that her bold enterprise.

At another time, many of devotion going to visit him, a young boy, taking little heed to his feet, and by reason the path was so straight upon the side of the mountain, fell down, and tumbled until he came to the bottom of the valley, which was very deep : for the mountain is so high, that huge trees growing beneath seem to them that be above nothing else but little shrubs. The people present were at this chance much dismayed, and very diligently did they seek, to see where they could find his dead body : for who would have thought any otherwise but that he **was** slain, or once imagined that his body could ever have come safe to the ground, so many rocks being in the way to tear it in pieces ? yet for all this, he was found in the valley, not only alive, but also without

KING TOTILA AND ST. BENEDICT

Uffi Gallery, Florence)

Nevaccio di Bartolommeo Landi

any harm at all. Then they perceived very well, that the reason why he was not hurt was because Marcius' prayers did preserve him in his falling.

Over his cave there was a great rock, which seemed to hang but by a little piece unto the mountain, and therefore daily was it feared that it would fall, and so kill the servant of God. For preventing of which mischief, the honourable man Mascatus, nephew to Armentarius, came thither with a great number of country people, desiring him to leave his cave so long until they had removed that rock, to the end he might afterward continue there without any danger: but the man of God could not by any means be persuaded to come forth, bidding them notwithstanding do what they thought convenient, only he retired himself to the farthest part of his cell : yet none made any doubt, but that if so huge a rock as that was did fall, but that it would both spoil his cave and kill himself. Wherefore they laboured what they might, to see if they could remove that mighty stone without any danger to the man of God, and forthwith, in the sight of them all, a strange thing happened: for that rock, severed by their labour from the rest of the mountain, not touching Marcius' cave, did skip clean over, and avoiding, as it were, to hurt God's servant, it fell far off : which thing no man can doubt but that it was done by the hands of Angels, at the commandment of almighty God.

At such time as this holy man came first to inhabit that mountain, and had not yet made any door for his cave, he fastened the one end of an iron chain to the stony wall, and the other he tied to his leg, to the end he might go no farther than the length of that chain did give him leave: which thing the reverent man Bennet hearing of, sent him this word by one of his monks: " If thou be God's servant, let the chain of Christ, and not any chain of iron, hold thee ": upon this message Marcius forthwith loosed his chain, yet did he keep still the same compass, and go no farther than he did before. Living afterward in the same cave, he began to entertain certain disciples, which dwelt apart from his cell, who, having no other water but that which with a rope and a bucket they drew out of a well, great trouble they had, because their rope did often break: and therefore they came unto him, craving that chain which he had loosed from his leg, that they might tie the rope to that, and fasten the bucket upon it: and from that time forward, though the rope was daily wet with water, yet did it break no more; for having touched the holy man's chain, it became strong like unto iron, so that the water did not wear it, nor do it any harm.

Peter. These worthy acts of his do please me, seeing they are strange, and that very much, because they were so lately done, and be yet fresh in memory.

Chapter Seventeen: how a Monk of Mount Argentario raised up a dead man. ¶ Gregory.

Not long since in our time, a certain man called Quadragesimus was subdeacon in the church of Buxentin, who in times past kept a flock of sheep in the same country of Aurelia: by whose faithful report I understood a marvellous strange thing, which is this. At such time as he led a shepherd's life, there was an holy man that dwelt in the mountain of Argentario: whose religious conversation and inward virtue was answerable to the habit of a monk, which outwardly he did wear. Every year he travelled from his mountain to the church of St. Peter, Prince of the Apostles: and in the way took this Quadragesimus' house for his lodging, as himself did tell me. Coming upon a day to his house, which was hard by the church, a poor woman's husband died not far off, whom when they had, as the manner is, washed, put on his garments, and made him ready to be buried, yet it was so late, that it could not be done that day: wherefore the desolate widow sat by the dead corpse, weeping all night long, and to satisfy her grief she did continually lament and cry out. The man of God, seeing her so pitifully to weep and never to give over, was much grieved, and said to Quadragesimus the subdeacon · "My soul taketh compassion of this woman's sorrow, arise, I beseech you, and let us pray": and thereupon they went to the church, which, as I said, was hard by, and fell to their devotions. And when they had prayed a good while, the servant of God desired Quadragesimus to conclude their prayer; which being done, he took a little dust from the side of the altar: and so came with Quadragesimus to the dead body; and there he began again to pray, and when he continued so a long time, he desired him not, as he did before, to conclude their prayers, but himself gave the blessing, and so rose up: and because he had the dust in his right hand, with his left he took away the cloth that covered the dead man's face; which the woman seeing, earnestly withstood him, and marvelled much what he meant to do: when the cloth was gone, he rubbed the dead man's face a good while with the dust, which he had taken up; and at length, he that was dead received his soul again, began to open his mouth and his eyes, and to sit up, and as though he had awakened from a deep sleep, marvelled what they did about him; which when the woman, that had wearied herself with crying, beheld, she began then afresh to weep for joy, and cry out far louder than she did before: but the man of God modestly forbad her, saying: "Peace, good woman, and say nothing, and if any demand how this happened, say only, that our Lord Jesus Christ hath vouchsafed to work his pleasure." Thus he spake, and forthwith he departed from Quadragesimus, and never came to his house again. For, desirous to avoid all temporal honour, he so handled the matter, that they which saw him work that miracle, did never see him more so long as he lived.

Peter. What others think I know not: but mine opinion is, that it is a miracle above all miracles, to raise up dead men, and secretly to call back their souls, to give life unto their bodies again.

Gregory. If we respect outward and visible things, of necessity we must so believe ; but if we turn our eyes to invisible things, then certain it is that it is a greater miracle, by preaching of the word and virtue of prayer, to convert a sinner than to raise up a dead man : for in the one, that flesh is raised up which again shall die : but in the other, he is brought from death which shall live for ever. For I will name you two, and tell me in which of them, as you think, the greater miracle was wrought. The first is Lazarus, a true believer, whom our Lord raised up in flesh ; the other is Saul, whom our Lord raised in soul. For of Lazarus' virtues after his resurrection we read nothing : but after the raising up of the other's soul, we are not able to conceive what wonderful things be in holy scripture spoken of his virtues : as that his most cruel thoughts and designments were turned into the bowels of piety and compassion ; that he desired to die for his brethren, in whose death before he took much pleasure ; that knowing the holy scriptures perfectly, yet professed that he knew nothing else but Jesus Christ and him crucified ; that he did willingly endure the beating of rods for Christ, whom before with sword he did perse-cute ; that he was exalted to the dignity of an Apostle, and yet willingly became a little one in the midst of other disciples ; that he was rapt to the secrets of the third heaven, and yet did turn his eye of compassion to dispose of the duty of married folks, saying : *Let the hus-band render debt to the wife, and likewise the wife to the husband ;*[1] that he was busied in contemplating the quires of Angels, and yet contemned not to think and dispose of the facts of carnal men ; that he rejoiced in his infir-mities, and took pleasure in his reproaches ; that for him to live is Christ, and gain to die ; that although he lived

[1] 1 Cor. 7, 3.

in flesh, yet was he wholly out of the flesh. Behold how this blessed Apostle lived, who from hell returned in his soul to the life of virtue : wherefore less it is for one to be raised up in body, except perchance, by the reviving thereof, he be also brought to the life of his soul, and that the outward miracle do serve for the giving of life to the inward spirit.

Peter. I thought that far inferior, which I perceive now to be incomparably superior : but prosecute, I beseech you, your former discourse, that we spend no time without some spiritual profit to our souls.

Chapter Eighteen : of Bennet the Monk. ¶

Gregory. A certain monk lived with me in mine Abbey, passing cunning in holy scripture, who was elder than I, and of whom I learned many things which before I knew not. By his report I understood that there was in Campania, some forty miles from Rome, a man called Bennet, young in years, but old for gravity : one that observed the rule of holy conversation very strictly. When the Goths in the time of King Totilas found him, they went about to burn him, together with his cell ; and fire for that end was put to, which consumed all things round about, but no hold would the fire take upon his cell : which when the Goths saw, they became more mad, and with great cruelty drew him out of that place, and espying not far off an oven made hot to bake bread, into those flames they threw him, and so stopped the mouth. But the next day he was found so free from all harm, that not only his flesh, but his very apparel also, was not by the fire anything touched at all.

Peter. I hear now the old miracle of the three children, which were thrown into the fire, and yet were preserved from those furious flames.[1]

Gregory. That miracle, in mine opinion, was in some thing unlike to this : for then the three children were

[1] Daniel 3.

bound hand and foot, and so thrown into the fire, for whom the King looking the next day, found them walking in the furnace, their garments being nothing hurt by those flames : whereby we gather that the fire into which they were cast, and touched not their apparel, did yet consume their bands, so that at one and the same time, for the service of the just, the fire had force to bring them comfort, and yet had none to procure them torment.

Chapter Nineteen : of the church of blessed Zeno the Martyr : in which the water ascended higher than the door, and though it were open, yet entered not in. ¶ Like unto this ancient miracle we had in our days another, but yet in a divers element : for not long since John the Tribune told me that, when the Earl Pronulphus was there, and himself also with Antharicus the king, how there happened at that time a strange miracle, and he affirmeth that himself doth know it to be true. For he said that, almost five years since, when the river of Tiber became so great that it ran over the walls of Rome, and overflowed many countries : at the same time in the city of Verona, the river Athesis did so swell, that it came to the very church of the holy martyr and Bishop Zeno ; and though the church doors were open, yet did it not enter in. At last it grew so high, that it came to the church windows, not far from the very roof itself, and the water standing in that manner, did close up the entrance into the church, yet without running in : as though that thin and liquid element had been turned into a sound wall. And it fell so out, that many at that time were surprised in the church, who not finding any way how to escape out, and fearing lest they might perish for want of meat and drink, at length they came to the church door, and took of the water to quench their thirst, which, as I said, came up to the windows, and yet entered not in ; and so for their necessity they took water, which yet, according to the nature of water, ran not in : and in that manner it

Girolamo dai Libri

Anderson

HE MADONNA AND CHILD WITH ST ZENO (AND ST LAURENCE JUSTINIAN)

(San Giorgio, Verona)

stood there before the door, being water to them for their comfort, and yet not water to invade the place : and all this to declare the great merit of Christ's martyr. Which miracle I said truly, that it was not unlike to that ancient one of the fire : which burnt the three children's bands, and yet touched not their garments.

Peter. Marvellous strange are these acts of God's saints which you tell ; and much to be admired of us weak men, that live in these days. But because I understand now, by your relation, what a number of excellent and virtuous men have been in Italy, desirous I am to know whether they endured any assaults of the devil, and did thereby more profit in the service of God.

Gregory. Without labour and fighting, none can obtain the crown of victory : whence, then, come so many conquerors but from this, that they fought valiantly, and resisted the assaults of the old enemy ? For the wicked spirit doth continually watch our thoughts, words, and works : to find something whereof to accuse us before the eternal Judge. For proof whereof I will now let you understand, how ready he is always to entrap and deceive us.

Chapter Twenty : of a Priest called Stephen, in the province of Valeria : whose stockings the devil would have drawn off. ¶ Some that are yet living with me, affirm this to be true which I will now speak of. A man of holy life there was, called Stephen, who was a Priest in the province of Valeria, nigh of kindred to my deacon Bonifacius : who, coming home upon a time from travel, spake somewhat negligently to his servant, saying : " Come, sir devil, and pull off my hose " : at which words, straightways his garters began to loose in great haste, so that he plainly perceived that the devil indeed, whom he named, was pulling off his stocking : whereat being much terrified, he cried out aloud, and said : " Away, wretched caitiff, away : I spake not to thee, but to my servant." Then the devil gave over, leaving his garters almost quite off. By which we may learn, that if the devil be so officious in things concerning our body, how ready and diligent he is to observe and note the cogitations of our soul.

Peter. A very painful thing it is and terrible, always to strive against the temptations of the devil, and, as it were, to stand continually armed ready to fight.

Gregory. Not painful at all, if we attribute our preservation not to ourselves, but to God's grace; yet so notwithstanding, that we be careful what we may for our parts, and always vigilant under God's protection. And it falleth out sometime by God's goodness, that when the devil is expelled from our soul, that he is so little of us to be feared, that contrariwise he is rather terrified by the virtuous and devout life of good people.

Chapter Twenty-one: of a Nun that, by her only commandment, dispossessed a devil. ¶ For the holy man, old father Eleutherius, of whom I spake before, told me that which I will now tell you: and he was himself a witness of the truth thereof: this it was. In the city of Spoleto, there was a certain worshipful man's daughter, for years marriageable, which had a great desire to lead another kind of life: whose purpose her father endeavoured to hinder: but she, not respecting her father's p , took upon her the habit of holy conversation: for which cause her father did disinherit her, and left her nothing else but six little pieces of ground. By her example many noble young maids began under her to be converted, to dedicate their virginity to almighty God, and to serve him. Upon a time, the virtuous Abbot Eleutherius went to bestow upon her some good exhortation: and as he was sitting with her, discoursing of spiritual matters, a country man came from that piece of ground which her father had left her, bringing a certain present: and as he was standing before them, suddenly a wicked spirit possessed his body ; so that straightways he fell down before them, and began pitifully to cry and roar out. At this the Nun rose up, and with angry countenance and loud voice, commanded him to go forth, saying : "Depart from him, thou vile wretch, depart." "If I depart," quoth the devil, speaking by the mouth of the possessed man, "into whom shall I go ?" By chance there was at that time a little hog hard by : into which she gave him leave to enter, which he did, and so, killing it, went his way.

Peter. I would gladly be informed, whether she might bestow so much as that hog upon the devil.

Gregory. The actions of our Saviour be a rule for us, according to which we may direct our life : and we read in the scripture, how the legion of devils that possessed a man said unto our Saviour : *If thou dost cast us forth, send us into the herd of swine :*[1] who cast them out, and permitted them to enter in as they desired, and to drown that herd in the sea. By which fact of our Saviour we learn also this lesson, that, except almighty God giveth leave, the devil cannot have any power against man, seeing he cannot so much as enter into hogs, without our Saviour's permission. Wherefore, necessary it is that we be obedient to him, unto whom all our enemies be subject, that we may so much the more be stronger than our enemies, by how much through humility we become one with the author of all things. And what marvel is it, if God's chosen servants, living yet upon earth, can do many strange things, when as their very bones, after they be dead, do oftentimes work miracles ?

Chapter Twenty-two : of a Priest in the province of Valeria, who detained a thief at his grave.

¶ For, in the province of Valeria, this strange thing happened : which I had from the mouth of Valentius, mine Abbot, who was a blessed man. In that country

[1] Matt. 8, 31.

there was a Priest, who in the company of divers other clerks served God, and led a virtuous and holy life : who, when his time was come, departed this life, and was buried before the church. Not far off, there belonged to the church certain sheep-cotes : and the place where he lay buried was the way to go unto the sheep. Upon a night, as the Priests were singing within the church, a thief came to the said place, took up a wether, and so departed in all haste : but as he passed where the man of God was buried, there he stayed, and could go no farther. Then he took the wether from his shoulders, and would fain have let it go, but by no means could he open his hand : and therefore, poor wretch, there he stood fast bound, with his prey before him ; willingly would he have let the wether go, and could not ; willingly also have carried it away, and was not able. And so very strangely the thief, that was afraid to be espied of living men, was held there against his will by one that was dead ; for his hands and feet were bound in such sort, that away he could not go. When morning was come, and the Priests had ended their service, out they came : where they found a stranger, with a wether in his hand. And at the first they were in doubt, whether he had taken away one of theirs, or else came to give them one of his own : but he that was guilty of the theft told them in what manner he was punished : whereat they all wondered, to see a thief, with his prey before him, to stand there bound by the merits of the man of God. And straightways they offered their prayers for his delivery, and scarce could they obtain that he, which came to steal away their goods, might at least find so much favour as to depart empty as he came : yet in conclusion, the thief that had long stood there with his stolen wether, was suffered to go away free, leaving his carriage behind him.

Peter. By such facts almighty God doth declare, in what sweet manner he doth tender us, when he vouchsafeth to work such pleasant miracles.

Chapter Twenty-three: of the Abbot of Mount Preneste, and his Priest. ¶ Gregory.

Above the city of Preneste there is a mountain, upon which standeth an Abbey of the blessed Apostle, St. Peter : of the monks of which place, whiles I lived in an Abbey myself, I heard this miracle : which, those religious men said, they knew to be very true. In that monastery they had an Abbot of holy life, who brought up a certain monk, that became very virtuous, whom he perceiving to increase in the fear of God, he caused him in the same monastery to be made Priest : who, after his taking of orders, understood by revelation that his death was not far off ; and therefore desired leave of the Abbot to make ready his sepulchre, who told him that himself should die before him : "but yet for all that," quoth he, "go your way, and make your grave at your pleasure." Away he went, and did so. Not many days after, the old Abbot fell sick of an ague, and drawing near to his end, he bad the foresaid Priest that stood by him, to bury his body in that grave which he had made for himself : and when the other told him that he was shortly to follow after, and that the grave was not big enough for both, the Abbot answered him in this wise : "Do as I have said, for that one grave shall contain both our bodies." So he died, and according to his desire, was buried in that grave which the Priest had provided for himself. Straight after, the Priest fell sick, and lay not long before he departed this life ; and when his body was by the monks brought to the grave, which he had provided for himself, they opened it, and saw that there was not any room, because the Abbot's corpse filled the whole place : then one of them, with a loud voice, said : "O father, where is your promise, that this grave should hold you both?" No sooner had he spoken those words, than the Abbot's body, which lay with the face upward, did, in all their sight, turn itself upon one side, and so left place enough for the burial of the Priest: and so after his death he performed what he promised alive, concerning the lying of both their bodies in that one grave. But because we have now made mention of St. Peter's Abbey in the city of Preneste, where this miracle happened, are you content to hear something of the keepers of his church which is in this city where his most holy body remaineth?

Peter. Most willing I am, and beseech you that it may be so.

Chapter Twenty-four: of Theodorus, Keeper of St. Peter's Church, in the City of Rome.

¶ Gregory. There be yet some alive that knew Theodorus, keeper of that church: by whose report a notable thing that befell him came to my knowledge. For rising somewhat early one night to mend the lights that hung by the door, and was upon the ladder (as he used) to pour oil into the lamps, suddenly St. Peter the Apostle in a white stole, standing beneath upon the pavement, appeared unto him, and spake to him in this manner: "Theodorus, why hast thou risen so early?" and when he had said so, he vanished out of his sight: but such a fear came upon him, that all the strength of his body did forsake him, so that he was not able to rise up from his bed for many days after. By which apparition what meant the blessed Apostle else, but to give those which serve him to understand by that his presence, that whatsoever they do for his honour, himself for their reward doth always behold it?

Peter. I marvel not so much at his apparition: as that being before very well, he fell sick upon that sight.

Gregory. What reason have you, Peter, to marvel at that? for have you forgotten how the prophet Daniel, when he beheld that great and terrible vision at which he trembled, speaketh thus of himself: *I became weak, and was sick for very many days;*[1] for the flesh cannot conceive such things as pertain to the spirit, and therefore sometimes when a man's mind is carried to see somewhat beyond itself, no remedy but this earthly and frail vessel of ours, not able to bear such a burthen, must fall into weakness and infirmity.

Peter. Your reason hath taken away that scruple which troubled my mind.

Chapter Twenty-five: of Abundius, Keeper of the same Church of St. Peter. ¶ Gregory. Not very

many years since (as old men say) there was another keeper of the same church, called Abundius, a grave man, and of great humility: who served God so faithfully, that the blessed Apostle St. Peter did by miracle declare what opinion he had of his virtue. For a certain young maid, that frequented his church, was so pitifully sick of the palsy, that she crept upon her hands, and, for very weakness, drew her body upon the ground. Long time had she prayed to St. Peter for help of this her infirmity: who upon a night in a vision, stood by her and spake thus: "Go unto Abundius, and desire his help, and he shall restore thee to thine health." The maid, as she made no doubt of the vision, so not knowing this Abundius, up and down she crept through the church, enquiring for the man, and suddenly met with him whom she sought for; and asking for him of himself, he told her that he was Abundius. Then quoth she: "Our pastor and patron, blessed St. Peter the Apostle, hath sent me, that you should help me of this my disease." "If you be sent by him," quoth Abundius, "then rise up": and taking her by the hand, he forthwith lifted her up upon her feet: and from that very hour, all the sinews and parts of her body became so strong, that no sign of her former malady remained. But if I should recount all the miracles in

[1] Daniel 8, 27.

particular, which are known to have been done in his church, questionless no time would be left for the relation of any other ; wherefore I will speak no more of them, but come to such holy men as have been famous in divers other places of Italy.

Chapter Twenty-six: of a solitary Monk called Menas. ¶ Not long since, in the province of Samnium, there was a reverent man called Menas, who some ten years since led a solitary life, and was known to many of our friends : and for the truth of such his notable acts as I shall report, I will not name any one author, because I have so many witnesses as there be men that know that province of Samnium. This holy man had no other wealth to live upon, but a few hives of bees, which a certain Lombard would needs have taken away : for which cause the holy man reprehended him, and by and by he fell down before him, and was tormented of a devil : upon which accident his name became famous, both to his neighbours and also to that barbarous nation : so that none durst after that but in humility come into his cell. Oftentimes also there came certain bears out of the wood which was hard by, to devour up his honey, whom he strook with a little stick which he carried in his hand ; and the bears so feared his stripes, that they would roar out and run away, and they which little feared naked swords were now afraid to be beaten by him with a small wand. He desired not to possess aught in this world, nor to seek for any thing ; and his manner was, by heavenly talk to inflame all such as of charity came to visit him, with the desire and love of eternal life. And if at any time he understood that others had committed any great sin, he would never spare them, but with true love to their souls reprehend them for their faults. His neighbours, and others also that dwelt farther off, used upon a custom, every one upon certain days in the week, to send him their presents and offerings, to the end he might have somewhat to bestow upon such as came to visit him. A certain man there was, called Carterius, who, overcome of filthy concupiscence, violently took away a Nun, and by unlawful matrimony made her his wife : which thing so soon as the man of God understood, he sent him by such as he could that message which his fact deserved. The man, guilty in his conscience of that wickedness which he had committed, durst not himself go unto God's servant, fearing lest, as his manner was, he would sharply have rebuked him : and therefore he sent his offerings among others, that at least through ignorance he might receive what he sent him. But when all the offerings were brought before him, he sat still, viewing them all in particular, and laying the rest aside, he took those which Carterius sent, and cast them away, saying : "Go and tell him : Thou hast taken away God's offering, and dost thou send me thine ? I will none of thy offering, because thou hast taken from God that which was his." By which fact all that were present fell into a great fear, perceiving that he could certainly tell what they did which were absent.

Peter. Many such men as he was might, in mine opinion, have been martyrs, if they had lived in times of persecution.

Gregory. There be, Peter, two kinds of martyrdoms, the one secret, the other open : for if a man hath a burning zeal in his mind to suffer death for Christ, although he endureth not any external persecution, yet hath he in secret the merit of martyrdom. For that one may be a martyr without suffering death openly, our Lord doth teach us in the Gospel : who said unto the sons of Zebedeus, desiring as then, through infirmity of soul, the principal places to sit upon in his kingdom : *Can you drink the chalice which I shall drink?* and when they answered that they could, he said to them both : *My chalice verily shall you drink, but to sit at my right hand* *or left, is not mine to give you:*[1] in which words what is signified else, by the name of *chalice*, but the cup of passion and death? And seeing we know that James was put to death for Christ, and that John died when the Church enjoyed peace: undoubtedly we do gather that one may be a martyr without open suffering: for as much as he is said to have drunk our Lord's chalice, who yet in persecution was not put to death. But concerning those notable and excellent men of whom I have made mention before, why may we not truly say, that if they had fallen into a time of persecution, they might have been martyrs, when as by enduring the secret assaults of the devil, and by loving their enemies in this world, by resisting all carnal desires, and in that they did in their heart sacrifice themselves to almighty God, they were also martyrs in the time of peace? seeing that now in our days we see that mean men and of secular life, yea, and even those of whom one would have supposed that they did little think of heaven, have by occasion of persecution obtained the glorious crown of martyrdom.

Chapter Twenty-seven : of forty country husbandmen that were slain by the Lombards, because they would not eat flesh sacrificed to idols.

¶ For about fifteen years since, as they report who might very well have been present, forty husbandmen of the country were taken prisoners by the Lombards, whom they would needs have enforced to eat of that which was sacrificed to idols: but when they utterly refused so to do, or so much as once to touch that wicked meat, then they threatened to kill them, unless they would eat it : but they, loving more eternal than transitory life, continued constant, and so they were all slain. What then were these men ? what else but true martyrs, that made choice rather to die than, by eating of that which was unlawful, to offend their Creator ?

[1] Matt. 20, 22-23.

Chapter Twenty-eight: of a great number of prisoners that were slain, because they would not adore a goat's head. ¶ At the same time, the Lombards, having almost four hundred prisoners in their hands, did, after their manner, sacrifice a goat's head to the devil: running round about with it in a circle, and by singing a most blasphemous song did dedicate it to his service. And when they had themselves with bowed heads adored it, then would they also have enforced their prisoners to do the like. But a very great number of them choosing rather by death to pass unto immortal life, than by such abominable adoration to preserve their mortal bodies, refused utterly to do what they commanded them ; and so would not by any means bow down their heads to a creature, having always done that service to their Creator : whereat their enemies, in whose hands they were, fell into such an extreme rage, that they slew all them with their swords, which would not join with them in that sacrilegious fact. What marvel then is it, that those notable men before mentioned might have come to martyrdom, had they lived in the days of persecution, who in the time of peace, by continual mortification, walked the straight way of martyrdom : when as we see that, in the storm of persecution, they merited to obtain the crown of martyrdom, who, the Church being quiet, seemed to walk the broad way of this world ? Yet that which we say concerning the elect servants of God, is not to be holden for a general rule in all. For when open persecution afflicteth the Church, as most true it is that many may arrive to martyrdom, who, when no such tempest did blow, seemed contemptible, and of no account : so likewise sometimes they fall away for fear, who before persecution, and when all was quiet, seemed to stand very constant : but such holy men as before have been mentioned, I dare boldly say that they might have been martyrs, because we gather so much by their happy deaths : for they could not have fallen in open persecution, of whom it is certain that, to the very end of their lives, they did continue in the profession of piety and virtue.

Peter. It is as you say : but I much wonder at the singular providence of God's mercy, which he sheweth to us unworthy wretches, in that he doth so moderate and temper the cruelty of the Lombards, that he suffereth not their wicked priests to persecute the faith of Christians : when as they see themselves, as it were, the conquerors and rulers of Christian people.

Chapter Twenty-nine : of an Arian Bishop that was miraculously strooken blind. ¶ Gregory.

Many, Peter, have attempted that, but miracles from heaven have stayed the course of their cruelty : and one will I now tell you, which I heard three days since of Bonifacius, a monk of my Abbey, who, until these four years last past, remained amongst the Lombards. An Arian Bishop of theirs coming to the city of Spoleto, and not having any place where to exercise his religion, demanded a church of the Bishop of that town : which when he constantly denied him, the Arian prelate told him, that the next day he would by force take possession of St. Paul's church, which was hard by his lodging. The keeper of the church, understanding this news, in all haste ran thither, shut the doors, and with locks and bolts made them as fast as he could : and when it was night he put out all the lamps, and hid himself within. The next morning, very early, the Arian Bishop came thither with many in his company : meaning by force to break open the doors. But suddenly by miracle the locks were cast far off, and the doors of themselves, making a great noise, flew open : and all the lamps, before put out, were lightened again by fire descending from heaven : and the Arian Bishop that came to enter the church by violence, was suddenly strooken blind, so that other men were fain to lead him back again to his own lodging. Which strange accident when the Lombards there about understood, they durst not any more presume to violate Catholic places : and so it fell out wonderfully, by God's providence, that for as much as the lamps in St. Paul's church were by reason of him put out : that at one and the self same time, both he lost the light of his eyes, and the church received her former light again.

Chapter Thirty : how a church of the Arians in Rome was hallowed according to the Catholic manner. ¶ Neither is that to be passed over in silence which God of his mercy vouchsafed, two years since, to shew in this city, to the great condemnation of the Arian heresy : for part of that which I intend now to speak of, many of the people know to be true : part the Priest and keepers of the church affirm that they saw and heard. A church of the Arians, in that part of the city which is called Subura, remained until two years since with the doors shut up ; at which time, being desirous that it should be hallowed in the Catholic faith, we brought with us thither the relics of the blessed martyrs St. Stephen and St. Agatha : and so with great multitudes of people, singing of praises to almighty God, we entered the church : and when the solemnity of mass was in celebrating, and the people, by reason of the straight place, thrust one another, some of them that stood without the chancel heard an hog running up and down through their legs, and each one perceiving it told it to his next fellow : but the hog made towards the church door to go forth, striking all those into great admiration by whom he passed ; but though they heard him, yet none there was that saw him : which strange thing God of piety vouchsafed to shew, to the end we should understand how that the unclean spirit, which before possessed that place, was now departed and gone. When mass was done we went away, but the night following such a noise was heard in the top of the church, as though somebody had there run up and down ; and the next night after that a far greater, and withal, of a sudden, such a terrible crack there was, as though the whole church had been quite falling down : which forthwith vanished away, and never after was the church troubled any more by the old enemy : but by the great stir which he kept before his departure, he made it apparent that he went very unwillingly from that place, which so long time he had possessed.

Not many days after, in a passing fair and clear day, a cloud miraculously descended upon the altar of the same church : covering it as it had been with a canopy : and filled the church with such a kind of terror and sweetness, that though the doors were wide open, yet none durst presume to enter in. The Priest also and the keepers of the church, and those which were come thither to say mass, beheld the self same thing, yet could they not go in, although they felt the sweetness of that strange perfume.

Likewise upon another day, the lamps hanging without light, fire came from heaven and set them a burning : and a few days after, when mass was ended, and the keeper of the church had put out the lamps, and was departed, yet returning back again, he found them burning which before he had put forth ; but thinking that he had done it negligently, he did it now more carefully the second time, and so departed the church and shut the door ; but returning three hours after, he found them again burning as before : to the end that by the very light the world might manifestly know, how that place was from darkness translated to light.

Peter. Although we be in great miseries and tribulations, yet these strange miracles, which God vouchsafeth to work, do plainly declare that he hath not utterly forsaken and given us over.

Gregory. Albeit I was determined to recount unto you only such strange things as were done in Italy, are you for all that content, to the further condemnation of the said Arian heresy, that I turn a little my speech to Spain, and so by Africk return back again to Italy?

Peter. Go whither you will, willingly will I travel with you, and joyfully return home again.

Chapter Thirty-one: of King Hermigildus, son to Leuigildus, King of the Visegoths: who was, for the Catholic faith, put to death by his father.

¶ **Gregory.** Not long since, as I have learned of many which came from Spain, king Hermigildus, son of Leuigildus, king of the Visegoths, was from Arian heresy lately converted to the Catholic faith by the most reverent man Leander, Bishop of Seville, with whom I was not long since familiarly acquainted ; which young Prince, upon his conversion, his father, being an Arian, laboured both by large promises and terrible threats to draw again to his former error : but when most constantly his son answered, that he would never forsake the true faith which he had once embraced, his father in great anger took away his kingdom, and beside deprived him of all wealth and riches ; and perceiving that, with all this, his mind was nothing moved, he committed him to straight prison, laying irons both upon his neck and hands. Upon this, the young king Hermigildus began now to contemn his earthly kingdom, and to seek with great desire after the kingdom of heaven : and lying in prison fast bound, he prayed to almighty God in hair-cloth to send him heavenly comfort : and so much the more did he despise the glory of this transitory world, by how much he knew himself in that case that he had now nothing that could be taken from him.

When the solemn feast of Easter was come, his wicked father sent unto him in the dead of the night an Arian Bishop, to give him the communion of a sacrilegious consecration, that he might thereby again recover his father's grace and favour : but the man of God, as he ought, sharply reprehended that Arian Bishop which came unto him, and giving him such entertainment as his deserts required, utterly rejected him ; for albeit outwardly he lay there in bands, yet inwardly to himself he stood secure in the height of his own soul. The father, at the return of the Arian prelate, understanding these news, fell into such a rage that forthwith he sent his officers of execution to put to death that most constant confessor, in the very prison where he lay : which unnatural and bloody commandment was performed accordingly : for so soon as they came into the prison, they clave his brains with an hatchet, and so bereaved him of mortal life, having only power to take that from him which the holy martyr made small account of. Afterward, for the publishing of his true glory to the world, there wanted not miracles from heaven : for in the night time singing was heard at his body : some also report that, in the night, burning lamps were seen in that place : by reason whereof his body, as of him that was a martyr, was worthily worshipped of all Christian people. But the wicked father and murtherer of his own son, albeit he was sorry that he had put him to death, yet was not his grief of that quality that it brought him to the state of salvation. For although he knew very well that the Catholic faith was the truth, yet, for fear of his people, he never deserved to be a professor thereof.

At length, falling sick, a little before his death, he commended his son Recharedus, who was to succeed him in the kingdom, and was yet an heretic, unto Bishop Leander, whom before he had greatly persecuted : that by his counsel and exhortation, he might likewise make him a member of the Catholic Church, as he had before made his brother Hermigildus ; and when he had thus done, he departed this life. After whose death, Rec-

haredus the king, not following the steps of his wicked
father, but his brother the martyr, utterly renounced
Arianism : and laboured so earnestly for the restoring
of religion, that he brought the whole nation of the
Visegoths to the true faith of Christ, and would not
suffer any that was an heretic in his country to bear
arms and serve in the wars. And it is not to be admired that he became thus to be a preacher of the true
faith, seeing he was the brother of a martyr, whose
merits did help him to bring so many into the lap of
God's Church : wherein we have to consider that he
could never have effected all this, if king Hermigildus
had not died for the testimony of true religion ; for, as
it is written : *Unless the grain of wheat falling into the earth
doth die, itself remaineth alone ; but if it die, it bringeth forth
much fruit.*[1] This we see to prove true in the members,
which before was verified in the head : for one died
amongst the Visegoths that many might live, and of one
grain that was sown for the faith, a great crop of faithful
people sprung up.

Peter. A wonderful thing, and much to be admired in
these our days.

**Chapter Thirty-two : of certain Bishops of Africk,
who had their tongues cut out by the Vandals,
that were Arian heretics, for the defence of the
Catholic faith; and yet spake still as perfectly as
they did before. ¶ Gregory.** Likewise, in the time
of Justinian the Emperor, when as the Vandals, that were
Arian heretics, did grievously persecute the Catholic
faith, certain Bishops, continuing constant, were openly
examined : whom when the king of the Vandals saw
that he could neither by any words or rewards draw to
embrace his heretical religion, yet he thought that by
torments he might do it : and therefore, when he commanded them not to speak in defence of truth, and they

[1] John 12, 24.

157

refused to obey his precept, lest by silence they might
seem to give consent unto wicked heresy, in a great
fury he commanded their tongues to be cut out by the
roots. A miraculous thing, and yet known to many
old men : they did as perfectly afterward speak in defence of true religion, as they did before, when they had
their tongues safe and sound.

Peter. You tell me of a marvellous strange thing, and
greatly to be admired.

Gregory. It is written, Peter, of the only Son of the
eternal Father : *In the beginning was the Word, and the
Word was with God.*[1] Of whose virtue and power it
straightways followeth : *All things were made by him.*
Why then should we marvel, if that eternal Word could
speak without a tongue, which made the tongue ?

Peter. What you say pleaseth me very well.

Gregory. These Bishops, therefore, flying at that time
from the persecution, came unto the city of Constantinople : and at such time as myself, about the affairs of
the Church, was sent thither unto the Emperor, I found
there a Bishop of good years, who told me that he saw
them himself speak without tongues : for they opened
their mouths, and said : " Behold and see how we have
no tongues, and yet do speak " ; for, as he said, their
tongues being cut off by the roots, there seemed as it
were a deep hole in their throat : and yet, though their
mouths were empty, they pronounced their words very
plain and distinctly. One of which, falling afterward in
that place into carnal sin, was forthwith deprived of that
supernatural gift : and that by the just judgment of almighty God, seeing reason requireth that he which was
careless to preserve the continency of his body which
he had, should not any longer utter the words of truth
without the tongue of his body which he had not. But
because I have now spoken sufficient for the condemna-

[1] John I, I.

tion of Arianism, therefore I will return to entreat of such other miracles as have lately fallen out here in Italy.

Chapter Thirty-three: of the servant of God, Eleutherius.

¶ Eleutherius, of whom I made mention before, father of the Abbey of the Evangelist St. Mark, which is in the suburbs of the city of Spoleto, lived long time together with me in this city in my monastery, and there ended his days. Of whom his monks do report that by his tears he raised up one that was dead : for he was a man of such simplicity and compunction, that no doubt but those tears, coming from his humble and simple soul, were of force to obtain many things of almighty God. One miracle of his I will now tell you, which himself, being demanded by me, did with great simplicity confess. As he was travelling upon a certain day, and not finding at night any other place to lodge in, he went to a Nunnery, wherein there was a little boy which the wicked spirit did usually every night torment. The Nuns, giving entertainment to the man of God, desired him that the said little boy might remain with him all night : wherewith he was well content. In the morning, the Nuns diligently enquired of the father, if the child had not been sore troubled and tormented that night : who, marvelling why they asked that question, answered that he perceived not any such thing. Then they told him how a wicked spirit did every night pitifully afflict the child, and earnestly desired him that he would take him home to his own Abbey, because their hearts could not endure to behold any such misery. The old man yielded to their request, and so carried away the boy home to his own monastery : where he remained long time safe and sound, the devil not presuming to touch him. Whereupon the old man, seeing him to continue so well, was immoderately glad thereof, and therefore, in

159

the presence of the monks, he spake thus : "The devil did dally with those sisters : but now he hath to do with the servants of God, he dare not come near this boy." He had scarce uttered these words, when as in that very instant the poor child was, in the presence of them all, possessed, and pitifully tormented : which the old man beholding, straightways lamented and fell a weeping, and persevering so a long time, the monks came to comfort him ; but he answered them, saying : "Believe me," quoth he, "none of you shall this day eat any bread, unless this boy be dispossessed." Then, with the rest of the brethren, he fell prostrate to his prayers, and there they continued so long, until the boy was delivered from his former torments, and besides so perfectly cured, that the wicked spirit never after presumed to molest him any more.

Peter. I verily suppose that he sinned a little in vain glory : and that God's pleasure was, that the other monks should co-operate to the dispossessing of the devil.

Gregory. It is even so as you say : for seeing he could not alone bear the burthen of that miracle, it was divided amongst the rest of his brethren. Of what force and efficacy this man's prayers were, I have found by experience in myself : for being upon a time, when I lived in the Abbey, so sick that I often swooned : and was by means thereof, with often pangs, continually at death's door, and in such case that, unless I did continually eat something, my vital spirit was going away : Easter day was at hand, and therefore when I saw that upon so sacred a vigil I could not refrain from often eating, in which not only old persons, but even children use to fast, I was more afflicted with grief, than grieved with mine infirmity : yet at length my sorrowful soul quickly found out a device, and that was, to carry the man of God secretly into the oratory, and there to

160

entreat him that he would by his prayer obtain for me of God so much strength and ability as to fast that day · which fell out accordingly : for so soon as we came into the oratory, with humility and tears he fell to his prayers, and after a while (having made an end) he came forth, and upon the words of his blessed prayers, my stomach grew so strong, that I did not so much as think of any meat, nor feel any grief at all. Then I began to marvel at myself, and to think in what case I was before, and how I felt myself now : and when I thought upon my former sickness, I found none of those pangs with which before I was troubled : and when my mind was busied about the affairs of the Abbey, my sickness was quite out of my memory ; yea, and as I said, if I did think thereof, yet feeling myself so well and strong, I began to doubt whether I had eaten or no. When evening was come, I found myself so lusty that I could very well have fasted until the next day. And by this means, having experience of his prayers in myself, I made no doubt but those things also were true which in other places he did, though myself was not then present.

Peter. Seeing you told me that he was a man of great compunction, desirous I am to be better informed touching the efficacy of compunction and tears : and therefore I pray you, let me understand how many kinds of compunction there be.

Chapter Thirty-four : of the divers kinds of compunction. ¶ Gregory. Compunction is divided into many kinds : to wit, when every sin is of penitent men in particular bewailed : whereof the prophet Jeremy, in the person of penitent sinners, speaketh thus : *Mine eye hath brought forth divisions of waters.*[1] But speaking more properly, there be especially two kinds of compunction for the soul that thirsteth after God is first sorrowful in

[1] Lamentations 3, 48.

heart for fear, and afterward upon love. For first it is
grieved and weepeth, because, calling to mind former
sins committed, it feareth to endure for punishment of
them everlasting torments: but when long anxiety and
sorrow hath banished away that fear, then a certain
security of the hope of pardon doth follow: and so the
soul is inflamed with the love of heavenly delights, and
whereas before it did weep for fear of eternal pain, afterward it poureth out tears, that it is kept from everlasting
joys. For the soul doth then contemplate those glittering
quires of Angels, that heavenly company of those blessed
spirits, that great majesty of the eternal beholding the
face of God; and doth lament so much more now,
because it wanteth that everlasting felicity, than it wept
before at the fear of eternal punishment. Which thing
in scripture is mystically set down, in an holy and true
history: for there we read how Axa, the daughter of
Caleb, riding upon an ass, did sigh: and when her
father demanded what the matter was, she answered
him thus: *Give me your blessing, a southern and dry land
you have given me, join also a watery : and he gave her a
watery ground above and beneath.*[1] For Axa then rideth
upon the ass, when our soul doth subdue and govern
the sensual motions of the flesh: which sighing doth
crave wet ground of her father, when it doth with contrition and sorrow of heart desire of our Creator the
grace of tears and weeping. For some there be, upon
whom God hath bestowed such a gift, that they will
speak freely in defence of justice, help them that be
oppressed, give alms to the poor, and be zealous in
religion, but yet have they not obtained the grace of
tears: these be they, that have ground towards the
south, and that which is dry: but yet do they want
that which is moist and wet: because, albeit they be
diligent and fervent in good works, yet requisite it is

[1] Joshua 15, 19.

that they should also, either for fear of hell or the love of heaven, bewail the sins of their life past. But because, as I said, there be two kinds of compunction, therefore her father gave her that which was wet above and also wet beneath : for our soul doth then receive that which is wet above, when it is grieved, and doth weep for the desire of heaven ; and it doth then possess that which is wet beneath, when it is afraid, and poureth forth tears for the fear of hell fire : and albeit that which is wet beneath is bestowed upon our soul, before that which is wet above, yet because the compunction of love is the more excellent, convenient it was that the ground which was wet above should be first named, and afterward that which was wet beneath.

Peter. Your discourse pleaseth me very well : but seeing you have now told me of that reverent man Eleutherius, and his great grace of compunction, desirous I am to know whether there be now any such men living in the world.

Chapter Thirty-five : of Amantius, a Priest in the Province of Tuscania. ¶ Gregory. Floridus, Bishop of Tivoli, a man (as yourself knoweth very well) of holy life, and worthy to be credited, told me that he had dwelling with him a certain Priest called Amantius, of marvellous simplicity : who, like unto the Apostles, had such a grace given him of God, that, laying his hand upon them that were sick, he restored them to their former health ; and although the disease were very great and dangerous, yet upon his touching did it forthwith depart. Moreover he said that he had also this miraculous gift, that wheresoever he found any serpents or snakes, though never so cruel, yet did he with the sign of the cross dispatch and kill them : for by virtue of the cross, which the man of God made with his hand, their bowels did break, and they suddenly die : and if by chance the snake gat into any hole, then did he with the sign of the cross bless the mouth thereof, and it wrought the same effect ; for any might straightways find it there dead. Myself having understanding of this great grace bestowed upon him, was desirous to see him : and when he was brought unto me, I caused him to be lodged in a chamber amongst the sick men : thereby to try what his gift was in curing of diseases. At that time, there was one amongst them beside himself, being fallen into a phrensy : who one night did so cry out like a mad man, that with his noise he disquieted all the rest that were sick, so that they could not sleep or take any rest : and so it fell out very strangely that, one being ill, all the rest fared the worse. But as I had before learned of the reverent Bishop Floridus, who was at that time there present with the said Priest, and afterward also plainly understood of him that attended that night upon the sick persons, the foresaid venerable Priest, rising out of his bed, went softly to the place where the mad man lay, and there prayed, laying his hands upon him ; whereupon the man became somewhat better. Then he carried him away unto the higher part of the house, into the oratory : where more plentifully he prayed unto God for his recovery : and straight after he brought him back again to his own bed safe and sound, so that he cried out no more, neither troubled any of the other sick persons. By which one fact of his, I had sufficient reason to give credit to all the rest that before had been told me.

Peter. A great edification it is, to see men working such notable miracles : and to behold, as it were upon earth, heavenly Jerusalem in her citizens.

Chapter Thirty-six: of Marimianus, Bishop of Syracusis. ¶ Gregory. Neither is that miracle to be passed over with silence, which almighty God vouchsafed to work by his servant Maximianus, now Bishop of Syracusis, but then the father and governor of mine Abbey. For at such time as I was, upon the commandment of my Bishop, sent to Constantinople to the Emperor, about affairs of the Church, the same reverent man, Maximianus upon charity, with other of his monks, came thither unto me : who in his return homeward to Rome, fell into a great tempest upon the Adriake sea : in which both himself and all those that were in his company, after a most strange and miraculous manner, tasted both of the indignation and favour of almighty God. For the sea did so rage with the fury of the winds, that they had spent their mast : the sails floated upon the waves : and the ship, beaten and torn with boisterous billows, did leak water so fast, that it was now come to the upper deck, in such sort that the ship seemed not so much to be in the waters, as the waters in the ship.

The mariners and passengers, troubled with the fear of death, not as a thing far off, but even present before their eyes, void of all hope of this life, prepared themselves for the next : and so, mutually giving the pax or kiss of peace one to another, they received the body and blood of our Saviour : commending themselves to almighty God, that he would vouchsafe mercifully to receive their souls, who had delivered their bodies to so fearful a death : but God, who had wonderfully terrified their minds, did more wonderfully preserve their lives. For the same ship although full of water, yet did it hold on her course for eight days together, and upon the ninth, it arrived at the port of Cothronum : and when all the rest were safely gone out, then last of all the reverent man Maximianus went also forth : and no sooner was he upon land, than the ship sunk in the haven : as though, by their departure, it had wanted that which did preserve it : and whereas before, being at sea, it was full of men, and carried also abundance of water, and yet sailed onward : now when Maximianus with his monks were landed, it could not in the haven carry the waters alone : whereby God gave them to understand, that, when it was laden, himself with his divine hand did govern and preserve it : seeing when it was empty it could not for a small time continue above the water.

Chapter Thirty-seven : of Sanctulus, a Priest in the Province of Nursia.

¶ About forty days since, you saw with me one called Sanctulus, a reverent Priest, who every year came unto me out of Nursia : but three days ago, a certain monk, coming from those parts, brought me very heavy news of his death. The holy life and virtue of which man was such, that although I can not but fetch sweet sighs when I remember it, yet now I may without all fear report and publish to the world such miracles as I have learned by the relation of very virtuous and holy Priests, that were his neighbours : and as amongst dear friends familiarity causeth one to presume much in charity, oftentimes myself did so courteously urge him, that he was enforced to tell me some small miracles which himself had done.

Certain Lombards being upon a time pressing of olives to make oil, Sanctulus, as he was both merry in countenance and heart, came unto them, and saluted them pleasantly : and shewing them his bottle which he brought, rather willed than desired them to fill it with oil. But they being infidels, and having laboured all day in vain, and not pressed out any oil at all, took his words in ill part, and gave him very bad speech : but the man of God, notwithstanding this, spake unto them yet with a more merry countenance, and said : " If you desire to do me a good turn, you will fill this bottle for Sanctulus, and so he will depart from you very well contented." But they, seeing no oil to run forth, and hearing him yet for all that so earnest to have his bottle filled, fell into a great rage, and railed mightily upon him. Then the man of God, seeing that no oil came from the press, called for water, which he blessed before them all, and with his own hands cast it upon the press : and forthwith, by virtue

166

of that benediction, such plenty of oil ran forth, that the Lombards, who before had long laboured in vain, did not only fill their own vessels, but also his bottle : giving him thanks for that, coming to beg oil, by his blessing he bestowed that upon them which himself had demanded.

At another time, when a great dearth was in the country, the man of God being desirous to repair the church of St. Lawrence, burnt before by the Lombards, he hired for that end many cunning workmen and divers other labourers, who of necessity were daily to be maintained : but so great was the scarcity, that he wanted bread to relieve them ; whereupon his workmen cried out for meat, because they were faint and could not labour. The man of God, hearing this, gave them comfortable words, promising to supply their want ; yet inwardly very much was he grieved, being not able to perform what he had said. Going therefore up and down in great anxiety, he came to an oven, wherein the neighbours that dwelt by had the day before baked bread : and stooping down, he looked in, to see whether they had by chance left any bread behind them, where he found a loaf both greater and whiter than commonly they used : which he took away, but yet would he not by and by give it to his workmen, lest perhaps it belonged to some other body, and so might as it were, of compassion to other, have committed a sin himself : and therefore he did first shew it to all the women there about, enquiring whether it were any of theirs : but all denied it, saying that they had all received their just number of loaves. Then the man of God in great joy went with that one loaf to many workmen, wishing them to give thanks to almighty God, telling them how his goodness had provided them of necessary food ; and forthwith he set that loaf before them, whereof, when they had satisfied themselves, he gathered up more pieces of bread which remained, than the whole loaf itself was before in quantity. The day following, again he set it before them, and again the pieces remaining were far more than the former fragments: and so, for the space of ten days together, all those artificers and workmen lived upon that one loaf, and were very well satisfied: some thing remaining every day for the next, as though the fragments had by eating increased.

Peter. A strange thing, and not unlike to that notable miracle of our Saviour; and therefore worthy to be admired of all.

Gregory. Our Saviour at this time, Peter, vouchsafed by his servant to feed many with one loaf, who in times past, by himself, fed five thousand with five loaves: and doth daily of a few grains of corn produce innumerable ears of wheat: who also out of the earth brought forth those very grains; and more than all this, created all things of nothing. But to the end you should not marvel any longer, what by God's assistance the venerable man Sanctulus wrought outwardly: I will now tell you what, by our Lord's grace, he was inwardly in his soul. Upon a certain day, the Lombards had taken a Deacon, whom they kept in prison, with a purpose to put him to death. When evening was come, the man of God, Sanctulus, entreated them to set him at liberty, and to grant him his life: but when he saw that he could not obtain that favour at their hands, but that they were fully resolved to have his life: then he beseeched them, that they would at least commit him to his keeping: wherewith they were content, but with this condition, that if he scaped away, that then himself should die for him. The man of God was very well content, and so he received the Deacon into his own charge and custody.

The midnight following, when he saw all the Lombards fast asleep, he called up the Deacon, willing him quickly to rise up and to run away as fast as he could: "and almighty God," quoth he, "deliver thee out of their hands." To whom the Deacon (knowing what he had promised) said : "Father, I can not run away, for if I do, out of all doubt they will put you to death." Yet for all this, Sanctulus enforced him to be gone with all speed, saying : "Up, and away : and God of his goodness defend and protect you : for I am in his hands, and they can do no more unto me than his divine Majesty shall give them leave." Upon these words away went the Deacon ; and he that had undertaken his safe keeping, as one that had been deceived, remained behind.

In the morning the Lombards demanded of Sanctulus for their prisoner : who told them that he was run away. "Then," quoth they, "you best know what is convenient for you to have." "Yea, marry, that do I," answered the servant of God, with great constancy. "Well," quoth they, "thou art a good man, and therefore we will not by divers torments take away thy life ; but make choice of what death thou wilt." To whom the man of God answered in this manner : "Here I am, at God's disposition and pleasure, kill me in such sort, as he shall vouchsafe to give you leave." Then all the Lombards that were present agreed to have him beheaded : to the end an easy and quick death might soon dispatch him. When it was given out abroad that Sanctulus was to die, whom for his virtue and holiness they greatly honoured, all the Lombards that were in those parts repaired thither, being glad (such cruel minds they have) to behold him put to death : and when all the army was gathered together, they brought him forth to execution, and the strongest man amongst them was chosen out, to cut off his head at one blow.

The venerable man, beset with armed soldiers, betook himself to his usual weapons : for he desired them to give him a little leave to pray : which when he had obtained, he cast himself prostrate upon the earth, and fell to his devotions : in which after he had continued for a good space, the executioner spurned him up with his foot, bidding him rise, kneel down, and to prepare himself for death. The man of God rose up, bowed down his knee, and held forth his head, and beholding the drawn sword ready to dispatch him, these only words they said that he spake aloud: "O Saint John, hold that sword." Then the foresaid executioner, having the naked weapon in his hand, did with all his force lift up his arm to strike off his head; but by no means could he bring it down again, for it became suddenly so stiff that it remained still above, the man being not able once to bend it downward. Then all the Lombards who came to feed their eyes with the lamentable sight of his death, began with admiration to praise God's name, and with fear to reverence the man of God: for they now saw apparently of what great holiness he was, that did so miraculously stay the arm of his executioner above in the air.

Then they desired him to rise up, which he did; but when they required him to restore his executioner's arm to his former state, he utterly refused, saying: "By no means will I once pray for him, unless beforehand he swear unto me, that he will never with that arm offer to kill any Christian more." The poor Lombard, who, as we may truly say, had stretched out his arm against God, enforced with this necessity, took an oath never more to put any Christian to death. Then the man of God commanded him to put down his arm, which forthwith he did; he commanded him also to put up his sword, which in like manner he performed. All the Lombards, by this perceiving him to be a man of rare virtue, began in all haste to present him with the gifts of such oxen and other cattle as before they had taken from others: but the man of God utterly refused all such kind of presents, desiring them rather, if they meant to bestow anything upon him worth the giving, that they would deliver unto him all such prisoners as they had in their keeping : that he might have some cause in his prayers to commend them to almighty God. To which request of his they condescended, and so all the poor captives were discharged : and thus, by God's sweet providence, one offering himself to die for another, many were delivered from death.

Peter. A strange thing it was : and although I have heard the same story by the relation of others, yet I cannot deny, but so often as I hear it repeated, it seemeth still unto me as though it were fresh news.

Gregory. There is no cause why you should admire Sanctulus for this thing : but ponder with yourself, if you can, what manner of spirit that was, which possessed his simple soul, and did advance it to so high a perfection of virtue. For where was his mind, when he offered himself with such constancy to die for his neighbour ; and to save the temporal life of his brother, contemned his own, and put his head under the executioner's sword ? What force of true love did then harbour in that heart, when he nothing feared death to preserve the life of another ? Ignorant I am not, that this venerable man Sanctulus could scant read well, and that he knew not the precepts of the law : yet because charity is the fulfilling of the law, by loving God and his neighbour, he kept the whole law : and that which outwardly lacked in knowledge, did inwardly by charity live in his soul. And he, perhaps, who never read that which St. John the Apostle said of our Saviour, to wit, that *as he yielded his life for us, so we likewise should yield our lives for our brethren :*[1] yet that great and high precept of the Apostle he knew more by action than by speculation. Let us here, if you please, compare his learned ignorance with our unlearned knowledge : where our kind of learning is nothing worth, his is of great price and estimation : we, destitute of virtue, do speak thereof, and, as it were in the midst of plentiful

[1] 1 John 3, 16.

trees smell of the fruit, but do not eat thereof. He knew full well how to gather and taste of the fruit itself, although he lacked the smell of words and vain speech.

Peter. What, I pray, do you think, is the cause that good men are still taken away; and such as for the benefit and edification of many, might live still in this world, either are not to be found at all, or at least very few can be heard of?

Gregory. The malice and wickedness of them that remain behind in the world deserveth that those should quickly be taken away, who by their life might much help us: and for as much as the world draweth towards an end, God's chosen servants are taken out of it, that they fall not into more wicked times: and therefore from hence it cometh that the prophet saith: *The just man doth perish, and there is none that doth ponder it in his heart: and men of mercy are gathered together, because there is none that hath understanding.*[1] And from hence also it proceedeth that the scripture saith: *Open ye, that they may go forth which do tread it under foot.*[2] Hence, likewise, it is that Solomon saith: *There is a time of casting stones abroad, and a time of gathering them together.*[3] And therefore the nearer that the world draweth to an end, so much the more necessary it is that the living stones should be gathered together, for the heavenly building: that our celestial Jerusalem may arrive to the full measure of his whole perfection. And yet do I not think that all God's elect servants are so taken out of the world, that none but the wicked remain behind: for sinners would never be converted to the sorrow of true penance, if they had not the examples of some good people to provoke them forward.

Peter. Without cause do I complain of the death of good men, when as daily I see them also that be wicked in great numbers to depart this life.

[1] Isai. 57, 1.   [2] Jerem. 50, 26.   [3] Eccles. 3, 5.

172

Redemptus of Ferenti
Chapter Thirty-eight : of the vision of Redemptus, Bishop of the City of Ferenti. ¶ Gregory. Wonder
nothing at this, Peter, for you knew very well Redemptus,
Bishop of the city of Ferenti, a man of venerable life,
who died almost seven years since : with whom I had
familiar acquaintance, by reason that he dwelt not far from
the Abbey in which I lived. This man, when I asked him
(for the matter was very well known far and near), told
me that which by divine revelation he had learned concerning the end of the world, in the time of John the
younger, who was my predecessor. For he said that upon
a certain day, as he was, according to his manner, visit-
ing of his diocese, he came to the church of the blessed
martyr Euthicius : and when it was night he would needs
be lodged nigh to the sepulchre of the martyr, where
after his travel he reposed himself. About midnight,
being, as he said himself, neither perfectly waking, nor
yet sleeping, but rather heavy of sleep, he felt his waking
soul oppressed with great sorrow : and being in that case,
he saw the same blessed martyr Euthicius standing before
him, who spake thus : "Art thou waking, Redemptus?"
to whom he answered, that he was. Then the martyr
said : "The end of all flesh is come : the end of all flesh
is come" : which words after he had repeated thus three
times, he vanished out of his sight.

Then the man of God rose up, and fell to his prayers
with many tears : and straight after, those fearful sights
in heaven followed ; to wit, fiery lances, and armies
appearing from the north. Straight after likewise the
barbarous and cruel nation of the Lombards, drawn as a
sword out of a sheath, left their own country, and invaded
ours : by reason whereof the people, which before for the
huge multitude were like to thick corn-fields, remain
now withered and overthrown : for cities be wasted, towns
and villages spoiled, churches burnt, monasteries of men
and women destroyed, farms left desolate, and the country

The Dialogues of St. Gregory

remaineth solitary and void of men to till the ground, and destitute of all inhabitants : beasts possessing those places, where before great plenty of men did dwell. And how it goeth in other parts of the world I know not, but here in this place where we live, the world doth not foretell any end, but rather sheweth that which is present and already come. Wherefore so much the more zealously ought we to seek after eternal things, by how much we find all temporal so quickly to be fled and gone. Surely this world were to be contemned, although it did flatter us, and with pleasant prosperity contented our mind : but now, seeing it is fraught with so many miseries and divers afflictions, and that our sorrows and crosses do daily increase and be doubled, what doth it else but cry unto us that we should not love it?

Many more things yet remain of the worthy acts of God's servants, but because I have resolved now upon another course, I will now pass them over with silence.

Peter. For as much as I perceive that many Christians do doubt of the immortality of the soul, after the dissolution of the body : I beseech you for the spiritual good of many, to set down some reasons for proof thereof : or the examples of some souls which have testified the same, if you remember any : to the end that those which be troubled with any such temptations, may learn that the soul doth not die together with the body.

Gregory. This is a work of great labour, especially for one that is busied with other affairs, and hath other things to attend unto : yet if any profit by my means may redound to others, willingly do I prefer that before mine own will and pleasure : and therefore, God's grace assisting me, in this fourth book following, I will clearly show that the soul doth live after the death of the body.

The end of the Third Book

174

The Dialogues of St. Gregory
The Fourth Book

St. Gregory's Dialogues

The Fourth Book

Chapter One : how carnal men give the less credit to those things which be eternal and spiritual : because they know not by experience, what they hear others to speak of. ¶ After that the first Parent of mankind was for his sin banished from the joys of Paradise, he fell into the misery of this ignorance and banishment, which to this very day we do all endure : for his sin was the cause that he could not any longer see those joys of heaven, which before by contemplation he possessed : for during the time of his residence in Paradise, he usually heard God talking with him, and by purity of heart and heavenly vision, was present with the quires of the blessed Angels. But after his fall he lost that light of soul, which before abundantly he enjoyed. From whom we being by carnal propagation derived, that live now in this dark ignorance of banishment, do hear indeed of an heavenly country, and how it is inhabited by the Angels of God ; and that the souls of just and perfect men do there keep them company. But yet such as be carnal, because they can not by experience know those invisible creatures, doubt whether there be any such, seeing with their corporal eyes they cannot behold them : from which doubt our first Parent was altogether free : for although he was exiled from the joys of Paradise, yet did he still keep in memory what he had lost, because he had before beheld the same : but these men can not by any means call to mind such things as they hear others speak of, because they never had of them any former experience as our first father Adam had.

For it is in this case as if a woman big with child should be put in prison, and be there delivered of a son, which never went forth, but were there continually brought up : for if his mother should tell him of the sun, moon, stars, mountains : and speak of the fields, the flying of birds, and running of horses ; her child, that had continually been brought up in the prison, and acquainted with nothing else but black darkness, might well hear what she said, but with a doubt whether it were true or no, because experience taught him not any such thing. Even so, men that are born in this dark world, the place of their banishment, do hear that there be wonderful, strange, and invisible things : but because they are not acquainted with any else but terrestrial creatures, which only be visible, they doubt whether there be any such invisible things as are reported of, or no : for which cause the Creator himself of all things both visible and invisible, and the only begotten Son of the eternal Father, came into this world, for the redemption of mankind : and sent the holy Ghost unto our hearts, that quickened by him and his grace, we should believe those things which as yet by sense or experience we cannot possibly understand : and therefore so many of us as have received this spirit, the heavenly pledge of our inheritance, make no doubt of God's invisible and immortal creatures : and whosoever as yet is not settled in this belief, out of all question, he ought of reason to give credit to the words of them that be more learned and holy, and believe them that, through the grace of God's holy Spirit, have experience of those things that be invisible : for he were a very foolish child, that thought his mother lied, when she spake of light in other places, because himself, where he was, beheld nothing else but the darkness of the prison.

Peter. That you say doth wonderfully content me : yet he who believeth not that there be any invisible things, out of question in mine opinion is an infidel : and he that is an infidel, in that thing whereof he doubteth seeketh not for faith, but for reason.

Chapter Two: that an infidel liveth not without faith. ¶ **Gregory.** I speak boldly yet truly, that an infidel liveth not without faith : for if I demand of him, who is his father or mother, straightways he will tell me, such a man and such a woman : and if I press him further, whether he doth remember the time when he was first conceived, or the hour when he was born into this world, he will answer me, that he never knew or saw any such thing : and yet for all this doth he believe that which he never beheld, seeing he believeth, without all doubt, that such a man was his father, and such a woman his mother.

Peter. I must needs confess, that I never knew before this time that an infidel had any faith.

Gregory. Infidels have faith, but not in God, for then they were not infidels : but worthily are they by the former reason to be blamed, and thereby also to be provoked to embrace true faith : for if concerning their visible body, they believe that which they never saw, why do they not also believe some things which with their corporal eyes they cannot behold ?

Chapter Three: that God created three kinds of spirits with life. ¶ For that our soul doth live after the death of the body, reason doth teach us, assisted and holpen with faith : for almighty God created three kinds of spirits having life. One altogether spiritual without body : another with a body, but yet which dieth not with the body : the third that which is both joined with the body, and also together with the body doth die. The spirits that have no bodies be the Angels : they that have bodies but die not with them, be the souls of men : those

179

that have bodies and die together with them, be the souls of cattle and brute beasts. Man, therefore, as he is created in the middle state, inferior to Angels and superior to beasts, so doth he participate of both : having immortality of soul with the Angels, and mortality of body with beasts, until the day of doom : for then the glory of the resurrection shall take away and consume the mortality of the body : for being then reunited to the soul, it shall be preserved for ever : as the soul joined to the body is preserved for God. Neither shall the bodies of the damned, lying in torments, ever perfectly perish : for though they always decay, yet for ever shall they continue : and as they sinned both with soul and body, so living always in body and soul, they shall always die without end.

Peter. All your discourse is consonant to that reason which Christian religion teacheth : but I beseech you, if there be so great difference betwixt the souls of men and beasts as you affirm, why doth Solomon speak in this manner ? *I have said in mine heart of the sons of men, that God would prove them, and shew them to be like unto beasts : therefore there is one death of men and beasts, and their state is both alike :* and prosecuting afterward more exactly that opinion of his, thus he writeth : *As a man dieth, so do beasts die: all things breathe alike, and man hath nothing more than beasts.* After which words, he addeth also this general conclusion : *All things are subject to vanity, and all things go to one place : of the earth they were made, and into the earth they return again.*[1]

Chapter Four : of Solomon's question, to wit : The death of men and beasts is all one. ¶ Gregory. Solomon's book, in which these sayings are found, is called *Ecclesiastes :* as much to say properly as *The Preacher.* And in a sermon the manner is to have an opinion set down, by means whereof the tumultuous

[1] Eccles. 3, 17-20.

sedition of common people may be appeased : and whereas divers have divers opinions, yet are they all, by the Preacher's arguments and reasons, brought to unity and agreement: and therefore this book is called *The Preacher:* because in it Solomon doth as it were take upon him the person and words of the unruly vulgar sort, and by way of inquisition speaketh those things, which haply ignorant men through temptation do verily think : and therefore so many questions as he doth by way of enquiry propound, so many divers persons doth he in a manner take upon himself : but the true Preacher doth, as it were with his hand, compound all their doubts and disagreements, and bring them all to concord and unity of opinion, when as in the end of his book he saith : *Let us all together hear an end of speaking : Fear God, keep his commandments, for this is every man.*[1] For if in that book he had not by his discourse taken upon him the person of divers, why did he admonish all to make an end of speaking, together with him, and to hear ?

He, therefore, that in the conclusion of the book saith: *Let us all together hear :* doth give evident testimony of himself, that he took many persons upon him, and that he spake not at all as of himself : and therefore some things there be in that book, which are moved by way of disputation, and other some which by reason give satisfaction : some things which he uttereth in the person of one that is tempted, and who as yet followeth the pleasures of the world : and some other things, in which he disputeth them according to the rule of reason, and to draw the mind from vain pleasure and delight : for as there he saith : *This, therefore, seemeth unto me good, that a man should eat and drink, and take joy of his labour*[2]: so afterward he addeth : *It is better to go unto the house of mourning, than to the house of feasting.*[3] For if it be good to eat and drink, it seemeth better to go unto the house of feasting

[1] Eccles. 12, 13.   [2] *Ibid.* 5, 18.   [3] *Ibid.* 7, 2.

181

The Dialogues of St. Gregory

than to the house of mourning : and therefore by this it is evident, that he uttered that former saying in the person of frail men, and pronounced this latter according to the rule of reason : and therefore doth he straightways set down the grounds of his reason, and sheweth what commodity is gotten by going to the house of mourning, saying thus : *For in that we are put in mind of the end of all men, and the living man thinketh what he shall be.*[1] Again there we find it written : *O young man, rejoice in thy youth :*[2] and yet a little after is added : *for youth and pleasure be vain things.*

Seeing, therefore, he doth afterward reprove that for vain, which before he seemed to allow : plainly doth he declare that he spake those words as it were of carnal concupiscence, and the other of a right and true judgment. Therefore as he doth, in the first place, express the delight of carnal things, and pronounceth it to be good to cast away all care, and to eat and drink : so afterward, with reason and judgment doth he reprove that, when he saith that it is better to go unto the house of mourning, than to the house of feasting : and though he saith that a young man ought to rejoice in his youth, yet doth he utter that as proceeding from the resolution of a carnal mind ; seeing afterward, by definitive sentence, he reproveth both youth and pleasure, as vain things. Even so and in like manner, doth our Preacher set down the opinion of man's suspicion, as it were in the person of those that be weak, and subject to temptation, when he saith : *The death of man and beasts is one, and their condition both alike : as man dieth, so they also die : all things do breathe alike, and a man hath not any more than beasts :* who, notwithstanding, afterward putteth down his own opinion, proceeding from judgment and reason, in these words : *What hath a wise man more than a fool, and what a poor man, but that he may go thither where life is ?*[3] He there-

[1] Eccles. 7, 2.   [2] Ibid. 11, 9.   [3] Ibid. 6, 8.

182

fore that said : *A man hath no more than beasts* : said also with mature deliberation, that a wise man hath not only more than a beast, but also more than a foolish man, to wit, that he goeth to that place where life is : in which words he doth also teach us, that man's life is not in this world, seeing he affirmeth it to be elsewhere : wherefore man hath this more than beasts, because they after death do not live : but he doth then begin truly to live, when by mortal death he maketh an end of this transitory life and therefore long after he saith : *Whatsoever thy hand can do, instantly work : because with them in hell whither thou goest, there shall be neither work, nor reason, nor knowledge, nor wisdom :*[1] how then is the death of man and beasts all one, and how is their condition and state alike ? or how hath not a man more than beasts, when as they after death live not, and the souls of men, after the death of their bodies, be for their wicked deeds carried to hell, and do not die when they depart this life ? But in both these sayings, which seem contrary each to other, it is made manifest that the Preacher speaketh the truth : uttering the one of carnal temptation, and yet afterward, upon deliberation and according to truth, resolutely setteth down and defineth the contrary.

Peter. Glad I am, that ignorant I was of that question which I demanded : seeing I have, by means thereof, come to so exact an understanding of that which before I knew not. But I beseech you to take it patiently, if I also, like to this our Preacher, take upon me the person of weak and frail men : that I may the better, as it were by their demanding of questions, be profitable to them in their weakness and infirmities.

Gregory. Why should I not bear with you, condescending to the infirmities of your neighbours ? when as Paul saith : *To all men I became all things, that I might save all :*[2] and surely you are the more to be reverenced, for

[1] Eccles. 9, 10.   [2] 1 Cor. 9, 22.

condescending to their weakness upon charity, and therein do you imitate the steps of an excellent preacher.

Chapter Five: of a question concerning the soul, which goeth invisibly out of the body: to wit, whether there be any such thing, seeing it can not be seen. ¶ Peter.

It chanced so, that I was present when one departed this life. Who suddenly, as he was a speaking, gave up the ghost ; and whom before I heard talking with me, in an instant I saw dead : but whether his soul went out of the body or no, that I did not see : and it seemeth very hard to believe that thing, which no man can behold.

Gregory. What marvel is it, Peter, that you saw not the soul departing out of the body, seeing you behold it not when it remaineth in the body? What? do you believe me to have no soul, because, whiles you now talk with me, you can not see it? The nature of the soul is invisible, and therefore invisibly doth it depart out of the body, as it doth invisibly remain in the body.

Peter. That the soul hath life, so long as it remaineth in the body, easily do I perceive by the motion thereof : for if the body were destitute of the soul, the members could not possibly move at all : but that the soul liveth when it is out of the body, by what motions or actions I should gather, desirous I am to be informed by you : to the end that by such things as I do see, I may know that thing which I can not see.

Gregory. Though not with any great subtlety of discourse, yet confidently do I affirm it to be most true, that as the power of the soul doth quicken and move the body, so the power of God doth fill all things which he hath created ; and to some things doth he give life by breathing it into them ; to other things he vouchsafeth life in another manner : and upon some other things he bestoweth only a being, without any life at all. Seeing, therefore, you doubt not but that God is the creator and preserver of all things, that he doth fill and embrace all things, that he doth excel all things, and also maintaineth them, that he is incircumscriptible and invisible : so neither ought you to doubt, but that he is served with invisible creatures, seeing they that serve ought to be somewhat like unto him upon whom they attend, and so, consequently, that we ought not to doubt, but for as much as he is invisible in himself, that they also be of the same nature : and what creatures can these be else but his holy Angels, and the souls of just men ? Wherefore, as you know, when you see the body move, that the soul remaineth in the body, and you gather this from the body which is lowest : so ought you to think of the life of the soul that departeth from the body, deducing a reason from God who is the highest : to wit, that the soul liveth invisibly, seeing it is to remain in the service of the invisible Creator.

Peter. All this is very well said : yet our mind can hardly be brought to believe that, which with our corporal eyes we can not behold.

Gregory. Seeing St. Paul saith, that *faith is the substance of things to be hoped for, the argument of things not appearing :* [1] truly are we said to believe that which can not be seen, and by no means to believe that which with our eyes we do behold : yet in few words to bring you home again to yourself, I say, that no visible things be seen but by the means of invisible : for although your bodily eye beholdeth all sensible creatures, yet could it not behold any such thing, did it not receive force from that which is invisible : for take away the soul, which none doth see, and in vain be the eyes opened to look upon anything. Take away the soul from the body, and the eyes, out of all question, may remain still open as before. If, then, our eyes did see of themselves, how cometh it to pass, that now the soul is gone, they see nothing at all ? Learn

[1] Hebr. 11, 1.

then by this, that visible things themselves are not seen, but by means of them that be invisible. Let us also imagine that we saw before us the building of houses, huge timber and stones to be lifted up, great pillars to hang upon engines : what, I pray you, effecteth all this ? the visible body that with hands draweth and moveth those huge and massy things, or the invisible soul that giveth life to the body ? for take away that which is not seen in the body, and straightways all those things, which before did move, will remain without any motion at all. By which we may easily gather, that nothing can be disposed of in this visible world, but by another creature which is invisible : for as almighty God either by inspiration, or by replenishing those creatures which have reason, doth both quicken and move those things which be invisible, so, in like manner, those things which be invisible do give motion and sense to carnal bodies which are visible.

Peter. Willingly overcome with these reasons alleged, I confess that I am enforced almost to think that these visible things are nothing : whereas before, taking upon me the person of weak and unlearned men, I doubted whether there were any invisible creatures or no ; wherefore your whole discourse doth very well please me : yet, as l am assured of the life of the soul by the motion of the body, so desirous I am to know by some sure and certain demonstrations, that the soul doth also live, after it is departed from the body.

Chapter Six: that as the life of the soul remaining in the body, is gathered by the motion of the members : so the life of the soul, after death in holy men, is to be found out by the virtue of miracles.

¶ **Gregory.** Herein most ready I am to satisfy your request ; and for proof of this point, no difficulty do I find : for think you that the holy Apostles and martyrs of Christ would have contemned this present life, and

Giotto   Alinari

FAITH
(Madonna dell' Arena, Padua)

offered their bodies to death, had they not known that their souls did most assuredly live for ever? You confess that you know the life of the soul remaining in the body by the motion thereof: behold, then, how these that lost their lives for Christ, and believed that souls lived after death, be renowned for their daily miracles. For sick persons come unto their dead bodies, and be cured: perjured persons repair thither, and be possessed with devils: possessed with devils visit them, and are delivered: lepers come, and be cleansed: dead folk are brought, and they be raised up again. Consider then in what sort their souls do live in those places where they live, whose dead bodies live also in this world by so many miracles. If then you gather the life of the soul remaining in the body by the motion of the members: why do you not likewise, by the dead bones which work miracles, infer that the soul doth live after the death of the body?

Peter. No solution, as I think, can overthrow the force of this reason alleged: by which we are constrained through visible things to believe those which we see not and be invisible.

Chapter Seven: of the departure of men's souls.

¶ Gregory. A little before, you complained for that you could not see the soul of one when it departed out of his body: but that was your fault, who desired with corporal eyes to behold an invisible thing, for many of us, that by sincere faith and plentiful prayer, have had the eye of our soul purified, have often seen souls going out of their bodies: and therefore now I think it necessary to set down both how, and in what sort, men's souls departing out of their bodies have been seen: and also what wonderful things have been revealed unto them, at the time of their departure: that by this means examples may satisfy our wavering and doubtful minds, which reason can not so fully persuade. Wherefore to begin. I remember that, in the second book of this work,

I told you how venerable Bennet (as by relation of his own monks I learned) being far distant from the city of Capua, beheld the soul of Germanus (Bishop of the same place) at midnight to be carried to heaven in a fiery globe : who, seeing the soul as it was ascending up, beheld also, in the largeness of his own soul, within the compass of one sunbeam, the whole world as it were gathered together.

Chapter Eight: of the departure of the soul of Speciosus, a Monk.

¶ By the relation also of the same monks, his disciples, I understood how two noble men that were brethren, and very well learned in humanity, the one called Speciosus, the other Gregory, entered into religion, there to live virtuously under the direction of his rule : whom the venerable father placed in a Monastery of his, hard by the city of Teracina. These men, whiles they remained in the world, were very rich, but for the redemption of their own souls, they had given all to the poor, and led their life in the same Monastery. One of these twain, to wit Speciosus, being sent upon business of the Monastery to the city of Capua : his natural brother Gregory in the meantime, sitting at table at dinner amongst the other monks, rapt in spirit, beheld his brother's soul, though so far distant, departing out of his body : which forthwith he told unto the other monks, and straight after in all haste took his journey to Capua, where he found his brother newly buried ; and there understood how he died at that very hour, in which he saw his soul going out of his body.

Chapter Nine: of the soul of a certain Anchoret.

¶ A certain religious man, and one of great credit (at such time as I lived in the Monastery), told me that certain sailing from Sicily to Rome, as they were in the midst of the sea, beheld the soul of a certain servant of God carried to heaven, who had been an Anchoret in the land of Samnium. Landing afterward in the same place, and making enquiry of that thing, they understood that holy man to have departed this life upon that very day in which they saw his soul ascending to heaven.

Chapter Ten: of the Departure of Abbot Hope's soul. ¶ Whiles I lived as yet in my Monastery, I understood, by the relation of a very reverent man, a certain thing which I will now tell you. A venerable father there was, called Hope, who had built an Abbey in a place called Cample, distant almost six miles from the old city of Nursia. This man almighty and merciful God, by temporal affliction, preserved from everlasting misery, and gave him great grace and quiet of mind : for how dearly he loved him, yea, at that very time when he sent him affliction, was afterward made apparent to the world, when he vouchsafed perfectly to restore him to his former health. This man therefore was, for the space of forty years, punished with such a continual blindness of his eyes, that he could not so much as behold any light at all. But because none in adversity can without the help of God's grace stand and unless the same merciful father, who sendeth punishment, giveth also patience : straightways his chastising of our sins doth by impatience more increase them : and so it pitifully falleth out, that our sin is by that very thing made greater, by which an end of all sin might very well have been expected. God therefore seeing our infirmity, together with affliction, by his sweet providence keepeth and preserveth us ; and is in his correction which he sendeth his chosen children in this world, so just with mercy, that they may become such to whom afterward he may justly shew mercy : and therefore, though he did lay his cross of blindness upon this venerable man, yet did he not leave him destitute of inward light : for as his body was wearied with pain, so, by the providence of God's holy Spirit, his soul was refreshed with heavenly comfort.

At length when he had continued forty years in this kind of blindness, our good Lord restored him to his former sight, giving him also to understand that he was shortly to leave this world : and therefore admonished him to preach the word of life unto all such Abbeys as were about him ; and that for as much as himself had received the light of his body, he would go and open unto them the spiritual light of the soul : who forthwith obeying God's commandment, visited the foresaid Abbeys, and preached unto them such precepts of good life as himself before had in conversation practised. Returning after fifteen days to his own Abbey, he called his monks together, and in their presence received the Sacrament of the body and blood of our Lord, and straightways began, together with them, the mystical hymns of the Psalms : afterward, falling with attention to his prayers, whiles they continued on their singing, he gave up the ghost : at which very time all the monks saw a dove coming out of his mouth, which in their sight flying forth through the top of the oratory being then opened, ascended up into heaven. And surely it is to be thought, that his soul, by divine providence, did in that manner appear in the likeness of a dove, that almighty God might thereby shew with what a true and simple heart that holy man had always served him.

Chapter Eleven : of the departure of a Priest's soul, called Ursinus.

¶ Neither must I forget that which the reverent Abbot Stephen (who not long since died in this city, and whom you knew very well) told me to have happened in the same province of Nursia. For he said that a Priest dwelt in that country, who in the fear of God governed the church committed to his charge : and although, after he had taken orders, he did still love his old wife as his sister, yet did he avoid her as his enemy : and never would he permit her to come near him upon any occasion, abstaining wholly from all intercourse of familiarity. For this is a thing proper to holy men, oftentimes to deprive themselves of those things which be lawful, to the end they may remain the more free from such as be unlawful : and therefore this man, not to fall into any sin, utterly refused all necessary and requisite service at her hands.

When this reverent man had long lived in this world, the fortieth year after he was made priest, by a great and vehement ague [he] was brought to the last cast : his old wife, beholding him so far spent, and to lie as though he had been dead, put her head near unto him, to see whether he did breathe or no: which he perceiving, having yet a little life left, enforced himself to speak as well as he could, and in great fervour of spirit brake out into these words : " Get thee away, woman : a little fire is yet left, away with the straw." After she was gone, his strength somewhat increasing, he began with great joy to cry out : " Welcome, my Lords, welcome, my Lords · why have you vouchsafed to visit me, your unworthy servant ? I come, I come : I thank you, I thank you " and when he did often repeat these and the like words, his friends that were present asked him to whom he spake, to whom with a kind of admiration he answered : " What ? do you not here behold the holy Apostles ? Do you not see the chief of them, St. Peter and St. Paul ?" And so, turning himself again towards them, he said : " Behold I come, behold I come " : and in speaking those words, he gave up his happy ghost. And that he did indeed verily behold the holy Apostles, he testified by that his departure with them. And thus it doth often fall out, by the sweet providence of God, that good men at their death do behold his Saints going before them, and leading as it were the way, to the end they should not be afraid at the pangs thereof; and that whiles their souls do see the Saints in heaven, they may be discharged from the prison of this body, without all fear and grief.

Chapter Twelve : of the soul of Probus, Bishop of the City of Reati. ¶ Concerning which thing I must also tell you that which the servant of God, Probus (who now in this city liveth in an Abbey), gave me to understand of an uncle of his, called also Probus, who was Bishop of the city of Reati. For he said that, being grievously sick and in great extremity of death, his father, whose name was Maximus, caused many physicians to be sent for, to see whether by their skill he could any ways be holpen ; who all upon the feeling of his pulse, gave sentence of speedy death. When dinner time was come, and the day somewhat far spent, the venerable Bishop, more careful of their health than of his own, desired them that they would go up with his old father into the higher part of his palace ; and after their great pains, to refresh themselves with a poor dinner. Whereupon all went up, and none remained with him, but a little young boy, who, as Probus saith, is yet living. The little boy, standing by his bedside, suddenly saw certain men coming in to the man of God, apparelled in white stoles, whose faces were far more beautiful and bright than the whiteness of their garments : whereat being amazed and afraid, he began to cry out, and ask who they were : at which noise the Bishop also looking up, beheld them coming in and knew them, and thereupon comforted the little boy, bidding him not to cry, or be afraid, saying that they were the holy martyrs St. Juvenal and St. Eleutherius that came to visit him : but he, not acquainted with any such strange visions, ran out at the doors as fast as he could, carrying news hereof both to his father and the physicians ; who, going down in all haste, found the Bishop departed : for those Saints, whose sight the child could not endure, had carried his soul away in their company.

Chapter Thirteen : of the death of a Nun called Galla. ¶ Neither will I conceal that which I received by the relation of those that are grave and of good credit. In the time of the Goths, an honourable young maid called Galla, daughter to Symmachus the Consul, was bestowed in marriage : whose husband, before the year came about, departed this life : and though both plenty of wealth and her young years were great allurements to a second marriage, yet she made choice rather to be married spiritually to God, in which after mourning everlasting joy doth follow : than to become again subject to carnal matrimony, which always beginneth with joy, and in conclusion endeth with sorrow. But because she had a passing high colour, the physicians told her that, unless she did marry again, that she would through abundance of heat, contrary to nature, have a beard like unto men : which afterward fell so out indeed : but the holy woman little regarded outward deformity, which inwardly in her soul was enamoured with the beauty of the heavenly spouse ; and feared not if that in her became foul, which she knew that her celestial spouse did nothing love. Wherefore straight upon the death of her husband, casting off her secular habit and attire, she rendered herself for the service of God to that Nunnery which is by the church of the blessed Apostle St. Peter ; where she lived for the space of many years in prayer and simplicity of heart, and bestowed alms plentifully upon needy and poor people.

At length, when almighty God determined to bestow upon her an everlasting reward, he sent her a cancer in one of her breasts. Two candles she had usually in the night time burning before her bed ; for loving light, she did not only hate spiritual darkness, but also corporal. One night, lying sore afflicted with this her infirmity, she saw St. Peter standing before her bed, betwixt the two candlesticks, and being nothing afraid, but glad, love giving her courage, thus she spake unto him : "How is it, my Lord ? what ? are my sins forgiven me?" To whom (as he hath a most gracious countenance) he bowed down a little his head, and said: "Thy sins are forgiven thee; come and follow me." But because there was another Nun in the Monastery which Galla loved more than the rest, she straightways beseeched him that sister Benedicta might go with her: to whom he answered that she could not then come, but another should: "and as for her," quoth he, "whom you now request, thirty days hence shall she follow you": and when he had thus said, he vanished out of her sight. After whose departure, she straightways called for the mother of the Convent, and told her what she had seen and heard: and the third day following, both she and the other before mentioned departed this life: and she also, whose company Galla desired, the thirtieth day after did follow them. The memory of which thing continueth still fresh in that Monastery, so that the Nuns which now live there (receiving it by tradition from their predecessors) can tell every little point thereof, as though they had been present at that time when the miracle happened.

Chapter Fourteen: of the Departure of a poor man, sick of the palsy, called Servulus. ¶ Here also we have to know that oftentimes, at the death of God's servants, heavenly musick is heard, to the end that whiles they give willing ear to that melody, the soul may have no leisure to feel, when it departeth from the body. For I remember that, in my Homilies [1] upon the Gospel, I told how in that porch which is in the way to St. Clement's Church, there lay a certain man called Servulus, whom I doubt not but you also do remember: who, as he was poor in wealth, so rich in merits. This man had long been afflicted with sickness: for from the first time that I knew him, to the very last hour of his life, never can I remember but that he was sick of the palsy, and that

[1] Homelia 15.

so pitifully, that he could not stand, nor sit up in his bed : neither was he ever able to put his hand unto his mouth, or to turn from one side to the other. His mother and brethren did serve and attend him, and what he got in alms, that by their hands he bestowed upon other poor people. Read he could not, yet did he buy the holy scriptures, which very carefully he caused such religious men as he entertained to read unto him : by means whereof, according to his capacity, though, as I said, he knew not a letter of the book, yet did he fully learn the holy scripture. Very careful he was in his sickness always to give God thanks, and day and night to praise his holy name.

When the time was come, in which God determined to reward this his great patience : the pain of his body strook inwardly to his heart, which he feeling, and knowing as his last hour was not far off, called for all such strangers as lodged in his house, desiring them to sing hymns with him, for his last farewell and departure out of this life : and as he was himself singing with them, all on a sudden he cried out aloud, and bad them be silent, saying : "Do ye not hear the great and wonderful musick which is in heaven ?" and so whiles he lay giving of ear within himself to that divine harmony, his holy soul departed this mortal life : at which time, all that were there present felt a most pleasant and fragrant smell, whereby they perceived how true it was that Servulus said. A monk of mine, who yet liveth, was then present, and with many tears useth to tell us, that the sweetness of that smell never went away, but that they felt it continually until the time of his burial.

Chapter Fifteen : of the Departure of a Nun called Romula.

¶ In the same Homilies, I remember likewise, how I told a certain thing, which Speciosus, my fellow-Priest, doth also verify to be most true. At such time as I entered into religion, there dwelt in this city,

near to the church of our blessed Lady, a certain old
woman, called Redempta, living in the habit of a Nun,
a disciple of that Hirundina, which was famous for
virtue, and led an eremitical life (as they say) in the
mountains by the city of Preneste. This foresaid Redempta had two scholars, which wore the same habit
that she did: the one called Romula, and the name of the
other, which yet liveth, I can not tell, though by sight
I know her very well. These three together in one little
house lived a poor life, yet rich for piety and virtue :
and of these twain Romula far excelled the other in merit
of life : for she was a woman of marvellous patience,
passing obedient, a great observer of silence, and one
that with great zeal bestowed her time in continual
prayer.

But because it often falleth out, that they whom the
world think to be perfect, have yet in the eyes of almighty God some imperfection (as many times unskilful
men do commend seals of arms as excellently well en-
graven, which yet the cunning workman doth better consider, and laboureth to make more perfect), this foresaid
Romula fell into such a pitiful palsy, that she was fain to
keep her bed : where she lay, deprived almost of all the
use of her members : which great cross, notwithstanding,
drew her not to any impatience, but rather the sickness
of her body was the health of her soul, and the cause of
her greater increase in virtue : for the less she could do
in other things, the more she did in prayer and devotion.
Upon a certain night she called for Redempta (who, as
I said, brought them both up as her daughters), saying :
" Come, mother, come, mother " : who straightways with
her other disciple rose up, and (as myself and many more
have heard it from their own mouths) when they were
about midnight by her bedside, suddenly there came a
light from heaven, which filled all that cell : and such
a brightness there appeared, that it put them both into a

wonderful fear, and, as themselves did afterward report, all their body became cold, in such sort, that there they stood amazed : for they heard a noise, as it were of many that came in, and the cell door shaken and thrust open, as though there had been a great press of people : and as they said, they heard a great company come in, yet they saw nobody, and that by reason of great fear and much light : for both fear did make them to hold their eyes downward, and the brightness of such plenty of light did so dazzle them, that they could not behold anything.

Straight after that light followed a wonderful pleasant smell, which did greatly comfort their fearful hearts. Romula, perceiving that they could not endure that abundance of light, with sweet words comforted Redempta, that stood trembling by her bedside, saying : " Be not affeard, mother ; for I shall not die at this time " : and when she had often repeated those words, by little and little the light vanished away, but yet the sweet smell remained still, and so continued both the next and the third day after. Upon the fourth night, again she called for that her mother, and when she was come, she desired to receive the Sacrament, and so she did ; and behold, before Redempta or her other disciple departed from her bedside, suddenly they heard two quires singing before the door without : and as they said, they perceived by their voices that the one was of men, that began the psalms, and the other of women that answered: and whiles these heavenly funerals were in celebrating before the cell door, that holy soul departed this life, and was carried in that manner up into heaven : and the higher those two quires did ascend, the less did they hear that celestial musick, until at length they heard no more : and beside that sweet and odoriferous smell, which before they felt, vanished quite away.

Chapter Sixteen : of the departure of the holy virgin Tarsilla. ¶ Sometime also for the comfort of

the soul that departeth, there appeareth unto it the author himself of life, and rewarder of all virtue : for proof whereof I will here report that which I remember also to have spoken of in mine Homilies, concerning mine aunt Tarsilla : who, in the company of two others of her sisters, had for continuance in prayer, gravity of life, singularity in abstinence, arrived to the top of perfection. To this woman, Felix, my great-grandfather, sometime Bishop of this see of Rome, appeared in vision, and shewed her the habitation of everlasting light, speaking thus : "Come with me, and I will entertain you in this dwelling place of light" Shortly after, taken with an ague, she was brought to the last cast : and as when noble men and women lie a dying, many do visit them for the comfort of their friends : so divers both men and women, at the time of her departure, were come, which stood round about her bed : at what time she, suddenly casting her eyes upward, beheld our Saviour coming : whereupon, looking earnestly upon him, she cried out to them that were present : "Away, away : my Saviour Jesus is come" : and so, fixing her eyes upon him, whom she beheld, her holy soul departed this life : and such a wonderful fragrant smell ensued, that the sweetness thereof gave evident testimony that the author of all sweetness was there present. Afterward, when her dead body, according to the manner, was made ready to be washed, they found that, with long custom of prayer, the skin of her arms and knees was, like a camel's, become hard : and so her dead body gave sufficient testimony, what her living spirit had continually practised.

Chapter Seventeen : of the departure of a young maid called Musa. ¶ Neither must that be forgotten, which the servant of God before mentioned, called Probus, used to tell of a little sister which he had, called Musa : for he said that one night our blessed Lady

T. GREGORY APPEARN TO THE DYNG FINA

Domenico Ghirlandaio

appeared unto her in vision, shewing her sundry young maids of her own years, clothed all in white : whose company she much desiring, but yet not presuming to go amongst them, the Blessed Virgin asked her whether she had any mind to remain with them, and to live in her service : to whom she answered that willingly she would. Then our blessed Lady gave her in charge, not to behave herself lightly, nor to live any more like a girl, to abstain also from laughing and pastime, telling her that after thirty days she should, amongst those virgins which she then saw, be admitted to her service.

After this vision, the young maid forsook all her former behaviour : and with great gravity reformed the levity of her childish years : which thing her parents perceiving, and demanding from whence that change proceeded, she told them what the blessed Mother of God had given her in commandment, and upon what day she was to go unto her service. Five and twenty days after, she fell sick of an ague ; and upon the thirtieth day, when the hour of her departure was come, she beheld our blessed Lady, accompanied with those virgins which before in vision she saw to come unto her, and being called to come away, she answered with her eyes modestly cast downward, and very distinctly spake in this manner : "Behold, blessed Lady, I come, behold, blessed Lady, I come" : in speaking of which words she gave up the ghost, and her soul departed her virgin's body, to dwell for ever with the holy virgins in heaven.

Peter. Seeing mankind is subject to many and innumerable vices, I think that the greatest part of heaven is replenished with little children and infants.

Chapter Eighteen: how certain young children are hindered from heaven by their parents' wicked education: as is shewed by the example of a blasphemous young boy. ¶ Gregory. Although we ought not to doubt, but believe that all infants which be baptized, and die in their infancy, go to heaven ; yet no point of our belief it is, that all little ones which can speak do come unto that holy place : because some little children are kept from heaven by their parents, which bring them up wickedly and in lewd life. For a certain man in this city, well known to all, some three years since had a child, as I think five years old, which upon too much carnal affection he brought up very carelessly : in such sort that the little one (a lamentable case to speak of) so soon as anything went contrary to his mind, straightways used to blaspheme the name of God.

This child, in that great mortality which happened three years since, fell sick, and came to the point of death : and his father holding him at that time in his arms, the child (as they say, which were then present) beheld with trembling eyes certain wicked spirits coming towards him : at which sight he began to cry out in this manner : " Keep them away, father, keep them away " : and crying so out, he turned away his face, and would have hid himself in his father's bosom : who demanding why he was so afraid, and what he saw : " O father," quoth he, " there be blackamoors come to carry me away " : after which words straightways he blasphemed God, and so gave up the ghost. For to the end God might make it known to the world for what sin he was delivered to such terrible executioners, he permitted him at his very death to iterate that sin, for which his father, whiles he lived, would not correct him : so that he which through God's patience had long lived a blasphemer, did at length, by his just judgment, blaspheming end his life, that the father might both know his own sin, and also how, by neglecting the soul of his little son, he nourished and brought up not a little sinner for hell fire. But now to surcease from further speech of this sad and melancholy matter, let us prosecute, as we have begun, our former joyful narration.

The Departure of Stephen

Chapter Nineteen: of the departure of the man of God called Stephen. ¶ By the relation of the same Probus, and other religious men, I came to the knowledge of such things as in my Homilies I told to mine auditors, concerning the venerable father Stephen. For he was a man, as Probus and many more affirm, who had no wealth in this world, nor cared for any, loving only poverty for God's sake : in adversity always did he keep patience : secular men's company did he avoid : and his desire was always to pray and serve God : of whom I will here report one excellent virtuous act, that by one, many other which he likewise did, each man may ponder with himself. This man, therefore, having upon a time carried his corn, which he reaped with his own hands, into the barn, being the only substance upon which he and his disciples were to live all the year : a certain wicked wretch, pricked forward by the devil, set it all on fire : which another perceiving, ran in all haste and told it to the servant of God : and after he had done his message, he added these words, saying : "Alas and woe, father Stephen, what an ill chance hath befallen you." To whom straightways, with a pleasant countenance and quiet mind, he answered : "Nay, what an ill chance and misery is befallen him that hath done this : for to me what hath happened?" By which words of his it appeareth, to what great perfection he was arrived, that took so quietly the loss of all his worldly wealth, and was more sorry for the other's sin than grieved for his own loss ; and more thought what his neighbour had inwardly lost in his soul, than what himself had outwardly lost in his substance. When this man lay a dying, many came to visit him, and to commend their souls to his, that was now leaving this world : and standing about his bed, some of them beheld Angels coming in, but yet were not able to tell it unto others then present : others there were that saw nothing, but yet such a great fear fell

201

upon them all, that none could endure to remain in that place, when his soul departed the body : and therefore all of them, terrified and wholly possessed with fear, fled away : by which they perceived of what power he was, that received his soul going out of this world : seeing at that time no mortal creature could endure to be there present.

Chapter Twenty: how sometime the merit of the soul is not so truly declared at the time of the departure as afterward. ¶ But here we have to understand, that sometime the merit of the soul is not so truly known at the time of the departure, as it is afterward : and therefore divers holy martyrs have suffered many great torments at the hands of infidels : who afterwards, at their dead bones, were famous for signs and miracles, as before hath been noted.

Chapter Twenty-one : of the two Monks of Abbot Valentinus. ¶ For the virtuous man Valentinus, who afterward, as you know, was in this city Abbot of my Monastery, having had before in the province of Valeria the government of another Abbey : into which, as he told me, the cruel Lombards entered in, and hung up two of his monks upon a tree, who in that manner ended their life. When evening was come, both their souls began in that place to sing so plainly and distinctly, that they also who had killed them, hearing that kind of musick, became wonderfully afraid. All the prisoners likewise that were there present heard it, and afterward witnessed the same : which strange melody God's providence would have known, to the end that mortal men living yet upon earth might thereby learn how that, if they serve him truly in this world, that they shall after death verily live with him in the world to come.

Chapter Twenty-two : of the departure of Abbot Suranus. ¶ At such time as I yet lived in the Monastery, I understood by the relation of certain religious men, that in the time of the Lombards, in this very province called Sura and not far off, there was an holy Abbot called Suranus, who bestowed upon certain prisoners, which had escaped their hands, all such things as he had in his Monastery : and when he had given away in alms all his own apparel, and whatsoever he could find either in the monks' cells or in the yards, and nothing was left : suddenly the Lombards came thither, took him prisoner, and demanded where his gold was : and when he told them that he had nothing, they carried him to an hill hard by, where there was a mighty great wood in which a certain prisoner that ran away from them had hid himself in an hollow tree. There one of the Lombards, drawing out his sword, slew the foresaid venerable Abbot, whose body as it fell to the ground, suddenly all the hill together with the wood did shake, as though the earth by that trembling had said, that it could not bear the weight of his holiness and virtue.

Chapter Twenty-three : of the departure of a Deacon belonging to the church of the Marsori.
¶ Another Deacon also there was in the province of the Marsori, a man of holy life, whom the Lombards had taken, and one with his sword had cut off his head. But as his body fell to the ground, he that slew him was possessed by a devil, and so he fell down at the holy man's feet, shewing thereby that he was delivered to the enemy of God, because he had so cruelly slain the friend of God.

Peter. What is the reason, I beseech you, that almighty God suffereth them to be put to death : whom afterward he doth make known to the world, that they were holy men and his dear servants ?

Chapter Twenty-four : of the death of the man of God, that was sent to Bethel. ¶ Gregory. Seeing we find it written, that what death soever the just man

dieth, that his justice shall not be taken from him : what
hurt cometh to God's elect servants (walking no question the way to everlasting life), if for a little while
they have some pitiful end ? and perhaps it proceedeth
from some small sin of theirs, which by such kind of
death God's pleasure is that it should be purged. And
hereof it cometh that reprobates receive superiority and
power over others, who at their death be so much the
more punished, for that they used their cruel authority
against God's servants : as the foresaid wicked and
wretched man, whom God suffered not to triumph over
that venerable Deacon, though he permitted him to kill
his body : which thing to be true we learn also out of
holy scriptures. For that man of God which was sent
against Samaria, because contrary to God's commandment he did eat in his journey, was slain by a lion ; and
yet in the same place we read, that the lion stood by the
man's ass, and did not touch his dead body.[1] By which
we perceive that his sin of disobedience was by that his
death pardoned : because the same lion that feared not
to kill him, presumed not yet to touch his dead carcass :
for licence he had for the one, but no leave was granted
for the other, because he that was culpable in his life,
having his sin of disobedience now punished, was just
by his death ; and therefore the lion that before slew
the body of a sinner, preserved afterward the corpse of
a just man.

Peter. Your discourse pleaseth me very well: yet
willing I am to know whether, before the resurrection,
the souls of just men do enter into the kingdom of
heaven.

Chapter Twenty-five : whether the souls of just
men be received into heaven, before the general
resurrection of our bodies. ¶ Gregory. This thing,
speaking generally of all just men, can neither be

[1] 3 Kings 13, 24-28.

affirmed nor denied : for the souls of some just men, remaining as yet in certain mansions, be deferred from heaven ; by which stay of theirs, what else do we learn, but that they lacked somewhat of perfect justice ? And yet is it more clear than day that the souls of them that be perfect, do, straight after death, possess the joys of heaven : the truth whereof Christ himself assureth us, when he saith : *Wheresoever the body shall be, thither will the eagles be gathered together ;*[1] for where our Saviour is present in body, thither, without all question, do the souls of just men assemble themselves ; and St. Paul saith : *I desire to be dissolved and to be with Christ.*[2] He, therefore, that doubteth not Christ to be in heaven, how can he doubt that St. Paul's soul is in the same place ? which Apostle speaketh also of the dissolution of his body, and his dwelling in heaven in these words : *We know that if our terrestrial house of this habitation be dissolved, that we have a building of God ; an house not made with hands, but everlasting in heaven.*[3]

Peter. If just men's souls be already in heaven : what then shall they receive for a reward of their virtuous and just life at the day of judgment ?

Gregory. Whereas now their souls be only in heaven, at the day of judgment this further increase of joy shall they have, that their bodies also shall be partakers of eternal bliss, and they shall in their flesh receive joy : in which, for Christ's sake, they suffered grief and torments. In respect of this their double glory, the scripture saith : *In their land, they shall possess double things ;*[4] and it is written of the souls of the just, that, before the day of resurrection : *To every one of them white stoles were given : and it was said to them : that they should rest yet a little time, until the number of their fellow-servants and brethren were complete.*[5] They, therefore, that now receive but

[1] Luke, 17, 37. [2] Philipp. 1, 23. [3] 2 Cor. 5, 1.
[4] Isai. 61, 7. [5] Rev. 6, 11.

one stole, in the day of judgment shall every one have two : because now they rejoice only for the felicity of their souls, but then shall they enjoy the endless glory of body and soul together.

Peter. I grant it to be as you say : but what, I beseech you, is the reason that oftentimes those which lie a dying do prophesy and tell of many things to come ?

Chapter Twenty-six : By what means it falleth out, that those which lie a dying do prophesy of things to come : and of the death of a certain advocate : of that also which was revealed to the monks Gerontius and Mellitus : of the death of a boy called Armentarius, and of the diversity of tongues. ¶ Gregory. Sometime the soul itself, by reason of the spiritual nature which it hath, doth foresee some thing which will so fall out ; and sometime souls, before their departure, come to the knowledge of future things by revelation ; sometime also, when they are straightways to leave the body, by heavenly inspiration they penetrate with their spiritual eyes the secrets of heaven. For that the soul, by reason of the spiritual nature which it hath, doth know things to come, certain it is, by that which happened to a certain advocate in this city, who died two days ago of a pain in his side. For a little before his death, he called for his boy, to give him his apparel, that he might rise up and walk : who, supposing him not to know what he said, refused to do what he willed him. Whereupon he rose up, put on his clothes, and said that he would go to the church of St. Sixtus, which is in the way called Appia : and when not long after, his sickness increasing, he departed this life, determined it was, that his body should be buried in the church of St. Januarius the martyr, which standeth upon the way called Prenestina. But because they which had the care of his burial thought it too far off, suddenly they resolved upon a new course : and so, going forth with his corpse by the way called Appia, not knowing what he had said, they buried him in that church which before he had mentioned : and seeing it is well known that he was a man given to the world, and one that sought after earthly gain, how could he know that which fell out, but that the force and spiritual nature of his soul did foresee what should become of his body ?

That those also, which lie a dying, do oftentimes by divine revelation foretell what shall happen afterward, we may learn by such things as have fallen out amongst us in divers Abbeys. For ten years since, there was a monk in my Monastery, called Gerontius, who, lying sore sick, saw by vision in the night time, certain white men beautifully apparelled to descend from above into the Monastery, and standing by his bed-side, one of them said : "The cause of our coming hither is to choose out certain of Gregory's monks, to send them abroad unto the wars": and forthwith he commanded another to write in a bill the names of Marcellus, Valentinian, Agnellus, and divers others, whose names I have now forgotten : that being done, he said further : "Put down also the name of him that now beholdeth us." By which vision he being assured of that which would come to pass, the next morning he told the monks, who they were that should shortly die out of the Monastery, adding also that himself was to follow them. The next day the foresaid monks fell more dangerously sick, and so died all in that very order which they were named in the bill. Last of all, himself also departed this life, who had foretold the departure of the other monks before him.

Likewise in that mortality which, three years since, lamentably afflicted this town, there was in the Monastery of the city of Portua, a young monk called Mellitus, a man of wonderful simplicity and humility, whose last day being come, he fell desperately sick of the common disease: which when venerable Felix, Bishop of the same place, understood (by whose relation myself have learned this story), very careful he was to visit him, and with sweet words to comfort him against death: adding, notwithstanding, that by God's grace he might live long in this world. To whom the sick man answered that his time was at hand, saying that there came unto him a young man with letters, willing him to open and read them: which when he had done, he said that he found both his own name, and all the rest of them which, the Easter before, had been baptized by that Bishop, written in letters of gold: and first of all he said that he found his own name, and afterward the rest of them that were christened at that time: by which he made no doubt but that both himself and the rest should shortly depart this life, and so it fell out, for he died that very day: and after him followed all those which had before been baptized, so that, within the space of a few days, no one of them was left alive. Of whom no question can be made, but that the reason why the foresaid servant of God saw them written in gold, was because their names were written in heaven in the everlasting sight of God.

And as these men, by divine revelation, knew and foretold such things as were to come: so sometimes souls, before their departure, not in a dream but waking, may have some taste of heavenly mysteries. For you were well acquainted with Ammonius, a monk of my Monastery, who whiles he lived in a secular weed and was married to the daughter of Valerianus, a lawyer in this city, continually and with all diligence he followed his business: by reason whereof he knew whatsoever was done in his father-in-law's house. This man told me, how, in that great mortality which happened in this city, in the time of that noble man Narsus, there was a boy in the house of the foresaid Valerianus, called Armentarius, who was very simple and passing humble: when, therefore, that mortal disease entered that lawyer's house, the foresaid boy fell sick thereof, and was brought to the point of death: who suddenly falling into a trance, and afterward coming to himself again, caused his master to be sent for, to whom he told that he had been in heaven, and did know who they were that should die out of his house. "Such and such," quoth he, "shall die, but as for yourself, fear nothing, for at this time die you shall not. And that you may be assured that I have verily been in heaven, behold I have there received the gift to speak with all tongues: you know well enough that ignorant I am of the Greek tongue, and yet will I speak Greek, that you may see whether it be true that I say or no." Then his master spake Greek, and he so answered him in that tongue, that all which were present did much marvel. In the same house there was a Bulgar, servant to the foresaid Narsus, who in all haste, being brought to the sick person, spake unto him in the Bulgarian tongue; and the boy that was born and brought up in Italy, answered him so in that barbarous language, as though he had been born and bred in that country. All that heard him thus talking wondered much, and by experience of two tongues which they knew very well that before he knew not, they made no doubt of the rest, though they could make no trial thereof. After this he lived two days, and upon the third, by what secret judgment of God none can tell, he tare and rent with his teeth his own hands and arms, and so departed this life. When he was dead, all those whom before he mentioned did quickly follow after; and besides them, none in that house died at that time.

Peter. A very terrible thing it is, that he which merited so great a grace, should be punished with so pitiful a death.

Gregory. Who is able to enter into the secret judgments of God? Wherefore those things which in divine examination we cannot comprehend, we ought rather to fear than curiously to discuss.

Capter Twenty-seven: of the death of the Earl Theophanius.

And to prosecute what we have already begun, concerning the prophetical knowledge of those that die, I will now tell you that which, when I was in the city of Centumcellis, I understood by the relation of many, touching Theophanius, Earl of that place. For he was a man of great mercy and compassion, and one that did many good works, but especially he was given to good housekeeping and hospitality. True it is that, following the affairs of his earldom, he spent much time about earthly and worldly business, but that rather of necessity and duty than according to his own mind and desire, as his virtuous end afterward declared. For when the time of his death was come, there arose a great tempest, which was likely to hinder the funerals; whereat his wife, pitifully weeping, asked him in this manner: "What shall I do? or how shall we carry you to be buried, seeing the tempest is so terrible, that none can stir out of doors?" To whom he answered thus: "Weep not, good wife, for so soon as I am dead you shall have fair weather": and when he had so said, he gave up the ghost: and straightways the air became clear, and the tempest ceased. After this miracle one or two more followed. For whereas his hands and feet were with the gout before swollen and festered, and by reason of much corrupt matter, did savour and smell: yet when he was dead, and his body after the manner came to be washed, they found his hands and feet so sound and whole, as though they had never been troubled with any such sores at all. Four days after his burial, his wife was desirous to have the marble stone that lay upon him changed: which being done, such a fragrant and pleasant smell came from his body, as though, instead of worms, spices had sprung out of that corrupt carcass: of which strange thing when I did in my Homilies make public mention, and certain incredulous persons doubted thereof: upon a day, as I was sitting in the company of divers noble men, those very workmen, which had changed the tombstone, came unto me about business of their own: whom in the presence of the clergy, nobility, and common people, I examined, touching that miracle: and they all affirmed it to be most true, saying that they were in a strange manner replenished with that sweet smell: and they added also certain other things concerning his sepulchre, that made the miracle greater, which, not to be over long, I mean to pass over with silence.

Peter. I perceive now that my former question is sufficiently satisfied: yet another remaineth which troubleth my mind, and that is, seeing you affirmed before that holy men's souls which depart this life be now in heaven, it followeth consequently that the souls of the wicked be also in hell: and yet ignorant I am whether it be so or no, for man's imagination cannot conceive how the souls of sinners can be tormented before the day of judgment.

Chapter Twenty-eight: that, as we believe the souls of just and perfect men to be in heaven: so we ought also to believe that the souls of the wicked, after their departure from the body, be in hell. ¶ Gregory. If, by the testimony of holy scripture, you believe that the souls of holy and perfect men be in heaven: by the same reason ought you also to believe that the souls of the wicked be in hell: for as just men do rejoice and be glad at the retribution of eternal justice, so necessary it is that the wicked at the same justice should be grieved and tormented: for as heavenly felicity doth glad the elect, so we ought to believe that, from the day of their departure, fire doth afflict and burn the reprobate.

Peter. With what reason can we believe, that corporal fire can hold and torment an incorporal thing?

Chapter Twenty-nine: the reason why we ought to believe, that corporal fire can hold and torment the spirits that be without bodies. ¶ Gregory. If a spirit without a body can be holden and kept in the body of a living man: why, likewise, after death, may not an incorporal spirit be holden and kept in corporal fire?

Peter. The reason why an incorporal spirit in every living man is kept in the body, is, because it doth quicken and give life to the body.

Gregory. If an incorporal spirit, Peter, may be kept in that to which it giveth life: why also, for punishment, may it not be kept there, where it continually dieth? And we say that a spirit is holden by fire, to the end that, in the torment thereof, it may both by seeing and feeling be punished: for the soul by seeing of the fire is afflicted, and burned it is, in that it seeth itself to be burned: and so it falleth out, that a corporal thing may burn that which hath no body, whiles that an invisible burning and sorrow is drawn from visible fire, and the incorporal soul by means of corporal fire may be tormented with a spiritual and incorporal flame: although out of the Gospel we also learn that the soul is not only tormented by seeing the fire, but also by the feeling thereof: for the rich glutton, as our Saviour saith, was buried in hell. And he giveth us to understand that his soul was kept in fire, in that he telleth us how he did beseech Abraham, speaking to him in this manner: *Send Lazarus, that he may dip the top of his finger into the water and may refresh my tongue: because I am tormented in this flame.*[1] Seeing, then, truth itself assureth us that the sinful rich man was condemned into fire, what wise man can deny that the souls of the reprobate be detained in fire?

Peter. Both reason and testimony of scripture draweth my mind to believe what you say: but yet, when I think

[1] Luke 16, 24.

KING THEODORICUS THE OSTROGOTH

(Franciscan Church, Innsbruck)

not of them, it returneth again to his former opinion : for I neither see, nor can perceive, how a corporal thing can hold and torment that which is incorporal and without body.

Gregory. Tell me, I pray you, whether do you think that those Angels which fell from heaven have bodies or no ?

Peter. What man that hath his wits will say that they have any bodies ?

Gregory. And whether do you think that the fire of hell is corporal or spiritual ?

Peter. I make no doubt but that it is corporal, seeing most certain it is that bodies be burned therewith.

Gregory. And as certain it is that, at the day of judgment, our Saviour shall say to the reprobate : *Go into everlasting fire, which is prepared for the devil and his angels.*[1] If, then, the devil and his angels, though without bodies, shall be tormented with corporal fire, what marvel is it that the souls after their departure, and before they be united again to their bodies, may in like manner suffer corporal torments ?

Peter. The reason you give is very plain, and therefore now there is not any further doubt touching this question, that doth trouble my mind.

Chapter Thirty : of the death of King Theodoricus, who was an Arian heretic. ¶ Gregory. Seeing with such difficulty you are brought to believe, I think it worth my labour to let you understand such things concerning this very point, as I have received from them that be of good credit.   Julian, who died almost seven years since, and had a worshipful office in this church of Rome, in which now by God's providence I serve, used often to visit me (living as yet in my Monastery) and to talk with me of spiritual things for the good of both our souls.   This man, upon a day, told me this story.

[1] Matt. 25, 41.

213

" In the time of king Theodoricus," quoth he, "my wife's father, being then in Sicily, was to return into Italy. The ship in which he came arrived at the island of Liparis · where he understood that there dwelt a certain solitary man of great virtue, whom he thought good, whiles the mariners were occupied about mending of their ship and tackling, to visit, to talk with him, and to commend himself to his prayers : and so he did in the company of others. When they were come to the man of God, amongst other talk which they had, he asked them this question : 'Do you,' quoth he, 'hear that king Theodoricus is dead ?' to whom they quickly answered : 'God forbid : we left him alive at our departure from Rome ; and before this present we never heard of any such thing.' Then the servant of God told them that certainly he was dead : ' for yesterday,' quoth he, ' at nine of the clock, he was without shoes and girdle, and his hands fast bound, brought betwixt John the Pope and Symmachus the Senator, and thrown into Vulcan's gulph, which is not far from this place.' When they heard this news, carefully they wrote down the time, and at their return into Italy, they understood that king Theodoricus died upon that very day, in which his unhappy passage out of this world and punishment was revealed to the servant of God." And for as much as he had, by miserable imprisonment, been the death of Pope John, and also killed Symmachus, justly did he appear to be thrown of them into fire, whom before in this life he had unjustly condemned.

Chapter Thirty-one : of the Death of Reparatus.

¶ At the same time, when I first desired to lead a solitary life, a certain old man called Deusdedit, passing well beloved of the whole city, and one also that was my friend and familiar acquaintance, told me that, in the time of the Goths, a certain worshipful man, called Reparatus, came to die ; who lying a long while with his countenance changed, and his body stiff, many thought in very deed that he had been dead : and when divers of his friends and family wept for his departure, all on a sudden he came to himself, to the great admiration of his mourning household. Being returned thus to life, he bad them in all haste to send a boy to the church of St. Lawrence in Damaso (so called of him that built it) and quickly to bring word what was become of Tiburtius the Priest. This Tiburtius, as the speech went, was much given to a dissolute and wanton life ; and Florentius, who at that time was a Priest in the same church, remembereth full well his conversation and manner of life. When the messenger was gone, Reparatus, that was returned to life, told them that in the place where he was, he saw a great wood-pile made ready, and Tiburtius brought forth and laid upon it, and there to have been burnt with fire. "Then another fire," quoth he, "was prepared, which was so high that it reached from earth to heaven": but although they demanded for whom it was, yet did he not tell them : for when he had spoken these words straightways he died : and the boy, which was sent to see what was become of Tiburtius, returned with news, that he found him, a little before his coming, departed this life. By which we may learn that, seeing this Reparatus was carried to the places of torments to see them, returned afterward to life to tell what he had there beheld, and straight after left this world : that he saw not all these things for himself, but for us that yet live, and have time granted to amend our wicked lives. And the reason why Reparatus saw that great wood-pile burning, was not that we should think that the fire of hell is nourished with any wood : but because he was to make relation of these things to them that remained still in this world, he saw that fire prepared for the wicked, to be made of the same matter of which our fire is, to the end that, by those things which we know and be acquainted with, we should learn to be afraid of those, which yet we have not seen nor have any experience.

Chapter Thirty-two: of the death of a Courtier: whose grave burned with fire.

¶ Maximianus, Bishop of Syracusis, a man of holy life, who for a long time in this city had the government of my Monastery, often told me a terrible story, which fell out in the province of Valeria. A certain courtier, upon Easter even, was godfather to a young maid, who, after the fast was ended, returned home to his house : where drinking more wine than enough, he desired that his god-daughter might tarry with him : whom that night, which is horrible to speak of, he did utterly undo. In the morning, up he rose, and with guilty conscience thought good to go unto the bath, as though the water of that place could have washed away the filthiness of his sin, yet he went and washed himself. Then he began to doubt, whether it were best to go unto the church or no ; fearing, on the one side, what men would say, if he went not upon that so great a festival day ; and on the other, if he did go, he trembled to think of God's judgment. In conclusion, shame of the world overcame him, and therefore to the church he went : where yet he remained with great fear and horror, looking every instant that he should have been delivered to the devil, and tormented before all the people. At that solemn mass, though he did wonderfully shake for fear, yet he scaped free from all punishment : and so he departed very joyfully from church : and the next day after, came thither without any fear at all : and so merrily and securely he continued for six days together, thinking with himself that either God saw not that his abominable sin, or else that mercifully he had pardoned the same. Upon the seventh day, by sudden death he was taken out of this world. And being buried, for a long time after, in the sight of the whole town, a flame of fire came out of his grave, which burnt his bones so long, until it consumed the very grave itself, in such sort that the earth which was raised up with a little bank, appeared lower than the rest of the ground. By which fact almighty God declared what his soul suffered in the other world, whose dead body flaming fire consumed in this. To us also he hath left a fearful example, that we may thereby learn what the living and sensible soul suffereth for sin committed, when as the sensible bones by such a punishment of fire were burnt to nothing.

Peter. Desirous I am to know whether in heaven the good know the good, and the wicked in hell know one another.

Chapter Thirty-three: that in heaven the good know the good: and in hell the wicked have knowledge of the wicked. ¶ Gregory. The truth of this question we find most clearly resolved in those words of our Saviour before alleged: in which, when it is said that: *There was a certain rich man, and he was clad with purple and silk, and he fared every day magnifically: and there was a certain beggar called Lazarus, that lay at his gate full of sores, desiring to be filled of the crumbs that fell from the rich man's table, and none did give him, but the dogs also came and licked his sores;* straightways it is there also said, that: *Lazarus died, and was carried of the Angels into Abraham's bosom: and the rich man also died, and was buried in hell: who, lifting up his eyes, being in torments, saw Abraham afar off, and Lazarus in his bosom, and he cried saying: Father Abraham, have mercy on me, and send Lazarus that he may dip the tip of his finger into water for to cool my tongue, because I am tormented in this flame.* To whom Abraham answered: *Son, remember that thou diddest receive good things in thy lifetime, and Lazarus likewise evil.*[1] By which words, the rich man, having no hope of salva-

[1] Luke 16, 19-25.

tion for himself, beginneth to make suit for his friends, saying : *Father, I beseech thee, that thou wouldest send him unto my father's house, for I have five brethren, for to testify unto them, lest they also come into this place of torments.* In which words we see plainly, that the good do know the good, and the bad have knowledge of the bad. For if Abraham had not known Lazarus, never would he have spoken to the rich man being in torments, and made mention of his affliction and misery past, saying : *that he had received evil things in his life.* And if the bad did not know the bad, never would the rich man in torments have remembered his brethren that were absent : for shall we think that he knew not them that were present with him, who was so careful to pray for them that were absent ?

By which we learn also the answer to another question, which you demanded not : and that is, that the good do know the bad, and the bad the good. For Abraham knew the rich man, to whom he said : *Thou hast received good things in thy life* : and Lazarus, God's elect servant, was also known to the rich reprobate, whom by name he desired that he might be sent unto him, saying : *Send Lazarus that he may dip the tip of his finger into water, and cool my tongue :* by which mutual knowledge on both sides, the reward likewise to both parts increaseth, for the good do more rejoice, when they behold them also in felicity whom before they loved : and the wicked seeing them, whom in this world not respecting God they did love, to be now punished in their company, tormented they are, not only with their own pains, but also with the pains of their friends. Beside all this, a more wonderful grace is bestowed upon the Saints in heaven : for they know not only them with whom they were acquainted in this world, but also those whom before they never saw, and converse with them in such familiar sort as though in times past they had seen and known one another:

and therefore when they shall see the ancient fathers in that place of perpetual bliss, they shall then know them by sight, whom always they knew in their lives and conversation. For seeing they do in that place with unspeakable brightness (common to all) behold God, what is there that they know not, that know him who knoweth all things?

Chapter Thirty-four: of a certain religious man, that at his death saw the Prophets.

¶ For a certain religious man of my Monastery, that lived a virtuous life, dying some four years since, saw at the very time of his departure (as other religious men do report, that were present) the Prophet Jonas, Ezechiel, and Daniel, and by their names called them his Lords, saying that they were come unto him: and as he was bowing his head downward to them for reverence, he gave up the ghost: whereby we perceive what perfect knowledge shall be in that immortal life, when as this man, being yet in corruptible flesh, knew the Prophets whom he never saw.

Chapter Thirty-five: how sometime souls ready to depart this world, that know not one another, know yet what torments for their sins, or like rewards for their good deeds, they shall receive. And of the death of John, Ursus, Eumorphius, and Stephen.

¶ And sometime it falleth out that the soul, before it departeth, knoweth them with whom, by reason of equality of sins or rewards, it shall in the next world remain in one place. For old Eleutherius, a man of holy life, of whom in the former book I spake much, saith that he had a natural brother of his, called John, who lived together with him in his Monastery, who, fourteen days beforehand, told the monks when he was to die: and three days before he departed this life, he fell into an ague, and when his time was come, he received the mystery of our Lord's body and blood : and calling for the monks about him, he willed them to sing in his presence, prescribing them a certain anthem concerning himself, saying : *Open unto me the gates of justice, and being gone into them, I will confess unto our Lord : this is the gate of our Lord, just men shall enter in by it ;*[1] and whiles the monks about him were singing this anthem, suddenly with a loud and long voice he cried out, saying : " Come away, Ursus " : straight after which words his soul departed this mortal life. The monks marvelled, because they knew not the meaning of that, which at his death he so cried for : and therefore after his departure, all the Monastery was in sorrow and affliction. Four days after, necessary business they had, to send some of their brethren to another Monastery far distant : to which place when they came, they found all the monks in great heaviness, and demanding the reason, they told them that they did lament the desolation of their house : " for four days since," quoth they, " one of our monks died, whose life kept us all in this place " : and when they inquired his name, they understood that it was Ursus : asking also at what hour he left this world, they found that it was at that very instant, when he was called by John who died with them. Out of which we may learn that the merits of either were alike ; and that in the next world they live familiarly together in one mansion, who at one time like fellows departed this life.

Here also will I tell you what I heard from the mouths of my neighbours, at such time as I was yet a layman, and dwelled in my father's house, which descended to me by inheritance. A certain widow there was not far from me, called Galla, which had a young man to her son, whose name was Eumorphius : not far from whom dwelt one Stephen called also Optio. This Eumorphius, lying sick at the point of death, called for

[1] Psalm 118, 19-20.

CORONATION OF THE BLESSED VIRGIN

(Uffizi, Florence)

Lorenzo Monaco

his man, commanding him in all haste to go unto Stephen Optio, and to desire him without all delay to come unto him, because there was a ship ready, to carry them both into Sicily. But because his man refused to go, supposing that through extremity of sickness he knew not what he spake, his master very earnestly urged him forward, saying : " Go thy way, and tell him what I say, for I am not mad, as thou thinkest." Hereupon away he went towards Stephen, but as he was in the midst of his journey, he met one that asked him whither he was going, and when he told him, that he was by his master sent to Stephen Optio : " You lose your labour," quoth the other, "for I come now from thence : and he died this very hour." Back again upon this news he returned to his master, Eumorphius : but before he could get home, he found him dead. And so, by con-conferring their meeting together, and the length of the way, apparent it was that both of them, at one and the self same instant, departed this mortal life.

Peter. Very terrible it is that you say : but what, I pray you, is the reason, that he saw a ship at his departure ? Or why did he say that he was to go into Sicily ?

Gregory. The soul needeth not anything to carry it : yet no wonder it is, if that appeared to the soul being yet in the body, which by means of the body it had oftentimes before seen : to the end that we should thereby understand whither his soul might spiritually be carried. And in that he said he was to go into Sicily, what else can be meant thereby, but that there be in the islands of that country more than in any place else, certain gaping gulphs of torments, casting out fire continually ? and as they say that know them, daily do they wax greater, and enlarge themselves : so that the world drawing to an end, and so, consequently, more coming thither to be burnt in those flaming dungeons, so much the more do those places of torments open and become wider. Which strange thing almighty God, for the terror and amendment of the living, would have extant in this world, that infidels which believe not the unspeakable pains of hell, may with their eyes see the places of torments, which they list not to credit when it is told them. And that both the elect and reprobate, whose life and conversation hath been alike, shall after death be carried to like places, the saying of our Saviour doth teach us, though we had no examples to prove the same ; for of the elect himself saith in the Gospel : *In the house of my Father there be many mansions.*[1] For if there were not inequality of rewards in the everlasting felicity of heaven, then were there not many mansions, but rather one : wherefore there be many mansions, in which divers orders and degrees of God's saints be distinguished, who in common do all rejoice of the society and fellowship of their merits, and yet all they that laboured receive one penny, though they remain in distinct mansions : because the felicity and joy which there they possess is one, and the reward, which by divers and unequal good works they receive is not one but divers : which to be true our Saviour assureth us, when, talking of his coming to judgment, he saith : *Then I will say to the reapers : Gather up the cockle, and bind it into bundles to burn.*[2] For the Angels, which be the reapers, do then bind up in bundles the cockle to burn, when like with like are put together in torment : as the proud to burn in hell with the proud, carnal with the carnal, covetous with the covetous, deceitful with the deceitful, envious with the envious, and infidels with infidels : when therefore those that were like in sinful life, be condemned to like torments, then be they as it were cockle bound together in bundles to be burnt.

Peter. You have given a sufficient reason for satisfaction to my demand : yet I beseech you to inform me

[1] John 14, 2. [2] Matt. 13, 30.

further, what the cause is, that some be called out of this world, as it were through error: who afterward return again to life, saying that they heard how they were not the men which were sent for out of this life.

Chapter Thirty-six: of those souls which seem as it were through error to be taken out of their bodies: and of the death and reviving of a monk called Peter: of the death, likewise, and raising up again of one Stephen: and of the strange vision of a certain soldier. ¶ Gregory.

When this happeneth, Peter, it is not, if it be well considered, any error, but an admonition. For God of his great and bountiful mercy so disposeth, that some after their death do straightways return again to life, that having seen the torments of hell, which before when they heard they would not believe, they may now at least tremble at, after they have with their eyes beheld them. For a certain Sclavonion, who was a monk and lived with me here in this city in my Monastery, used to tell me that at such time as he dwelt in the wilderness, that he knew one Peter, a monk born in Spain, who lived with him in the vast desert called Evasa: which Peter (as he said) told him how, before he came to dwell in that place, by a certain sickness he died, and was straightways restored to life again, affirming that he had seen the torments and innumerable places of hell, and divers, who were mighty men in this world, hanging in those flames; and that as himself was carried to be thrown also into the same fire, suddenly an Angel in a beautiful attire appeared, who would not suffer him to be cast into those torments: but spake unto him in this manner: "Go thy way back again, and hereafter carefully look unto thyself, how thou leadest thy life" after which words his body by little and little became warm, and himself, waking out of the sleep of everlasting death, reported all such things as happened about him: after which time he bound himself to such fasting and watching, that though he had said nothing, yet his very life and conversation did speak what torments he had seen and was afraid of: and so God's merciful providence wrought in his temporal death that he died not everlastingly.

But because man's heart is passing obdurate and hard, hereof it cometh that though others have the like vision, and see the same pains, yet do they not always reap the like profit. For the honourable man Stephen, whom you knew very well, told me of himself, that at such time as he was upon business resident in the city of Constantinople, that he fell sick and died ; and when they sought for a surgeon to bowel him, and to embalm his body, and could not get any, he lay unburied all the night following: in which space his soul was carried to the dungeon of hell, where he saw many things, which before when he heard he little believed. But when he was brought before the judge that sat there, he would not admit him to his presence, saying: " I commanded not this man to be brought, but Stephen the smith " : upon which words he was straightway restored to life, and Stephen the smith, that dwelled hard by, at that very hour departed this life: whose death did show that the words which he heard were most true. But though the foresaid Stephen escaped death in this manner at that time, yet three years since, in that mortality which lamentably wasted this city (and in which, as you know, men with their corporal eyes did behold arrows that came from heaven, which did strike divers), the same man ended his days : at which time a certain soldier being also brought to the point of death, his soul was in such sort carried out of his body, that he lay void of all sense and feeling, but coming quickly again to himself, he told them that were present, what strange things he had seen. For he said (as many report that know it very well) that he saw a bridge, under which a black and smoky river did run, that had a filthy and intolerable smell: but upon the farther side thereof there were pleasant green meadows full of sweet flowers, in which also there were divers companies of men apparelled in white: and such a delicate savour there was, that the fragrant odour thereof did give wonderful content to all them that dwelt and walked in that place. Divers particular mansions also there were, all shining with brightness and light, and especially one magnifical and sumptuous house which was a building, the brick whereof seemed to be of gold, but whose it was, that he knew not.

There were also upon the bank of the foresaid river certain houses, but some of them the stinking vapour which rose from the river did touch, and some other it touched not at all. Now those that desired to pass over the foresaid bridge, were subject to this manner of trial: if any that was wicked attempted to go over, down he fell into that dark and stinking river; but those that were just and not hindered by sin, securely and easily passed over to those pleasant and delicate places. There he said also that he saw Peter, who was steward of the Pope's family, and died some four years since, thrust into a most filthy place, where he was bound and kept down with a great weight of iron: and inquiring why he was so used, he received that answer, which all we that knew his life can affirm to be most true: for it was told him that he suffered that pain, because when himself was upon any occasion to punish other, that he did it more upon cruelty than to shew his obedience; of which his merciless disposition none that knew him can be ignorant. There also he said that he saw a Priest whom he knew: who coming to the foresaid bridge, passed over with as great security, as he lived in this world sincerely.

Likewise, upon the same bridge he said that he did

see this Stephen, whom before we spake of, who being about to go over, his foot slipped, and half his body hanging beside the bridge, he was of certain terrible men, that rose out of the river, drawn by the legs downward: and by certain other white and beautiful persons, he was by the arms pulled upward: and whiles they strove thus, the wicked spirits to draw him downward, and the good to lift him upward, he that beheld all this strange sight returned to life, not knowing in conclusion what became of him. By which miraculous vision we learn this thing concerning the life of Stephen, to wit, that in him the sins of the flesh did strive with his works of alms. For in that he was by the legs drawn downward, and by the arms plucked upward, apparent it is, that both he loved to give alms, and yet did not perfectly resist the sins of the flesh, which did pull him downward: but in that secret examination of the supreme judge, which of them had the victory, that neither we know, nor he that saw it. Yet most certain it is, that the same Stephen, after that he had seen the places of hell, as before was said, and returned again to his body, did never perfectly amend his former wicked life, seeing many years after he departed this world, leaving us in doubt whether he were saved or damned. Whereby we may learn, that when any have the torments of hell shewn them, that to some it is for their commodity, and to others for their testimony: that the former may see those miseries to avoid them, and these other to be so much the more punished, in that they would not take heed of those torments, which they both knew and with their eyes beheld.

Peter. What, I beseech you, was meant by the building of that house in those places of delight, with bricks of gold? For it seemeth very ridiculous, that in the next life we should have need of any such kind of metal.

Deusdedit the Shoemaker

What is meant by the building of the house in those pleasant places. And of one Deusdedit, whose house was seen to be built upon the Saturday.

¶ **Gregory.** What man of sense can think so? but by that which was shewn there, whosoever he was, for whom that house was built, we learn plainly what virtuous works he did in this world: for he that by plenty of alms doth merit the reward of eternal light, certain it is, that he doth build his house with gold. For the same soldier who had this vision said also, which I forgot before to tell you, that old men, and young, girls, and boys, did carry those bricks of gold for the building of that house: by which we learn that those to whom we shew compassion in this world, do labour for us in the next. There dwelt also hard by us a religious man, called Deusdedit, who was a shoemaker, concerning whom another saw by revelation that he had in the next world an house a building; but the workmen thereof laboured only upon the Saturday. Who afterward enquiring more diligently how he lived, found that whatsoever he got by his labour all the week, and was not spent upon necessary provision of meat and apparel, all that upon the Saturday he bestowed upon the poor in alms at St. Peter's church: and therefore see what reason there was, that his building went forward upon the Saturday.

Peter. You have given me very good satisfaction touching this one point: yet desirous I am further to know, what the reason was that some of those habitations were touched by the stinking vapour, and some were not; and what is meant by the bridge and river which he saw.

Gregory. By the representation of these things, Peter, are expressed the causes which they do signify. For the bridge, by which he beheld God's servants to pass unto those pleasant places, doth teach us that the path is very

227

strait which leadeth to everlasting life :[1] and the stinking river, which he saw running beneath, signifieth that the filthy corruption of vice in this world doth daily run to the downfall of carnal pleasure. And that some of the habitations were touched with the stinking vapour, and some were not, what is meant else, but that there be divers which do many good works, yet in their soul they are touched with the delight of carnal sins ? and therefore very great reason there is, that in the next world such should taste of a stinking vapour, whom filthy carnality did delight in this ; and therefore blessed Job, perceiving the pleasure of the flesh to be stinking, pronounceth this sentence of the wanton and carnal man : *His sweetness be worms.*[2] But those that do preserve their heart free from all pleasure of carnal thoughts, have not their houses touched with any such stinking vapour : and here we have also to note, that he saw one and the same thing both to be a vapour and also to have an ill savour, because carnal delight doth so obscure the soul which it hath infected, that it can not see the brightness of true light : for the more pleasure it hath in the inferior part, the more darkness it hath in the superior, which doth hinder it from the contemplation of heavenly mysteries.

Peter. Is there any text of holy scripture, to prove that carnal sins be punished with stinking and bad savours ?

Of the Punishment of the men of Sodom.

¶ Gregory. There is : for in *Genesis*[3] we read that our Lord rained fire and brimstone upon the city of Sodom : that both fire might burn them, and the stench of brimstone smother and kill them : for seeing they burnt with the unlawful love of corruptible flesh, by God's just judgment they perished both by fire and an unsavoury smell ; to the end they might know that they

[1] Matt. 7, 14.   [2] Job 24, 20.   [3] Gen. 19, 24.

had, by the pleasure of their stinking life, incurred the sorrows of eternal death.

Peter. Concerning those things which before I doubted of, I find myself now so fully satisfied, that I have not any further question to move.

Chapter Thirty-seven: how the souls of some men, being yet in their bodies, do see some spiritual punishment: and of that which happened to the boy Theodorus. ¶ Gregory. We have also to know that sometime the souls, whiles they are in their bodies, do behold some spiritual punishment : which yet happeneth to some for their own good, and to others for the edification of them that hear thereof. For there was one Theodorus (which story I remember that in mine Homilies to the people I have also spoken of) who was a very unruly lad, and, more upon necessity than of his own good will, in the company of his brother entered into my Monastery : and so little pleasure he took in spiritual talk, that it was death to him to hear anything tending to the good of his own soul, for he was so far from doing any good work, that he could not endure to hear thereof : and he would openly protest, sometimes by swearing, sometimes in anger, and sometimes in scoffing sort, that he never meant to take upon him the habit of a religious life. This untoward boy, in the late mortality which consumed the greatest part of this city, was grievously strooken : whereof he lay sore sick : and being at last come to the point of death, all the monks repaired to his chamber, to pray for the happy departure of his soul, which seemed not to be far off : for the one half of his body was already dead, and only in his breast a little life remained, and therefore the nearer they saw him to his end, the more fervently did they commend him to God's mercy. Whiles they were thus busied, suddenly he cried out to them, and with great clamour went about

229

to interrupt their devotions, saying : " Depart and away, for behold I am delivered over to a dragon to be devoured, and your presence doth let him, that he can not dispatch me. My head he hath already swallowed up in his mouth, and therefore go your ways, that my torments be not the longer, and that he may effect that which he is about to do : for if I be given him to devour, why do you keep me here in longer pain ? " At these fearful words the monks said unto him : " Why do you speak thus, good brother ? Bless your-self with the sign of the holy cross " : to whom he answered : " Willingly I would, but I can not, I am so loaden with this dragon's scales." Upon these words the monks fell prostrate upon the earth, and in great zeal with tears they prayed to God for his delivery out of the enemy's hands, who mercifully heard them, for upon a sudden the sick person began to cry out, and say : " God be thanked, behold the dragon that had me to devour, is fled away, and overcome with your prayers, here he could not tarry. Now, I beseech you, make intercession for my sins, for I am ready to turn unto God, and wholly to renounce all kind of secular life " : and thus he that was half dead, as before was said, re-served now to a longer life, turned to God with his whole heart: and so, after he had put on a new mind, and was a long time punished with affliction, then his soul departed from the miseries of this mortal life.

Chapter Thirty-eight : of the death of Chrisorius : and of a certain Monk of Iconia.

But Chrisorius on the contrary (as his kinsman Probus, of whom I made mention before, told me) was a substantial man in this world, but as full of sin as of wealth : for he was passing proud, given to the pleasures of the flesh, covetous, and wholly set upon scraping of riches to-gether. But when God determined to make an end of so many sins, he sent him a great sickness ; and when his last time drew near, in that very hour in which his soul was to leave the body, lying with his eyes open, he saw certain cruel men and black spirits stand before him, pressing upon him to carry him away to the pit of hell : at which fearful sight he began to tremble, to wax pale, to sweat, and with pitiful outcries to crave for truce : and often with faltering tongue to call for his son Maximus (whom, when I was a monk, I knew also to profess the same kind of life), saying : " Come away, Maximus, with all speed. Never in my life did I any harm to thee, receive me now in thy faith." His son, greatly moved at these outcries, came unto him in all haste : and his whole family lamenting and crying out, repaired also to his chamber : none of all which beheld those wicked spirits, which did so urge and vex him : but by his trouble of mind, by his paleness and trembling, they made no doubt of their presence : for he was so affrighted with their terrible looks, that he turned himself every way in his bed. Lying upon his left side, he could not endure their sight : and turning to the wall, there also he found them : at last, being very much beset, and despairing of all means to escape their hands, he cried out with a loud voice : " O truce till to-morrow, O truce till to-morrow " : and crying out in this sort he gave up the ghost. This being the manner of his death, certain it is that he saw this fearful sight not for himself, but for us : that his vision might do us good, whom God's patience doth yet with fatherly long sufferance expect to amendment. For what profit reaped he by seeing those foul spirits before his death, and by craving for that truce which he could not obtain ?

There is also now dwelling amongst us a Priest of Isauria called Athanasius, who telleth a very fearful story which in his time happened, as he saith, at Iconium. For there was in that place, as he reporteth, a Monastery called Thongolaton, in which there lived a monk that was had in great account: for he was of good conversation, and in his life very orderly: but, as the end declared, he was far otherwise than he outwardly appeared: for though he did seem to fast with the rest of the monks, yet did he secretly take his meat: which vice of his none of the other monks ever understood. But at length it came forth by this means: for falling grievously sick, so that no hope of life remained, he caused all the monks of the Convent to be called together, who all willingly came, verily thinking that, at the departure of so notable a man, they should have heard some sweet and good exhortation: but it fell out far otherwise, for with great trouble of mind, and trembling of body, he was enforced to tell them that he died in a damnable state, saying: "When you thought that I fasted with you, then had I my meat in secret corners: and behold, now I am delivered to a dragon to be devoured, who with his tail hath enwrapped fast my hands and feet: and his head he hath thrust into my mouth, and so he lieth sucking and drawing out of my breath": and speaking these words he departed this life, and had not any time given to deliver himself by penance from that dragon which he saw. By which we learn, that he had this vision only for the commodity of them that heard it, seeing himself could not escape from the enemy which he beheld, and into whose hands he was given to be devoured.

Peter. Desirous I am to be informed, whether we ought to believe that after death there is any fire of Purgatory.

Chapter Thirty-nine: whether there be any fire of Purgatory in the next world. ¶ Gregory. Our Lord saith in the Gospel: *Walk whiles you have the light:*[1] and by his Prophet he saith: *In time accepted have I heard thee, and in the day of salvation have I holpen thee:*[2] which the Apostle St. Paul expounding, saith: *Behold,*

[1] John 12, 35.   [2] Isai. 49, 8.

now is the time acceptable; behold, now the day of salvation.[1]
Solomon, likewise, saith : *Whatsoever thy hand is able to do,
work it instantly: for neither work, nor reason, nor knowledge, nor wisdom shall he in hell, whither thou dost hasten.*[2]
David also saith : *Because his mercy is for ever.*[3] By which
sayings it is plain, that in such state as a man departeth
out of this life, in the same he is presented in judgment
before God. But yet we must believe that before the
day of judgment there is a Purgatory fire for certain
small sins : because our Saviour saith, *that he which
speaketh blasphemy against the holy Ghost, that it shall not
be forgiven him, neither in this world, nor in the world to
come.*[4] Out of which sentence we learn, that some sins
are forgiven in this world, and some other may be
pardoned in the next : for that which is denied concerning one sin, is consequently understood to be granted
touching some other. But yet this, as I said, we have
not to believe but only concerning little and very
small sins, as, for example, daily idle talk, immoderate
laughter, negligence in the care of our family (which
kind of offences scarce can they avoid, that know in what
sort sin is to be shunned), ignorant errors in matters of
no great weight : all which sins be punished after death,
if men procured not pardon and remission for them in
their lifetime : for when St. Paul saith, that *Christ is the
foundation* : and by and by addeth : *And if any man build
upon this foundation gold, silver, precious stones, wood, hay,
stubble : the work of every one, of what kind it is, the fire
shall try. If any man's work abide which he built thereupon,
he shall receive reward; if any man's work burn, he shall
suffer detriment, but himself shall he saved, yet so as by fire.*[5]
For although these words may be understood of the fire
of tribulation, which men suffer in this world : yet if
any will interpret them of the fire of Purgatory, which

[1] 2 Cor. 6, 2.   [2] Eccles. 9, 10.   [3] Psalm 118, 1.
[4] Matt. 12, 32.   [5] 1 Cor. 3, 11–15.

shall be in the next life : then must he carefully consider, that the Apostle said not that he may be saved by fire, that buildeth upon this foundation iron, brass, or lead, that is, the greater sort of sins, and therefore more hard, and consequently not remissible in that place : but wood, hay, stubble, that is, little and very light sins, which the fire doth easily consume. Yet we have here further to consider, that none can be there purged, no, not for the least sins that be, unless in his lifetime he deserved by virtuous works to find such favour in that place.

Chapter Forty: of the soul of Paschasius the Deacon. ¶ For when I was yet in my younger years, and lived a secular life, I heard from the mouth of mine elders, who knew it to be true: how that Paschasius, a Deacon of this Roman church (whose sound and eloquent books of the holy Ghost be extant amongst us), was a man of a wonderful holy life, a marvellous giver of alms, a lover of the poor, and one that contemned himself. This man, in that contention which, through the exceeding hot emulation of the clergy, fell out betwixt Symmachus and Lawrence, made choice of Lawrence to be Bishop of Rome: and though he was afterward by common consent overcome, yet did he continue in his former opinion till his dying day : loving and preferring him, whom the Church, by the judgment of Bishops, refused for her governor. This Deacon ending his life in the time of Symmachus, Bishop of the Apostolic see : a man possessed with a devil came and touched his dalmatic, as it lay upon the bier, and was forthwith delivered from that vexation. Long time after, Germanus, Bishop of Capua (before mentioned), by the counsel of physicians, for the recovery of his health went to the baths: into which after he was entered, he found there standing in those hot waters the foresaid Paschasius, ready to do him service. At which

sight being much afraid, he demanded what so worthy a
man as he was did in that place : to whom Paschasius
returned this answer : "For no other cause," quoth he,
"am I appointed to this place of punishment, but for
that I took part with Lawrence against Symmachus : and
therefore I beseech you to pray unto our Lord for me,
and by this token shall you know that your prayers be
heard, if, at your coming again, you find me not here."
Upon this, the holy man Germanus betook himself to
his devotions, and after a few days he went again to the
same baths, but found not Paschasius there : for seeing
his fault proceeded not of malice, but of ignorance, he
might after death be purged from that sin. And yet we
must withal think that the plentiful alms which he bestowed in this life, obtained favour at God's hands, that
he might then deserve pardon, when he could work
nothing at all for himself.

Peter. What, I pray you, is the reason, that, in these
latter days, so many things come to light, which in times
past were not known : in such sort that by open revelations and manifest signs, the end of the world seemeth
not to be far off?

**Chapter Forty-one : why in latter times so many
things be known, concerning men's souls : which
in former ages were not heard of. ¶ Gregory.** So
it is, for the nearer that this present world draweth towards an end, so much the more the world to come is at
hand, and sheweth itself by more plain and evident
tokens. For seeing, in this world, we know not one
another's cogitations, and, in the next, men's hearts be
known to all, what fitter name can we give to this world
than to term it night, and what better to the next, than
to call it day? But as, when the night is almost spent,
and the day beginneth to break, darkness and light be in
a certain manner joined together, until the light of the
day following doth perfectly banish away the dark rem-

nants of the former night : even so, the end of this world
is, as it were, mingled together with the beginning of the
next, and with the darkness of this, some light of such
spiritual things as be in that doth appear : and so we see
many things which belong to that world, yet for all this,
perfect knowledge we have not any, but as it were in
the twilight of our soul behold them before the rising
of that sun of knowledge, which then abundantly will
cast his beams over all.

Peter. I like very well of your speech, yet, in so worthy
a man as Paschasius was, this doubt doth trouble me,
how he was after his death carried to any place of punishment, seeing the touching of his garment upon the bier
did dispossess a wicked spirit.

Gregory. Herein appeareth the great and manifold
providence of almighty God, by whose just judgment it
fell out, that Paschasius for some time entertained inwardly sin in his soul, and yet in the sight of the world
wrought miracles by his body after his death, who in his
lifetime did, as they know, many good works : to the end
that those which had seen his virtuous life, should not be
deceived concerning the opinion of his great alms ; and
yet himself should not without punishment have remission of his sin, which whiles he lived he thought to be
no sin, and therefore did not by tears wash it away.

Peter. I understand very well what you say, but by
this reason I am driven into such straights, that I must
stand in fear both of those sins which I know, and also
of those which I know not. But because a little before
you discoursed of the places of torments : in what part
of the world, I beseech you, are we to believe that hell
is, whether above the earth or beneath the same ?

**Chapter Forty=two : in what place of the world
we ought to believe that hell is. ¶ Gregory.** Touching this point I dare not rashly define anything : for
some have been of opinion that hell was in some place

upon the earth ; and others think that it is under the earth : but then this doubt ariseth, for if it be therefore called hell, or an infernal place, because it is below, then as the earth is distant from heaven, so likewise should hell be distant from the earth : for which cause, perhaps, the Prophet saith : *Thou hast delivered my soul from the lower hell;*[1] so that the higher hell may seem to be upon the earth, and the lower under the earth : and with this opinion that sentence of John agreeth, who, when he had said, *that he saw a book sealed with seven seals : and that none was found worthy, neither in heaven, nor in earth, nor under the earth, to open the book, and loose the seals thereof :*[2] he added forthwith : *and I wept much :* which book, notwithstanding, afterward he saith was opened by a lion of the tribe of Juda. By which book, what else can be meant but the holy scripture, which our Saviour alone did open : for being made man, by his death, resurrection, and ascension, he did reveal and make manifest all those mysteries which in that book were closed and shut up. And none in heaven, because not any Angel ; none upon earth, because not man living in body ; not any under the earth was found worthy : because neither the souls departed from their bodies could open unto us, beside our Lord himself, the secrets of that sacred book. Seeing, then, none under the earth is said to be found worthy to open that book, I see not what doth let, but that we should believe that hell is in the lower parts, under the earth.

Peter. I beseech you : Is there one fire in hell, or, according to the diversity of sinners, be there so many sorts of fire prepared in that place ?

Chapter Forty-three: whether there is one fire in hell, or many. ¶ Gregory. The fire of hell is but one : yet doth it not in one manner torment all sinners. For every one there, according to the quantity of his sin,

[1] Psalm 86, 13.   [2] Rev. 5, 1-3.

hath the measure of his pain. For as, in this world, many live under one and the same sun, and yet do not alike feel the heat thereof : for some be burnt more, and some less : so in that one fire, divers manners of burning be found, for that which in this world diversity of bodies doth, that in the next doth diversity of sins : so that although the fire be there all alike, yet doth it not in one manner and alike burn and torment them that be damned.

Peter. Shall those, I pray you, which be condemned to that place, burn always, and never have any end of their torments ?

Chapter Forty-four : whether those that be in hell shall burn there for ever. ¶ Gregory. Certain it is, and without all doubt most true, that as the good shall have no end of their joys, so the wicked never any release of their torments : for our Saviour himself saith : *The wicked shall go into everlasting punishment, and the just into everlasting life.*[1] Seeing, then, true it is, that which he hath promised to his friends : out of all question false it cannot be, that which he hath threatened to his enemies.

Peter. What if it be said that he did threaten eternal pain to wicked livers, that he might thereby restrain them from committing of sins ?

Gregory. If that which he did threaten be false, because his intent was by that means to keep men from wicked life : then likewise must we say that those things are false which he did promise : and that his mind was thereby to provoke us to virtue. But what man, though mad, dare presume so to say ? For if he threatened that which he meant not to put into execution : whiles we are desirous to make him merciful, enforced we are likewise (which is horrible to speak) to affirm him to be deceitful.

Peter. Willing I am to know how that sin can justly

[1] Matt. 25, 46.

be punished without end, which had an end when it was committed.

Gregory. This which you say might have some reason, if the just judge did only consider the sins committed, and not the minds with which they were committed : for the reason why wicked men made an end of sinning was, because they also made an end of their life : for willingly they would, had it been in their power, have lived without end, that they might in like manner have sinned without end. For they do plainly declare that they desired always to live in sin, who never, so long as they were in this world, gave over their wicked life : and therefore it belongeth to the great justice of the supreme judge, that they should never want torments and punishment in the next world, who in this would never give over their wicked and sinful life.

Peter. But no judge that loveth justice taketh pleasure in cruelty : and the end why the just master commandeth his wicked servant to be punished is, that he may give over his lewd life. If, then, the wicked that are tormented in hell fire never come to amend themselves, to what end shall they always burn in those flames ?

Gregory. Almighty God, because he is merciful and full of pity, taketh no pleasure in the torments of wretched men : but because he is also just, therefore doth he never give over to punish the wicked. All which being condemned to perpetual pains, punished they are for their own wickedness : and yet shall they always there burn in fire for some end, and that is, that all those which be just and God's servants may in God behold the joys which they possess, and in them see the torments which they have escaped : to the end that they may thereby always acknowledge themselves grateful to God for his grace, in that they perceive through his divine assistance, what sins they have overcome, which they behold in others to be punished everlastingly.

Peter. And how, I pray you, can they be holy and saints, if they pray not for their enemies, whom they see to lie in such torments ? when it is said to them : *Pray for your enemies.*[1]

Gregory. They pray for their enemies at such time as their hearts may be turned to fruitful penance, and so be saved : for what purpose else do we pray for our enemies, but, as the Apostle saith, *that God may give them repentance to know the truth, and recover themselves from the devil, of whom they are held captive at his will ?*[2]

Peter. I like very well of your saying : for how shall they pray for them, who by no means can be converted from their wickedness, and brought to do the works of justice ?

Gregory. You see, then, that the reason is all one, why, in the next life, none shall pray for men condemned for ever to hell fire : that there is now of not praying for the devil and his angels, sentenced to everlasting torments : and this also is the very reason why holy men do not now pray for them that die in their infidelity and known wicked life : for seeing certain it is that they be condemned to endless pains, to what purpose should they pray for them, when they know that no petition will be admitted of God, their just judge ? And therefore, if now holy men living upon earth take no compassion of those that be dead and damned for their sins, when as yet they know that themselves do some thing through the frailty of the flesh, which is also to be judged : how much more straightly and severely do they behold the torments of the damned, when they be themselves delivered from all vice of corruption, and be more nearly united to true justice itself : for the force of justice doth so possess their souls, in that they be so intrinsical with the most just judge, that they list not by any means to do that which they know is not conformable to his divine pleasure.

[1] Matt. 5, 44.   [2] 2 Tim. 2, 25-26.

Sacchi   Almari

THE MASS OF ST. GREGORY

(Vatican Gallery, Rome)

Peter. The reason you bring is so clear, that I cannot gainsay it: but now another question cometh to my mind, and that is, how the soul can truly be called immortal, seeing certain it is that it doth die in that perpetual fire.

Chapter Forty-five: how the soul is said to be immortal and never to die: if it be punished with the sentence of death. ¶ Gregory. Because there be two manner of lives, consequently also there be two manner of deaths. For one kind of life there is, by which we live in God, another which we received by our creation or generation : and therefore one thing it is to live blessedly, and another thing to live naturally. The soul, therefore, is both mortal and immortal : mortal, because it loseth the felicity of an happy life : and immortal, in that it always keepeth his natural life, which can never be lost, no, not when it is sentenced to perpetual death : for in that state, though it hath not a blessed life, yet it doth retain still the former being and natural life : by reason whereof it is enforced to suffer death without death, defect without defect, and end without end : seeing the death which it endureth is immortal, the defect which it suffereth never faileth, and the end which it hath is infinite, and without end.

Peter. What man is he, though never so holy, that, cometh to leave this mortal life, hath not just cause to fear the unspeakable sentence of damnation? for although he knoweth what he hath done, yet ignorant he is not, how straightly his works shall be examined and judged.

Chapter Forty-six: of a certain holy man that was afraid when he came to die. ¶ Gregory. It is even so, Peter, as you say. And yet sometime the only fear of death doth purge the souls of just men from their smaller sins, as you and I have often heard of a certain holy man that was very much afraid when he came to die : and yet, after he was dead, appeared to his disciples in a white stole, reporting to them in what excellent manner he was received, when he departed out of this world.

Chapter Forty-seven : how some by divine revelation are discharged from fear at their death. And of the manner how the monks Anthony, Merulus, and John departed this life. ¶ Sometime also almighty God doth by divine revelation strengthen the minds of them that be fearful, to the end that they should not be afraid of death. For a certain monk there was, called Anthony, that lived together with me in my Monastery, who by daily tears laboured to come to the joys of heaven : and when as he did very carefully and with great zeal of soul meditate upon the sacred scriptures, he sought not so much for cunning and knowledge, as for tears and contrition of heart, that by means thereof his soul might be stirred up and inflamed : and that by contemning all earthly things, he might with the wings of contemplation fly unto the kingdom of heaven. This man upon a night, by revelation, was admonished in this manner : "Make yourself ready, because our Lord hath given commandment for your departure" : and when he answered, that he had not wherewith to defray the charges of that journey : straightways he heard these comfortable words : " If you take care for your sins, they be forgiven you" ; which thing though he had heard once, and yet for all that was in great fear, another night he had again the same vision : and so after five days he fell sick of an ague, and as the other monks were praying and weeping about him, he departed this life.

Another monk there was in the same Monastery, called Merulus, who was wonderfully given to tears and bestowing of alms : and no time almost passed him, except it were when he was at meat or asleep, in which he did not sing psalms. This man, by vision in the night, saw a crown made of white flowers to descend upon his head : and straight after falling sick, he died with great quiet and joy of mind. Fourteen years after, when Peter, who now hath the government of my Monastery, went about to make a grave for himself hard by Merulus' sepulchre, such a fragrant and pleasant smell, as he saith, came out of it, as though it had been a storehouse of all manner of sweet flowers. By which it appeared plainly, that it was very true, which before he had seen by vision in the night.

Likewise in the same Monastery there was another, called John, who was a young man of great towardness, and one that led his life with great circumspection, humility, sweetness, and gravity. This man falling sore sick, saw in his great extremity by vision in the night an old man to come unto him, who touched him with a wand, saying: " Rise up, for you shall not die of this sickness : but make yourself ready, for you have not any long time to stay in this world " : and forthwith, though the physicians despaired of his health, yet he recovered, and became perfectly well. The vision which he saw he told to others, and for two years following, as I said, he served God in such sort, that his great devotion surpassed his young years. Three years since another monk died, who was buried in the churchyard of the same Monastery, and when we had ended all his funerals, and were departed, this John, as himself with pale face and great trembling told us, remained there still, where he heard that monk which was buried to call him out of the grave : and that it was so indeed, the end following did shew : for ten days after he fell sick of an ague and so departed this life.

Peter. Willingly would I learn whether we ought to observe such visions, as be revealed to us by night in our sleep.

Chapter Forty-eight: whether dreams are to be believed: and how many kind of dreams there be.

¶ **Gregory.** Concerning this point, Peter, you must understand that there are six kind of dreams. For sometime they proceed of too much fulness or emptiness of the stomach : sometime by illusion : sometime both by thought and illusion : sometime by revelation : and sometime both by thought and revelation. The two first all by experience know to be true : and the four latter we find mentioned in holy scripture. For if dreams did not sometime proceed by illusion from our secret enemy, never would the wise man have said : *Dreams have made many to err, and hoping in them have they been deceived :* [1] and again : *You shall not be sooth-sayers, nor observe dreams :* by which words we see how they are to be detested, that are compared with sooth-sayings. Again, if dreams did not sometime proceed both of thought together with illusion, the wise man would not have said : *Dreams follow many cares.* [2] And if sometime also they did not come by mystical revelation, Joseph had never known by dream that he should have been exalted above his brethren : [3] neither the Angel would ever in a dream have admonished the spouse of our Lady to fly away with the child into Egypt. [4] Again, if sometime they did not also proceed both from thoughts and divine revelation, never would the prophet Daniel, disputing of Nabuchodonosor's dream, have begun from the root of his former thoughts, saying : *Thou, O king, diddest begin to think in thy bed, what should happen in times to come ; and he that revealeth mysteries did shew thee what things should come :* and a little after : *Thou diddest see, and behold as it were a great statua : that great statua and high of stature did stand against thee, &c.* [5] Wherefore, seeing Daniel doth with reverence insinuate that the

[1] Ecclus. 34, 7.   [2] Eccles. 5, 2.   [3] Gen. 37, 5-10.
[4] Matt. 2, 13.   [5] Daniel 2, 29-31.

dream should come to pass, and also declareth from what cogitation it did spring, plainly do we learn that dreams sometimes do come both of thought and revelation together. But seeing dreams do grow from such divers roots, with so much the more difficulty ought we to believe them: because it doth not easily appear unto us, from what cause they do proceed. Holy men, indeed, by a certain inward spiritual taste, do discern betwixt illusions and true revelations, by the very voices or representations of the visions themselves: so that they know what they receive from the good spirit, and what they suffer by illusion from the wicked: and therefore, if our mind be not herein very attentive and vigilant, it falleth into many vanities, through the deceit of the wicked spirit: who sometime useth to foretell many true things, that, in the end, he may by some falsehood ensnare our soul.

Chapter Forty-nine: of one who in his dream had long life promised him, and yet died shortly after. ¶ As not long since it is most certain, that it befell to one that lived amongst us, who, being much given to observe dreams, had one night in a dream long life promised him: and when as he had made provision of great store of money for the maintenance of his many days, he was so suddenly taken out of this life, that he left it all behind him, without ever having any use thereof, and carried not with him any good works to the next world.

Peter. I remember very well who it was: but let us, I pray you, prosecute such questions as we began to entreat of: Doth any profit, think you, redound to men's souls, if their bodies be buried in the church?

Chapter Fifty: Whether the souls receive any commodity, if their bodies be buried in the church. ¶ **Gregory.** Such as die not in mortal sin receive this benefit by having their bodies buried in the church: for

when their friends come thither, and behold their
sepulchres, then do they remember them, and pray
unto God for their souls : but those that depart this
life in the state of deadly sin, receive not any absolution
from their sins, but rather be more punished in hell,
for having their bodies buried in the church : which
thing shall be more plain, if I do briefly tell you what
concerning this point hath chanced in our time.

Chapter Fifty-one: of a certain Nun that was buried in the church, which appeared with her body half burnt.

¶ Felix, Bishop of Portua, a man of
holy life, who was born and brought up in the province
of Sabina, saith that there lived in that place a certain
Nun, which, though she were chaste of her body, yet
had she an ungracious and foolish tongue : which
departing this life, was buried in the church : the keeper
whereof, the night following, saw her by revelation
brought before the holy altar, where she was cut in two
pieces, and the one half was burnt in the fire, and the
other was not touched at all. Rising up in the morning,
he told unto others what a strange vision he had seen,
and shewed them the very place in which she was burnt,
the marble whereof appeared with the very marks and
signs of a fire upon it, as though that woman had been
there burnt in very deed with corporal fire. By which
we may plainly see, that such as have not their sins
pardoned, can reap small benefit by having their bodies
after death buried in holy places.

Chapter Fifty-two : of the burial of Valerianus.

¶ John also, an honourable man, one of the governors
of this city, and one that is of great gravity and credit,
as all know, told me how one Valerianus, that was a
gentleman of the city of Bressa, departed this life, whose
body for money the Bishop was content should be buried
in the church. This Valerianus, even to his very old
age, led a light and wanton life : refusing utterly to give

over sin and wickedness. That very night in which he was buried, the blessed martyr Faustinus, in whose church his body lay, appeared to the keeper thereof, saying : "Go, and bid the Bishop cast out that stinking carcass which he hath here buried, and if he will not do it, tell him that thirty days hence he shall die himself." This vision the poor man was afraid to report unto the Bishop, and though he were admonished the second time to do it, yet he refused : and so upon the thirtieth day, the Bishop going safe and sound to bed (never fearing any such thing), suddenly departed this life.

Chapter Fifty-three: of the body of Valentinus, that was after his burial cast out of the church.

⁋ There be also at this time here in the city our venerable brother Venantius, Bishop of Luna, and Liberius, a noble man and one of very great credit : both which do say that themselves know it, and that their servants were present in the city of Genua, when this strange thing happened. One Valentinus, who had an office in the church of Milan, died there, a man in his life time given to wantonness and all kind of lightness, whose body was buried in the church of the blessed martyr Sirus. The midnight following, a great noise was heard in that place, as though some body by force had been drawn out from thence : whereupon the keepers ran thither, to see what the matter was, and when they were come, they saw two very terrible devils, that had tied a rope about his legs, and were drawing him out of the church, himself in the mean time crying and roaring out : at which sight they were so frighted, that they returned home again to their beds : but when the morning was come, they opened the grave in which Valentinus was buried, but his body they could not find, and therefore they sought without the church to see where it was, and so found it thrown into another place, with the feet still bound as it was drawn out of the church. Out of which, Peter, you may learn that such as die in mortal sin, and cause their bodies to be buried in holy ground, are punished also for that their presumption: the holy places not helping them, but rather the sin of their temerity accusing them.

Chapter fifty-four: of the body of a dyer buried in the church, which afterward could not be found.

¶ For another thing also which happened in this city, the company of dyers dwelling here do testify to be most true, and it is concerning one that was the chief of their profession, who departed this life, and was by his wife buried in the church of St. Januarius the martyr, near to the gate of St. Lawrence: whose spirit the night following, in the hearing of the sexton, cried out of his grave, saying: "I burn, I burn": and when he continued a long time crying so, the sexton told it to the dyer's wife, who thereupon sent certain of his own profession to the church, to see in what case his body was in the grave, who so cried out in that pitiful manner: and when they had opened it, there they found his garments safe and sound, which be still kept in the same church, for a perpetual memory of that which happened: but his body by no means could they find, as though it had never been buried there: by which we may gather to what torments his soul was condemned, whose body was in that sort turned out of the church. What profit, then, do holy places bring to them that be buried there, when as those, that be wicked and unworthy, be by God's appointment thrown out from those sacred places?

Peter. What thing is there, then, that can profit and relieve the souls of them that be departed?

Chapter fifty-five: what is available for the soul after death: and of a Priest of Centumcellis, who was desired by a certain man's spirit, to be holpen after his death, by the holy sacrifice: and of the

248

soul of a monk called Justus. ¶ Gregory. If the sins after death be pardonable, then the sacred oblation of the holy host useth to help men's souls : for which cause the souls sometime, of them that be dead, do desire the same : for Bishop Felix, whom we spake of before, saith that a virtuous Priest, who died some two years since, and dwelt in the diocese of the city of Centumcellis, and was pastor of the church of St. John in the place called Tauriana, told him that himself did use (when he had need) to wash his body in a certain place, in which there were passing hot waters : and that going thither upon a time, he found a certain man whom he knew not, ready to do him service, as to pull off his shoes, take his clothes, and to attend upon him in all dutiful manner. And when he had divers times done thus, the Priest, minding upon a day to go to the baths, began to think with himself that he would not be ungrateful to him that did him such service, but carry him somewhat for a reward, and so he took with him two singing breads : and coming thither he found the man there ready, and used his help as he was wont to do · and when he had washed himself, put on his clothes, and was ready to depart, he offered him for an holy reward that which he had brought, desiring him to take that courteously, which for charity he did give him. Then with a sad countenance, and in sorrowful manner, he spake thus unto him : "Why do you give me these, father ? This is holy bread, and I cannot eat of it, for I, whom you see here, was sometime lord of these baths, and am now after my death appointed for my sins to this place : but if you desire to pleasure me, offer this bread unto almighty God, and be an intercessor for my sins : and by this shall you know that your prayers be heard, if at your next coming you find me not here." And as he was speaking these words, he vanished out of his sight : so that he, which before seemed to be a man, shewed by that manner of departure that he was a spirit. The good Priest all the week following gave himself to tears for him, and daily offered up the holy sacrifice: and afterward returning to the bath, found him not there: whereby it appeareth what great profit the souls receive by the sacrifice of the holy oblation, seeing the spirits of them that be dead desire it of the living, and give certain tokens to let us understand how that by means thereof they have received absolution.

Here also I cannot but tell you that which happened three years since in mine own Monastery. A certain monk there was, called Justus, one very cunning in physic, and whiles I remained in the Abbey, served me very diligently, attending upon me in my often infirmities and sickness. This man himself at length fell sore sick, so that in very deed he was brought to the last cast. A brother he had, called Copiosus, that had care of him, who yet liveth. Justus perceiving himself past all hope of life, told this brother of his where he had secretly laid up three crowns of gold; but yet they were not so closely conveyed, that they could be concealed from the monks: for they, carefully seeking, and tossing up all his medicines and boxes, found in one of them these three crowns hidden. Which thing so soon as I understood, very much grieved I was, and could not quietly digest so great a sin at his hands, that lived with us in community, because the rule of my Monastery was that all the monks thereof should so live in common, that none in particular might possess anything proper to himself. Being, therefore, much troubled and grieved at that which had happened, I began to think with myself what was best to be done, both for the soul of him that was now dying, and also for the edification and example of those that were yet living. At length I sent for Pretiosus, Prior of the Monastery, and gave him this charge : " See," quoth I, " that none of our monks do so much as visit Justus in this his extremity, neither let any give him any comfort at all : and when his last hour draweth nigh, and he doth desire the presence of his spiritual brethren, let his carnal brother tell him that they do all detest him, for the three crowns which he had hidden : that, at least before his death, sorrow may wound his heart, and purge it from the sin committed : and when he is dead, let not his body be buried amongst the rest of the monks, but make a grave for him in some one dunghill or other, and there cast it in, together with the three crowns which he left behind him, crying out all with joint voice : 'Thy money be with thee unto perdition' ; and so put earth upon him." In either of which things my mind and desire was, both to help him that was leaving the world, and also to edify the monks yet remaining behind, that both grief of death might make him pardonable for his sin, and such a severe sentence against avarice might terrify and preserve them from the like offence : both which, by God's goodness, fell out accordingly. For when the foresaid monk came to die, and carefully desired to be commended to the devotions of his brethren, and yet none of them did either visit him, or so much as speak to him : his brother Copiosus told him for what cause they had all given him over : at which words he straightways sighed for his sin, and in that sorrow gave up the ghost. And after his death, he was buried in that manner, as I had given in commandment : by which fact all the monks were so terrified, that they began each one to seek out the least and basest things in their cells, and which by the rule they might lawfully keep : and very much they feared, lest some thing they had, for which they might be blamed.

Thirty days after his departure, I began to take compassion upon him, and with great grief to think of his punishment, and what means there was to help him · whereupon I called again for Pretiosus, Prior of my Monastery, and with an heavy heart spake thus unto him : " It is now a good while since that our brother which is departed remaineth in the torments of fire, and therefore we must shew him some charity, and labour what we may to procure his delivery : wherefore go your way, and see that for thirty days following sacrifice be offered for him, so that no one day pass in which, for his absolution and discharge, the healthful sacrifice be not offered " : who forthwith departed, and put my commandment in execution. In the mean time, my mind being busied about other affairs, so that I took no heed to the days how they passed : upon a certain night the same monk that was dead, appeared to his brother Copiosus : who, seeing him, enquired of his state in this manner : " What is the matter, brother ? and how is it with you ? " to whom he answered thus : " Hitherto have I been in bad case, but now I am well ; for this day have I received the communion " : with which news Copiosus straightways coming to the Monastery, told the monks : and they diligently counting the days, found it to be that in which the thirtieth sacrifice was offered for his soul : and so, though neither Copiosus knew what the monks had done for him, nor they what he had seen concerning the state of his brother, yet at one and the same time both he knew what they had done, and they what he had seen, and so the sacrifice and vision agreeing together, apparent it was that the dead monk was by the holy sacrifice delivered from his pains.

Peter. The things you report be passing strange, and yet full of joy and comfort.

Chapter Fifty-six : of the life and departure of Bishop Cassius. ¶ Gregory. And that we should

not call in question, or doubt of that which the dead

report, we have, for confirmation of the same thing, the facts of the living. For Cassius, Bishop of Narni, a man of holy life, who did usually every day offer sacrifice unto God (and whiles he was at the mysteries of those sacrifices, did also immolate himself in tears), received from our Lord this message by one of his Priests. "Do that thou doest: work that thou workest: let not thy foot cease, let not thy hand cease, upon the nativity of the Apostles thou shalt come unto me, and I will give thee thy reward." And so, seven years after, upon that very day of the Apostles, after he had ended the solemnity of Mass and received the mysteries of the sacred communion, he departed this life.

Chapter Fifty-seven: of one that was taken by his enemies and put in prison, whose irons fell off at the time of the sacrifice: and of one Baraca, a mariner, that was by the holy sacrifice delivered from drowning. ¶ That also which I have heard is known to many, to wit, how one was by his enemies taken and put in prison, with irons upon him: for whom his wife caused upon certain days sacrifice to be offered: who, long time after, returning home to his wife, told her upon what days his bolts used to fall off: by whose relation she found that it was upon those very days in which sacrifice had been offered for him. By another thing likewise, which happened seven years since, the very same truth is confirmed. For when Agathus, Bishop of Palermo (as many faithful and religious men both have and still do tell me), was, in the time of my predecessor of blessed memory, commanded to come to Rome, and in his journey fell into such a tempest at sea, that he despaired of ever coming to land: the mariner of the ship, called Baraca (who now is one of the clergy, and serveth in the same church), governed another small vessel, tied to the poop of the former ship: the rope whereof breaking in pieces, away it went with man

253

and all, and amongst the huge mountains of waters, quickly vanished out of sight. The ship in which the Bishop was, after many great dangers, at length arrived all weather-beaten at the island of Ostica : and when three days were past, and the Bishop could hear no news of the foresaid mariner that was so violently carried away with the storm, nor see him in any part of the sea, very sorry he was, and verily believed that he had been drowned : and so upon great charity bestowed one thing upon him being yet alive, which was not due unto him until he was dead : for he willed that the sacrifice of the healthful oblation should be offered unto almighty God for the absolution of his soul: which being done accordingly, and the ship new rigged, away he departed for Italy, where, arriving at Portua, he found the mariner alive, whom he verily supposed to have been drowned : upon which good chance altogether unlooked for, very glad he was, and demanded of him, how it was possible that he could escape so many days, in so great a danger and so terrible a tempest : who told him, how in that storm he was tossed with that little ship which he governed, and how he did swim with it being full of water : and so often as it was turned upside down, how he gat upon the keel, and held fast there : adding also that, by striving and labouring thus continually day and night, at length, with watching and hunger, his strength began to fail him : and then he told how, by the singular providence and mercy of God, he was preserved from drowning: for as even to this very day he still affirmeth, so then did he verify the same to the Bishop, telling him in this manner. "As I was," quoth he, "striving and labouring in the sea, and my strength began to fail me, suddenly I became so heavy of mind, that methought I was neither waking nor yet asleep: and being in that case in the midst of the sea, I saw one come, who brought me bread to refresh my tired body: which so soon as I had eaten, I recovered my strength again; and not long after, a ship passing by took me in, and so was I delivered from that danger of death and set safe a land. The Bishop, hearing this, enquired upon what day this strange thing happened, and he found by his relation, that it was that very day in which the Priest in the island of Ostica did sacrifice for him unto God, the host of the holy oblation.

Peter. That which you report, myself also heard at my being in Sicily.

Gregory. I, for my part, do verily believe, that the reason why, by God's providence, this thing falleth out thus apparently to them that be living, and think nothing thereof, is that all may know how, if their sins be not irremissible, that they may after death obtain pardon and absolution for them, by the oblation of the holy sacrifice. But yet we have here to note, that the holy sacrifice doth profit those kind of persons after their death, who in their life time obtained that such good works as were by their friends done for them might be available to their souls, after they were out of this world.

Chapter Fifty-eight: of the virtue and mystery of the holy sacrifice. ¶ And here also we have diligently to consider, that it is far more secure and safe that every man should do that for himself whiles he is yet alive, which he desireth that others should do for him after his death. For far more blessed it is, to depart free out of this world, than being in prison to seek for release: and therefore reason teacheth us, that we should with our whole soul contemn this present world, at least because we see that it is now gone and past: and to offer unto God the daily sacrifice of tears, and the daily sacrifice of his body and blood. For this sacrifice doth especially save our souls from everlasting damnation, which in mystery doth renew unto us the death of the Son of God: who although being risen from death, doth not now die any more, nor death shall not any further prevail against him: yet living in himself immortally, and without all corruption, he is again sacrificed for us in this mystery of the holy oblation: for there his body is received, there his flesh is distributed for the salvation of the people: there his blood is not now shed betwixt the hands of infidels, but poured into the mouths of the faithful. Wherefore let us hereby meditate what manner of sacrifice this is, ordained for us, which for our absolution doth always represent the passion of the only Son of God: for what right believing Christian can doubt, that in the very hour of the sacrifice, at the words of the Priest, the heavens be opened, and the quires of Angels are present in that mystery of Jesus Christ; that high things are accompanied with low, and earthly joined to heavenly, and that one thing is made of visible and invisible?

Chapter Fifty-nine: how we ought to procure sorrow of heart, at the time of the holy mysteries: and of the custody of our soul after contrition.

¶ But necessary it is that, when we do these things, we should also, by contrition of heart, sacrifice ourselves unto almighty God: for when we celebrate the mystery of our Lord's passion, we ought to imitate what we then do: for then shall it truly be a sacrifice for us unto God, if we offer ourselves also to him in sacrifice. Careful also must we be, that after we have bestowed some time in prayer, that, as much as we can by God's grace, we keep our mind fixed in him, so that no vain thoughts make us to fall unto dissolution, nor any foolish mirth enter into our heart: lest the soul, by reason of such transitory thoughts, lose all that which it gained by former contrition. For so Anne deserved to obtain that which she craved at God's hand, because after her tears she preserved herself in the former force of her soul: for of her thus it is written: *And her looks were not any more changed to divers things.*[1] She therefore, that forgot not what she desired, was not deprived of that gift which she requested.

Chapter Sixty: that we ought to pardon other men their sins, that we may obtain remission of our own. ¶ We have also further to know, that he doth rightly and in good sort demand pardon for his own sin, who doth forgive that which hath been done against himself. For our gift is not received, if, before, we free not our soul from all discord and lack of charity: for our Saviour saith: *If thou offer thy gift at the altar, and there thou remember that thy brother hath aught against thee, leave there thy offering before the altar, and go first to be reconciled to thy brother, and then coming thou shalt offer thy gift.*[2] Wherein we have to consider, that whereas all sin by a gift is loosed, how grievous the sin of discord is, for which no gift is received: and therefore we ought, in soul and desire, to go unto our neighbour though he be far off, and many miles distant from us, and there to humble ourselves before him, and to pacify him by humility and hearty good will, to the end that our Creator, beholding the desire of our mind, may forgive us our own sin, who receiveth a gift for sin. And our Saviour himself teacheth us, how that servant, which did owe ten thousand talents, by penance obtained of his Lord the forgiveness of that debt: but yet because he would not forgive his fellow-servant an hundred pence, which were due to him, that was again exacted at his hands, which before was pardoned.[3] Out of which sayings we learn, that if we do not from our heart forgive that which is committed against us, how that is again required at our hands, whereof before we were glad that by penance we had obtained pardon and remission.

[1] 1 Kings 1. 18.   [2] Matt. 5. 23-24.   [3] Matt. 18. 27.

Wherefore, whiles time is given us, whiles our judge doth bear with us, whiles he that examineth our sins doth expect our conversion and amendment : let us mollify with tears the hardness of our heart, and with sincere charity, love our neighbours : and then dare I speak it boldly, that we shall not have any need of the holy sacrifice after our death : if, before death, we offer up ourselves for a sacrifice unto almighty God.

¶ Here end the Dialogues of Saint Gregory.

Notes, &c.

Notes

Book I

INTRODUCTION, p. 4. Similarly in the letter addressed to Leander of Seville, prefixed to the *Moralia*, or *Exposition of the Book of Job* (composed before his elevation to the papacy), St. Gregory had written : " Now that the times are disturbed through multiplied evils, the end of the world being at hand, we ourselves, who are believed to be devoted to the inner mysteries, are involved in external cares." *Cf.* below, Bk. III. chap. 38 ; Bk. IV. chap. 41.

CHAPTER I. p. 7. Funda, more correctly *Fundi* (the translator is somewhat casual in his rendering of the Latin names of places), is the modern Fondi, in the province of Caserta, between Terracina and Formia. *Cf.* Horace, *Sat.* I. 5, 34–36. Honoratus is celebrated in the Roman Martyrology on January 16.

CHAPTER II. p. 9. For Totila, *see* below, Bk. II. chap. 14. He was king of the Ostrogoths in Italy from 541 to 552.

Ibid. p. 10. In 553, after the death of Totila's successor, Teias, Leuthar and Butilin (here called Buccellinus), chiefs of the Alamanni, who were subject to the king of the Franks, invaded Italy in support of the scattered remnants of the Goths. Butilin ravaged Campania in 554, until defeated and slain by Narses at the battle of Capua. *See* Hodgkin, *Italy and her Invaders*, V. bk. vi. chap. 1.

CHAPTER IV. p. 15. The province of Valeria included the cities of Reate (Rieti) and Tibur (Tivoli), and the modern province of Aquila (Abruzzi). St. Equitius is commemorated on March 7. It is uncertain whether the monastery *quod appellatur Balneum Ciceronis* was at Tusculum, or (as seems more probable from the context) on the site of the present abbey of San Domenico Abbate near Isola del Liri in the diocese of Sora.

Ibid. p. 16. Amiternum, an ancient Sabine town, the birthplace of Sallust, is some five miles from the modern city of Aquila ; its site is occupied by the village of San Vittorino. Two letters of Cassiodorus, written in the name of King Theodoric, refer to this Basilius, who, together with another Roman noble named Praetextatus, was imprisoned for practising magical arts, but made his escape. Theodoric ordered that he should be recaptured, and examined by a board of five persons, one of whom was the patrician Symmachus (*Cf.* Bk. IV. chaps. 13 and 30). *See* Hodgkin, *The Letters of Cassiodorus*, pp. 246, 247. Baronius places these events in the year 504 or thereabouts. Nothing is known of the subsequent fate of Basilius, to which St. Gregory refers ; he is evidently not the same person as the Basilius mentioned by Boëthius, in the *De Consolatione Philosophiae*, as one of his accusers.

Ibid. p. 18. Castorius (or Castus) was a military officer (*magister militum*), who shared in the defence of Rome against the Lombards, and is mentioned with high praise by St. Gregory himself in a letter of 595 to the Emperor Mauritius (*Registrum, Epist.* v. 36, ed. Ewald and Hartmann, i. p. 317). For " Bishop of Reatino " (*Reatinae antistes ecclesiae*) read " Bishop of Reate " (Rieti). The Bishop of Rome mentioned in this chapter is probably Pope Symmachus I. (498–514), for whom *see* below, Bk. IV. chap. 40.

Ibid. p. 19. Julianus is described in the Latin text as being then *defensor* (of the Church of Rome). The Defenders of the various Churches were ecclesiastical lawyers, clerics appointed to look after the interests of the Church. *See* Moroni, *Dizionario di Erudizione storico-ecclesiastica*, xx. pp. 38 *et seq.*, and St. Gregory, *Registrum, Epist.* v. 26, ed. Ewald and Hartmann, i. p. 307.

Ibid. p. 22. Valentinus was the second Abbot of Sant' Andrea, the monastery into which St. Gregory converted his palace on the Caelian Hill.

Ibid. p. 23. The Lombards came into the province of Valeria in 571, three years after their first appearance in Italy.

CHAPTER VII. pp. 26, 27. For Maximianus, Bishop of Syracuse, *see* Bk. III. chap. 36. The " Abbey which is hard by the city of Nepi " is the monastery " called Suppentonia," mentioned in the next chapter. There were a number of early mediæval monasteries on Mount Soracte ; the one presided over by Nonnosus was, perhaps, that traditionally associated with St. Sylvester, which was afterwards in the eighth century refounded by Carloman the Frank.

CHAPTER VIII. p. 29. Suppentonia is the modern Castel Sant' Elia, between Nepi and Civita Castellana. Anastasius is commemorated on January 11.

Ibid. p. 31. Tuscania, more properly Tuscia, is, of course, the modern Tuscany.

CHAPTER IX. p. 31. The place meant is apparently Ferentinum (Ferentino), near Frosinone, which, however, is in Latium not Tuscany. Bonifacius is commemorated on May 14.

CHAPTER X. p. 38. Tuder is now Todi in Umbria. Fortunatus died in 537, and is commemorated on October 14. The Julianus here mentioned, *nostrae ecclesiae defensor*, is not the same person as the Julianus connected with St. Equitius (Bk. I. chap. 4), who previously held the same office of "defender."

CHAPTER XII. p. 46. "In eo etiam loco *Interorina* vallis dicitur, quae a multis verbo rustico *Interocrina* nominatur." The place is apparently Interocrea, or Intocrium, the modern Antrodoco, between Rieti and Aquila.

Book II

INTRODUCTION, p. 51. St. Benedict was born at Nursia about 480. The date of his leaving Rome is disputed; it was probably a few years before 500. Constantinus and Simplicius were his two immediate successors, the second and third Abbots of Monte Cassino; Honoratus presided over the Abbey of Subiaco in St. Gregory's own days.

CHAPTER I., p. 52. For "Enside," read *Enfide,* which is identified with the mountain-village of Affile, between Olevano and Subiaco.

Ibid. p. 53. Sublacum, or Sublaqueum, now Subiaco, in the Apennines, above the river Anio. Here Nero had built a villa, with three artificial lakes, and it was over the ruins of the Emperor's "sylvan retreat" that the order of the Benedictines thus sprang into being. *Cf.* Lanciani, *Wanderings in the Roman Campagna,* pp. 350-352. The "strait cave," in which St. Benedict lived, is now the famous *Sagro Speco,* on the mountain-side, high above the town.

Ibid. p. 53. The name of this Abbot is variously given as Theodacus or Adeodatus.

CHAPTER II. p. 55. These thorns and nettles are piously said to have turned into the roses, the descendants of which are still seen in the garden of the monastery of the *Sagro Speco.*

CHAPTER III. p. 56. The monastery in question is said to have been at Varia (the modern Vicovaro), near Mandela. In the second chapter of the *Rule of St. Benedict,* we read that the Abbot "shall be acquitted in so far as he shall have shown all the watchfulness of a shepherd over a restless and disobedient flock; and if as their pastor he shall have employed every care to cure their corrupt manners, he shall be declared guiltless in the Lord's judgment, and he may say with the prophet, *I have not hidden Thy justice in my heart; I have told Thy truth and Thy salvation; but they contemned and despised me."* (Gasquet's translation.)

Ibid. p. 60. "That notable preacher of the world." This is, perhaps, a misprint in the edition of 1608 for "word." The Latin has simply: *ille quoque egregius praedicator.*

Ibid. p. 61. The name of the father of Maurus is variously written: Equitius, Evitius, Euticius; "Tertullius the senator" is simply *Tertullus patricius.* For the reception of children into the order, *cf.* chap. 59 of the *Rule.* According to the tradition, Maurus

became the Benedictine apostle of France, and died in 584, while
Placidus died a martyr's death in Sicily in 541, a few years before the
death of St. Benedict himself.

CHAPTER VI. p. 63. "If any one whilst engaged in any work,
either in the kitchen, in the cellar, in serving others, in the bake-
house, in the garden, or in any other occupation or place, shall do
anything amiss, break or lose anything, or offend in any way whatsoever,
and do not come at once to the abbot and community of his own
accord to confess his offence and make satisfaction, if afterwards it
shall become known by another he shall be more severely punished."
(*Rule of St. Benedict*, chap. 46, Gasquet's translation.)

CHAPTER VIII. p. 68. St. Benedict thus founded the great Abbey
of Monte Cassino in 528 or 529. Dante translates St. Gregory's
words in the *Paradiso* (xxii. 37-45), where he puts them into the
mouth of St. Benedict himself:

"Quel monte, a cui Cassino è nella costa,
Fu frequentato già in sulla cima
Dalla gente ingannata e mal disposta.
E quel son io che su vi portai prima
Lo nome di Colui, che in terra addusse
La verità che tanto ci sublima ;
E tanta grazia sopra me rilusse,
Ch'io ritrassi le ville circostanti
Dall' empio culto che il mondo sedusse."

CHAPTER XI. p. 70. "The son of a certain courtier" is hardly
the equivalent of *cujusdam curialis filius*. A *curialis*, or *decurio*, was
a member of the municipal council of some provincial town. See
Hodgkin, II. pp. 577 *et seq.*

CHAPTER XII. p. 71. "The brother who is sent on an errand,
and expects to return to his monastery the same day, shall not presume
to eat outside his house, even though he be asked to do so by any
one, unless he be so ordered by his abbot. If he do otherwise, let
him be excommunicated." (*Rule of St. Benedict*, chap. 51, Gasquet's
translation.)

CHAPTER XIII. p. 72. This Valentinian is probably the Abbot of
the Lateran mentioned on p. 52.

CHAPTERS XIV. and XV. pp. 73-75. Totila (Baduila) became
king of the Ostrogoths in Italy in 541, when Belisarius had won
back for Justinian and the Empire all the peninsula south of the Po.
His interview with St. Benedict took place probably in the following
year, 542. Of his four Gothic attendants here mentioned—Riggo,
Vult, Ruderic, and Bleda—the last two are also known in history as
having been sent by the king to besiege Florence in this same year.
(*Cf.* Hodgkin, *Italy and her Invaders*, II. p. 433). Totila recon-

quered almost all Italy, except Ravenna and Ancona ; he captured Rome twice (546 and 549), and overran Sicily ; but in 552 was defeated by Narses and killed in the rout of his army. It was naturally impossible for St. Gregory to take an impartial view of the Goths, and modern historians depict Totila in far more favourable colours. According to Dr. Hodgkin, he was " upon the whole one of the best types of the still future age of chivalry that the Downfall of the Empire can exhibit."

CHAPTER XV. p. 75. "Camisina" is Canusium, the modern Canosa di Puglia. The Bishop is the Sabinus spoken of below, Bk. III. chap. 5. Honoratus is the Abbot of Subiaco already mentioned on p. 52.

CHAPTER XVI. p. 75. Constantius, Bishop of Aquinum (Aquino), is commemorated on September 1.

CHAPTER XVII. p. 78. The Abbey of Monte Cassino was destroyed by the Lombards of the duchy of Beneventum in 589.

CHAPTER XIX. p. 80. " No one, without leave of the abbot, shall presume to give, or receive, or keep as his own, anything whatever. . . . All things are to be common to all, as it is written, *Neither did any one say or think that aught was his own.*" (*Rule of St. Benedict*, chapter 33, Gasquet's translation. *Cf.* also chapter 54.)

CHAPTER XX. p. 80. In chapter iv. of the *Rule*, among the instruments of good works, we read : " To dash at once against Christ (as against a rock) evil thoughts which rise up in the mind." According to the Latin text, this monk *cujusdam defensoris filius fuerat*. The *Defensores Civitatum* were the chief municipal authorities of the provinces, originally instituted to protect the people from the unjust extortions of the imperial officials. *Cf.* Hodgkin, *Italy and her Invaders*, I. pp. 625–628.

CHAPTER XXII. p. 82. Tarracina, the Volscian city of Anxur, now Terracina, the last town of the former Papal States before crossing the Neapolitan frontier.

CHAPTER XXXI. p. 91. The name of this Goth is more usually written Zalla.

CHAPTER XXXIII. p. 94. According to the tradition, St. Scholastica died on February 10, 543, and St. Benedict a month later, March 21, 543. Their bodies are supposed to lie together under the high altar of the abbey church at Monte Cassino ; but this is a little uncertain, as they are said to have been at one time translated (perhaps temporarily) to France.

CHAPTER XXXV. p. 96. This *Liberius quondam patricius* is probably the Liberius mentioned in the letters of Cassiodorus (Hodgkin, *The Letters of Cassiodorus*, pp. 178, 179) as a Roman noble who had been Praetorian Prefect under Theodoric. The monastery is referred to in St. Gregory's letters, *Registrum, Epist.* ix. 162, 164 (Ewald and

Hartmann, ii. pp. 162, 163). St. Germanus, Bishop of Capua, died in 540 or 541, and is commemorated on October 30.

Ibid. pp. 97, 98. This vision of the whole world, and St. Gregory's explanation, deeply impressed the mediæval mind. It was imitated by Marcus, the Irish Benedictine who wrote the Vision of Tundal (*Visio Tnugdali*, ed. Wagner, p. 52), and by Dante (*Par.* xxii. 133–153). St. Thomas Aquinas discusses it with a view to showing that St. Gregory's words do not imply that St. Benedict, still living in the present life, saw God in that vision *per essentiam*, in His Essence. (*Summa Theologiea*, II. ii. Q. 108, A. 5 ad 3.)

CHAPTER XXXVI. p. 99. "For he wrote a rule for his monks, both excellent for discretion and also eloquent for the style." The Latin runs: *Nam scripsit monachorum regulam, discretione praecipuam, sermone luculentam.* St. Gregory himself, in the epistle to Bishop Leander prefixed to the *Moralia*, professes to despise "literary style" (*ipsam loquendi artem, quam magisteria disciplinae exterioris insinuant*) ; "for I deem it most unworthy," he says, "to restrict the words of the heavenly oracle under the rules of Donatus" (*Epistola missoria ad Leandrum Hispalensem*, cap. 5). For the style and Latinity of the Rule, *cf.* especially E. Wölfflin, *Die Latinität des Benedikt von Nursia* in *Archiv für lateinische Lexikographie und Grammatik*, ix. Munich, 1896.

Book III

CHAPTER I. pp. 105–108. St. Paulinus (Meropius Pontius Anicius Paulinus) was born at Bordeaux in 353 or 354, of a noble house with vast estates in Gaul, Italy, and Spain. In middle life he left the world, and from 409 until his death in 431 was Bishop of Nola in Campania (a province of which he had been governor in early manhood). Many of his letters and poems (he had been a pupil of Ausonius) have been preserved. His feast is on June 22. The story here told by St. Gregory presents various chronological difficulties. The Vandals established their kingdom in Africa between 429 and 439 (in which latter year Gaiseric, or Genseric, took Carthage) ; their ravages in Italy (culminating in the sack of Rome by Gaiseric in 455) did not begin in the lifetime of Paulinus ; and Gaiseric himself, who is evidently the king here referred to, did not die until 477, more than forty years after the death of Paulinus. As a matter of fact, Alaric took Nola in 410, after his sack of Rome, and Paulinus, then newly appointed Bishop, was made prisoner. "Our Paulinus, Bishop of Nola," writes St. Augustine, "who from one most wealthy had become voluntarily poor and most abundantly holy, when the Barbarians sacked Nola, and he was held captive, prayed thus in his heart, as we afterwards learned from him : Lord, let me not be tormented on account of gold and silver, for Thou knowest where all I

Notes

have is " (*De Civitate Dei*, i. 10). Alaric died within the year. It seems not impossible, as M. André Baudrillart suggests (*Saint Paulin Évêque de Nole*, pp. 167–170), that the foundation for St. Gregory's story is some tradition connected with the taking of St. Paulinus in 410, and that the Vandals have been confused with the Visigoths, Gaiseric with Alaric. There is no evidence that St. Paulinus was ever a prisoner in Africa.

CHAPTER II. p. 109. For "Justinian the elder" read "Justin the elder" (the mistake is not the translator's, but due to the Latin text that he used). John I., a Tuscan by birth, was elected Pope in 523, in succession to Pope Hormisdas, whose reconciliation of the Roman See with the Eastern Empire, as represented by Justin I., had weakened the power of Theodoric in Italy. In 525 he was compelled by the Gothic king to go on an embassy to Justin, here recorded by St. Gregory, with a view of persuading the Emperor to adopt less vigorous methods against the Arians. At Constantinople he crowned the Emperor. On his return to Ravenna, Theodoric threw him into a dungeon, where he died in May, 526. He is the last Pope whom the Church of Rome venerates as a martyr. *Cf.* below, Bk. IV. chap. 30.

CHAPTER III. p. 109. Agapitus I., a Roman noble, was elected Pope in 535, when Justinian, the nephew and successor of Justin, was preparing to reconquer Italy from the Goths. He went to Constantinople, at once to make peace (in which he was unsuccessful) and to procure the deposition of the patriarch Anthimus, who adhered to the Monophysite heresy and was supported by the Empress Theodora. There the Pope suddenly died in April 536. Dante (*Par.* vi. 10–21) makes Justinian represent himself as converted from the Monophysites by the words of Agapitus :

> " Cesare fui, e son Giustiniano,
> Che, per voler del primo amor ch'io sento,
> D'entro le leggi trassi il troppo e il vano.
> E prima ch'io all'opra fossi attento,
> Una natura in Cristo esser, non piùe,
> Credeva, e di tal fede era contento ;
> Ma il benedetto Agapito, che fue
> Sommo pastore, alla fede sincera
> Mi dirizzò con le parole sue.
> Io gli credetti, e ciò che in fede sua era
> Veggio ora chiaro, sì come tu vedi
> Ogni contraddizion e falsa e vera."

CHAPTER IV. p. 110. Datius, Archbishop of Milan, a great champion of orthodoxy and an active ecclesiastical politician, was closely associated with Pope Vigilius in his struggle with Justinian

267

and Theodora. He died at Constantinople in 552. This legend probably refers to his earlier visit to the Byzantine Court, circa 544.

CHAPTER V. p. 111. Sabinus, Bishop of Canosa in Apulia, has been already mentioned, Bk. II. chap. 15. This story shows Totila in a different light from that in which he usually appears in Gregory's pages.

CHAPTER VIII. p. 116. The Pope in question is usually identified with John III. (561–574); but the previous reference to Constantius, Bishop of Aquino, as a contemporary of St. Benedict (cf. Bk. II. chap. 16), seems to point to John II. (533–535).

CHAPTER IX. p. 117. Frigidianus or Frigdianus (in Italian, San Frediano) was an Irishman. He died in 588, and is celebrated on March 18 and November 18. For "Anser" read *Auser*, now called the Serchio.

CHAPTER X. p. 118. Placentia is the modern Piacenza, in Lombardy.

CHAPTER XI. p. 119. Cerbonius died about 575. Populonium, or Populonia, a few miles from Piombino in the Maremma of Tuscany, was an important place in antiquity by reason of the smelting of the iron from Elba. It was the chief Etruscan seaport.

CHAPTER XII. p. 120. Otricoli (*Ocriculum*) is near Orte in Umbria. This St. Fulgentius (d. 540) is not to be confused with his contemporary, St. Fulgentius, Bishop of Ruspe (d. 533).

CHAPTER XIII. p. 121. The capture of Perusia (the modern Perugia) by the Goths and the martyrdom of St. Herculanus (Sant' Ercolano) took place in 549, after a siege of three years, during which the city was gallantly defended by a Greek imperial garrison under Cyprian. According to the legend, when the defenders were reduced to extremities, Herculanus ordered a lamb or an ox to be fed with all the store of grain that remained, and then hurled down from the walls, in order that the besiegers might suppose that supplies abounded, and abandon their hope of reducing the city by starvation. A young ecclesiastic, either accidentally or by treachery, revealed the trick to the Goths, who straightway took the city by storm.

CHAPTER XIV. p. 123. There were a number of Syrian monks in Italy during the sixth century (Herculanus of Perugia is said to have been a Syrian). Nothing more is known concerning this Isaac of Spoleto, who, if he lived "almost to the last days of the Goths," must have died about the middle of the century (Teias, the successor of Totila, and the last king of the Goths in Italy, was slain in 553). He is not to be confused with two other Syrians of the same name, the presbyter Isaac of Antioch (middle of fifth century) and Isaac of Nineveh, the Nestorian bishop of that city in the latter half of the seventh century. For the last-named, *see* J. B. Chabot, *De S. Isaaci Ninivitae vita, scriptis, et aoctrina* (Paris, 1892), and a more recent article by J. P. Arendzen in the *Catholic Encyclopedia*, vol. viii. (New York, 1910). The Latin *Liber de contemptu mundi* is a kind of collection from the writings of Isaac of Nineveh (translated from a Greek version of the Syriac original); upon this is based an Italian work of the fourteenth century, variously entitled *De la perfectione de la vita contemplativa* and *Collazione dell' Abate Isaac*, erroneously attributed to St. Gregory's Isaac of Spoleto, which has been several times reprinted (the latest edition is that of Bartolommeo Sorio, published at Rome in 1845, together with the letters of Giovanni dalle Celle).

CHAPTER XV. p. 128. Euthicius (better, Eutychius) died about 540; Florentins about 547.

CHAPTER XVI. p. 133. Marcius is called Martinus in the Latin text. Mons Marsicus is either Monte Marsicano in the Abruzzi, or the mountain of the same name near Marsico Nuovo in Basilicata. Pope Pelagius II., Gregory's immediate predecessor, reigned from 579 to 590.

CHAPTER XVII. p. 136. Buxentum, in Lucania, is either Pisciotta or Policastro on the coast of Calabria. Monte Argentario, in the Tuscan province of Grosseto (formerly a part of the republic of Siena) is famous in the annals of the order of the Passionists.

CHAPTER XVIII. p. 139. This monk Benedict (who, of course, is not the same person as his more famous contemporary, St. Benedict of Nursia) is commemorated on March 23.

CHAPTER XIX. p. 140. For "Antharicus" read *Autharicus.* Authari, king of the Lombards, reigned from 584 to 590. These great floods were in 589. Athesis is the modern Adige. St. Zeno, whose feast is on April 12, was Bishop of Verona in the fourth century, and, according to the legend, delivered the daughter of the Emperor Galienus from an unclean spirit. Nothing is known about his having suffered martyrdom. Cf. *Acta Sanctorum*, Aprilis Tom II., pp. 68-78. Two books of *Tractatus*, or *Sermones*, attributed to him are in Migne, P.L., XI.

CHAPTER XXII. p. 143. Valentius is the same person as the Valentinus mentioned on pp. 22, 202. He is variously called Valentinus, Valentius, or Valentio.

CHAPTER XXIII. p. 145. Praeneste is the mediæval Palestrina, near which St. Gregory's own ancestral lands lay. The mountain, upon the side of which the city stands, is crowned by Castel San Pietro, with a church probably occupying the site of the abbey here mentioned and a ruined castle of the Colonna.

CHAPTERS XXVII. and XXVIII. pp. 150-151. Dr. Hodgkin (VI. p. 97) conjectures that these atrocities were not committed by the Lombards properly so called, who were Arians, but by their barbarian auxiliaries, Bulgarians, Sarmatians, and Gepidae, who had come with them into Italy, and who were idolaters.

CHAPTER XXX. p. 153. The church in question is *Sancta Agatha in Subura*, now known as Santa Agata de' Goti. It had been built (or, perhaps, restored) as a church of the Arians by Ricimer, the Visigothic patrician, shortly before 472, and was taken for Catholic worship by St. Gregory in 591 or 592, and dedicated to St. Agatha, to whom he had a special devotion. In a letter written early in 594, St. Gregory commends the church to the acolyth Leo : "ecclesia sanctae Agathae sita in Subora, quae spelunca fuit aliquando pravitatis hereticae, ad catholicae fidei culturam, Deo propitiante, reducta est." (*Registrum, Epist.* iv. 19, ed. Ewald and Hartmann, i. p. 253) ; but makes no mention of any miracle. *Subura* is the district between the Esquiline, Quirinal, and Viminal hills, and had a bad repute in classical times. *Cf.* Horace, *Epod.* v., 57. For " St. Stephen," read " St. Sebastian." The Latin runs : "introductis illic beati Sebastiani et sanctae Agathae martyrum reliquiis."

CHAPTER XXXI. pp. 155–157. Leander, Bishop of Seville (to whom St. Gregory dedicated his *Moralia*), was the brother of Theodosia, the first wife of King Leovigild, the mother of Hermenigild and Rechared. Hermenigild, who had been converted from Arianism by his young wife Ingunthis (a Catholic Frank princess), was associated with his father in the kingdom, ruling at Seville, while Leovigild held his court at Toledo. He rebelled against his father in 583, and was either murdered or put to death by the latter (the circumstances are not clear) in 585. Leovigild died in 586, and his successor, Hermenigild's brother Rechared, became a Catholic in the following year. St. Leander died in 599, and was succeeded in the see of Seville by his more famous brother, St. Isidore, the great apostle of Latin culture and Catholic orthodoxy among the Visigoths of Spain.

CHAPTER XXXII. p. 157. St. Gregory's chronology is here at fault. The great persecutor of the Catholics in Africa, King Hunneric of the Vandals (the son and successor of Gaiseric), reigned from 477 to 484, in the time of the Emperor Zeno. Justinian did not ascend the imperial throne until 527.

CHAPTER XXXVI. p. 164. Maximianus, Bishop of Syracuse and formerly abbot of St. Gregory's abbey of Sant' Andrea on the Caelian Hill, was a constant friend and correspondent of the latter ; he died in 594. St. Gregory was sent to Constantinople as *apocrisiarius* or papal legate, by Pope Pelagius II., in 579, and stayed there until about 585. While there he composed his great *Moralia*.

Ibid. p. 165. "Cothronum" is Cotrone, on the east coast of Calabria.

CHAPTER XXXVIII. p. 173. For " Ferenti " (Ferentino), *cf.* Bk. I. chap. 9. " John the younger " is apparently Pope John III., who was Bishop of Rome from 561 to 574. The Lombards entered Italy in 568. Eutychius is the more usual form of this martyr's name.

Book IV

CHAPTER I. p. 178. There is a certain resemblance here with the famous opening of the seventh book of Plato's *Republic;* but Gregory, in spite of his residence at Constantinople, knew hardly any Greek, and the analogy is probably accidental.

CHAPTER III. p. 180. "Man, therefore, as he is created in the middle state." *Cf.* Dante in the *De Monarchia* (iii. 16).

CHAPTER VIII. p. 188. The monastery founded by St. Benedict at Terracina has been already mentioned, Bk. II. chap. 22.

CHAPTER X. p. 189. *Venerabilis pater nomine Spes.* "Cample" is, perhaps, Campello sul Clitunno, nearer Spoleto than Norcia.

CHAPTER XII. p. 192. For "Reati" (Reate) read "Rieti." A St. Juvenal was Bishop of Narni in the fourth century, but he was not a martyr; St. Eleutherius (not to be confused with St. Gregory's friend, the Abbot of that name), Pope and martyr, suffered death under the Emperor Commodus in 189.

CHAPTER XIII. pp. 192, 193. The Roman patrician and Christian philosopher, Quintus Aurelius Symmachus, was consul in 485, and afterwards Head of the Senate; he was put to death by Theodoric in 525 (*cf.* below, chapter 30). He was the father-in-law of Boëthius, and Galla was therefore the sister of the latter's wife, Rusticiana. It was to this Galla (*Ad Gallam viduam*) that St. Fulgentius of Ruspe addressed his treatise, *De Consolatione super morte mariti et de statu viduarum* (In Migne, P.L. LXV., coll. 311-323). Another Symmachus, the son of Boëthius, was consul in 522; but chronological considerations make it clear that his grandfather is the person whom St. Gregory means.

CHAPTER XIV. p. 194. The story of Servulus is told by St. Gregory in his 15th Homily. (*Homiliarum in Evangelia*, Lib. I. *Homilia* 15.)

CHAPTER XV. p. 195. *Homiliarum in Evangelia*, Lib. II. *Homilia* 40.

CHAPTER XV. p. 196. Praeneste, or Palestrina, was always a haunt for hermits and ascetics in the Middle Ages. For a later instance, that of the beata Margherita Colonna, *see* Maud F. Jerrold, *Vittoria Colonna*, pp. 32, 33.

CHAPTER XVI. p. 198. The story of Tharsilla, or Tarsilla, is told at greater length in the Homilies (Lib. II. *Homilia* 38). Tharsilla, Gordiana, and Emiliana were the three sisters of St. Gregory's father, Gordianus; one, Gordiana, returned to the world and married. The Pope Felix, whom St. Gregory describes as *atavus meus*, was probably the third Pope of that name, who was Bishop of Rome from 483 to

271

492, famous for his struggle with the patriarch Acacius of Constantinople. He was a married man before taking priest's orders, but his
exact relationship with St. Gregory is uncertain. This story curiously
suggests the apparition of St. Gregory himself to the dying Santa Fina,
painted by Domenico Ghirlandaio at San Gimignano.

CHAPTER XVIII. p. 200. He refers to the great pestilence that
devastated Rome at the beginning of 590, during which he was elected
Pope on the death of Pelagius II.

CHAPTER XIX. p. 201. In the Homilies (Lib. II. *Homilia* 35),
St. Gregory speaks of Stephen as " pater monasterii juxta Reatinae
urbis moenia constituti." *Cf.* above, Bk. IV. chap. 11.

CHAPTER XXI. p. 202. *Cf.* note on Bk. III. chap. 22.

CHAPTER XXII. p. 203. Sura is the present Sora in the valley of
the Liris (included in the modern province of Caserta), still famous
for the abbeys in its neighbourhood.

CHAPTER XXIII. p. 203. For " Marsori " read " Marsi " (*Ecclesia
Marsorum*). The district indicated is the modern Abruzzi.

CHAPTER XXV. p. 205. This appeal to these two texts in Isaiah
and the Revelation of St. John, for evidence of the resurrection of the
body, became a traditional one with mediæval theologians. Thus
Dante, answering St. James as to the object of the Christian's hope
(*Par.* xxv. 88–96) :

> " Le nuove e le scritture antiche
> Pongono il segno, ed esso lo mi addita.
> Dell' anime che Dio s'ha fatte amiche
> Dice Isaia che ciascuna vestita
> Nella sua terra fia di doppia vesta,
> E la sua terra è questa dolce vita.
> E il tuo fratello assai vie più digesta,
> Là dove tratta delle bianche stole,
> Questa rivelazion ci manifesta."

CHAPTER XXVI. p. 206. The church of San Sisto is on the Via
Appia within the city ; it was given by Honorius III. to St. Dominic
in the thirteenth century, and is now occupied by Dominican nuns.
The Via Praenestina runs from the Porta Maggiore (Porta Praenestina)
to Palestrina.

Ibid. p. 207. Portua (more properly Portus, the *Portus Traiani*) is
the modern Porto, an important commercial seaport under the Empire,
but now a village two miles from the sea.

Ibid. p. 208. *Patricii Narsae temporibus.* The Narses meant is
evidently the famous Armenian eunuch who reconquered Italy from the
Goths and governed Rome for the Empire from 552 to 567 ; not the
Narses, a contemporary of St. Gregory, to whom several of the Pope's
letters are addressed.

Notes

CHAPTER XXVII. p. 210. *Centumcellae* is the present Civita Vecchia. " Earl " is the translator's equivalent of *comes*, or " count," the chief military officer of a district. St. Gregory relates this story in his Homilies (Lib. II. *Homilia* 36).

CHAPTER XXX. p. 213. *Julianus hujus Romanae Ecclesiae secundus defensor* has already been mentioned, Bk. I. chap. 10. He was the second of this name to hold the office of "defender." *Cf.* note on Bk. I. chap. 4.

Ibid. p. 214. Theodoricus (Thiuda-reiks), whom we call Theodoric the Goth, was born in 454, invaded Italy as the delegate of the Emperor Zeno in 489, and, by his capture of Ravenna from Odoacer in 493, founded the short-lived Ostrogothic kingdom. In 500, he came to Rome as a pacific and beneficent sovereign, hailed by the Romans as a new Trajan, pledging himself to maintain the Roman laws for the benefit of the Roman People. He restored the walls and decreed the preservation of the monuments of the city. " King of the Goths and Romans in Italy," he ruled nominally as the representative of the Emperor at Byzantium. Himself an Arian, Theodoric during the greater part of his reign treated Arians and Catholics with the same impartial justice as he did Goths and Romans in the political field. But the reconciliation between the Byzantine Court and the Holy See in 519, the consequent tendency of the Roman Senate towards Constantinople rather than towards Ravenna, and the increasing bitterness between Arians and Catholics both in East and West, gradually alienated the King from his Catholic and Roman subjects, and he finally degenerated into a religious persecutor and suspicious tyrant. The philosopher Boëthius was tortured to death by his orders in 524 or 525; Symmachus, the Head of the Senate, was executed in 525; and Pope John I. (*cf.* above, Bk. III. chap. 2) died in the King's dungeons at Ravenna in May, 526. Theodoric followed his victims to the grave on August 30, 526, the day on which, according to his decree, all the Catholic churches in Italy were to have been surrendered to the Arians. At some uncertain date, his body was cast out of his magnificent tomb at Ravenna : Agnellus of Ravenna, who wrote in the first half of the ninth century, states that it had been done before his time (*Liber Pontificalis*, in Migne, P.L. cvi. col. 535); but there seems no foundation for the assertion of Fra Salimbene, the thirteenth-century chronicler of Parma (*Cronica*, ed. Holder-Egger, pp. 209, 210), that it was St. Gregory the Great himself who ordered this work of desecration to be carried out. The crater mentioned in this unpleasant legend is either that of Vulcano or Stromboli, two of the Lipari islands.

CHAPTER XXXI. p. 215. San Lorenzo in Damaso, the basilica of St. Lawrence near the site of Pompey's theatre, was founded by Pope St. Damasus (366-384).

CHAPTER XXXII. p. 216. "Courtier" is here, as before, the translator's equivalent for *curialis. Cf.* above, note on Bk. II. chap. 11.

CHAPTER XXXIII. p. 219. "For seeing that they do in that place with unspeakable brightness (common to all) behold God, what is there that they know not, that know him who knoweth all things?" *Cf.* Dante, *Par.* xv. 55–63, xxi. 82–102.

CHAPTER XXXV. p. 219. A "natural brother" (*germanus frater*) means a brother according to the flesh, not merely a fellow-monk.

Ibid. p. 220. Optio was not Stephen's name, but his military rank. The right reading is not *cui cognomen Optio fuit*, "whose surname was Optio," but *qui in numero optio fuit*, "who in rank was adjutant."

Ibid. p. 221. This allegorical ship is possibly the ultimate source of the boat that conveys the souls of the redeemed from the mouth of the Tiber in Dante's *Purgatorio.*

CHAPTER XXXVI. p. 223. Evasa appears to be the island of Iviza in the Balearic Archipelago.

Ibid. pp. 223–226. This famous and important chapter may be regarded as the germ of the later mediæval visions of Hell, Purgatory, and Heaven. The Bridge is the "Bridge of Dread," said to be of Oriental origin, which occurs in so many of the later visions of the other world (though not in the *Divina Commedia*) ; this is its first appearance in the West, the Latin version of the *Visio Sancti Pauli*, in which (though not in the original Greek) it also occurs, being later. The sumptuous house of gold, which is being built for an unnamed person, is the ultimate source of the empty throne seen preparing (probably for St. Bernard) in the vision of Tundal (*Visio Tnugdali*, ed. cit., p. 54), and for Henry VII. in the *Divina Commedia* (*Par.* xxx. 133–138). The episode of the priest, who passes safely over the bridge, is dramatically expanded in the vision of Tundal (ed. cit., pp. 15, 27).

Ibid. p. 227. In the usual version of the Latin text, the arrangement of the chapters is different. The story of Deusdedit forms chapter xxxvii., the story of the boy Theodorus being included with those of the deaths of Chrysaorius and the monk of Iconium as chapter xxxviii.

CHAPTER XXXVII. p. 229. The story of Theodorus (without his name) is told by St. Gregory in the Homilies (Lib. II. *Homilia* 38).

CHAPTER XXXVIII. p. 230. Chrysaorius in the Latin text.

Ibid. p. 232. St. Gregory calls this monastery in Greek Τῶν Γαλάτων, that is, "of the Galatians."

CHAPTER XL. pp. 234, 235. Pope Anastasius II., whom Dante (*Inf.* xi. 7–9) condemns as a heretic, died in November 498. Two rival conclaves met: the one, which represented the majority, was held in the Lateran, and elected the Sardinian deacon Symmachus to the papacy; the other, which favoured a reconciliation with the Emperor (Anastasius I.), in S. Maria Maggiore, chose for Pope the Archdeacon Laurentius, who was a Roman. After a violent struggle, an appeal to the arbitration of Theodoric resulted in the general recognition of Symmachus. The struggle was afterwards renewed, until Laurentius finally withdrew in 505. In the synod (*Synodus palmaris*) which was called in 501 to investigate the charges against Symmachus, the famous principle of the Church of Rome was established : *Summa sedes a nemine judicatur.* *Cf.* Grisar, *Geschichte Roms und der Päpste im Mittelalter,* nos. 308, 309. Paschasius died a few years before the death of Symmachus (514) ; he is venerated as a saint on May 31. A work on the Holy Ghost, *De Spiritu Sancto libri duo,* is attributed to him, and identified with the " rectissimi et luculenti de Sancto Spiritu libri," of which St. Gregory here speaks (Migne, P.L. lxii.) ; but its authenticity has been disputed, and it is included by Augustus Engelbrecht among the works of Bishop Faustus o. Riez (*Corpus Scriptorum Ecclesiasticorum Latinorum,* vol. xxi., Vienna, 1891.) A letter from Paschasius to Eugippius, the biographer of St. Severinus, is extant (In Migne, *tom. cit.,* and ed. Pius Knoell in *Corp. Script. Eccles. Lat.,* vol. ix. pars 2, Vienna, 1886). The scene of this apparition is laid by St. Gregory *in Angulanis thermis,* that is, the baths of Angulus, or Paterno, near the modern Castel Sant' Angelo in the Abruzzi. This story of Paschasius is cited by mediæval writers on the place of Purgatory as implying that souls are punished in the places on earth where they committed their faults. In his Commentary upon the *Sentences* of Peter the Lombard (*In Lib. IV. Sententiarum, dist. xx. pars i. art. i. q.* 6), St. Bonaventura combats this theory, declaring that the case of Paschasius was a special dispensation, and not according to the general purgatorial rule ; for " it appears altogether incredible, or at least improbable, that all the souls who sinned in Paris should be punished in Paris."

CHAPTER XLIV. p. 240. This doctrine of St. Gregory's, that the faithful do not pray for the souls of those whom they suppose to be in Hell, is more explicitly stated in the *Moralia* (lib. xxxiv. cap. 19) : " The Saints do not pray for the unbelieving and impious that are dead, because they shrink from the merit of their prayer, concerning those whom they already know to be condemned to eternal punishment, being made void before that countenance of the just Judge." This is curiously inconsistent with the popular legend, first heard in the eighth century, that St. Gregory, moved by the tale of the justice and humility of Trajan towards the poor widow whose son had been slain, prayed and obtained that the soul of the Emperor might return from Hell to his body to win his salvation. This inconsistency is noticed by St. Thomas Aquinas, who discusses the story at some length (*Summa Theologica*, III. supl. Q. 71, A. 5: *Utrum suffragia prosint existentibus in Inferno*). Dante speaks of the legend of Trajan and St. Gregory, in two famous passages (*Purg.* x. 73–93 ; *Par.* xx. 106–117).

CHAPTER XLV. p. 241. "Two manner of deaths," *duobus etiam modis mors debet intelligi*. *Cf.* Rev. xxi. 8 : "which is the second death." Thus Dante speaks of the souls of the lost, *che la seconda morte ciascun grida* (*Inf.* i. 117).

CHAPTER XLVIII. p. 245. This power of saints, to "discern betwixt illusions and true revelations," is emphasised by St. Catherine of Siena.

CHAPTER LII. p. 246. In the Latin text, this John is described as *in hac urbe locum praefectorum servans*, that is, vicar of the prefect or Rome. Bressa (Brixia) is the modern Brescia, of which St. Faustinus (martyred in the second century) is one of the patron saints.

CHAPTER LIII. p. 247. This Liberius, a contemporary of St. Gregory, is not to be confused with the Liberius mentioned in Bk. II. chap. 35. The office that Valentinus held was *ecclesiae Mediolanensis defensor* (*Cf.* Book I. chap. 4, notes). St Syrus, who is specially venerated at Genoa, was Bishop of Pavia, and was martyred about 96.

CHAPTER LV. p. 249. "Two singing breads," *duas oblationum coronas;* apparently, two unconsecrated hosts.

Ibid. p. 250. The monastery is, as usual, St. Gregory's convent of Sant' Andrea, on the Caelian Hill. In the *Rule of St. Benedict*, we read : "The beds shall be frequently searched by the abbot to guard against the vice of hoarding. And if any one be found in possession of something not allowed by the abbot, let him be subjected to the severest punishment" (chap. 55, Gasquet's translation).

CHAPTER LVI. p. 253. Cassius, Bishop of Narni, died in 558. The story of his death is told at greater length in the Homilies Lib. II. *Homilia* 37).

Index

Index

279

Index

Index

Index

Printed by
BALLANTYNE & COMPANY LTD
AT THE BALLANTYNE PRESS
Tavistock Street Covent Garden
London

THE COLOURED PLATES IN THIS WORK HAVE BEEN ENGRAVED
AND PRINTED BY HENRY STONE AND SON, LTD., BANBURY

Date Due

CPSIA information can be obtained at www.ICGtesting.com
Printed in the USA
BVOW06s1502150716

455393BV00007B/148/P